For Meyer Gold

THE GOOD
NEWS ABOUT
PANIC,
ANXIETY,
& PHOBIAS

BY

MARK S. GOLD, M.D.

BANTAM BOOKS
NEW YORK · TORONTO · LONDON · SYDNEY · AUCKLAND

THE GOOD NEWS ABOUT PANIC, ANXIETY, AND PHOBIAS
*A Bantam Book / published by arrangement with Villard Books,
a division of Random House, Inc.*

PRINTING HISTORY
Villard edition published April 1989

Bantam edition / August 1990

Library of Congress Cataloging-in-Publication Data

Gold, Mark S.
    The good news about panic, anxiety & phobias / by Mark S. Gold.
      p. cm.
    Includes bibliographical references.
    ISBN 0-553-34916-3
    1. Anxiety. 2. Panic disorders—Popular works. 3. Phobias—
Popular works. I. Title.
RC531.G62 1990
616.85′22—dc20   89-18488
                                              CIP

Published simultaneously in the United States and Canada

*Bantam Books are published by Bantam Books, a division of Bantam Double-
day Dell Publishing Group, Inc. Its trademark, consisting of the words
"Bantam Books" and the portrayal of a rooster, is Registered in U.S. Patent and
Trademark Office and in other countries. Marca Registrada. Bantam Books,
1540 Broadway, New York, New York 10036.*

PRINTED IN THE UNITED STATES OF AMERICA

BVG 0 9 8 7 6 5 4

THE GOOD NEWS ABOUT PANIC, ANXIETY, & PHOBIAS

Also by Mark S. Gold, M.D.

THE 800-COCAINE BOOK
THE GOOD NEWS ABOUT DEPRESSION
THE FACTS ABOUT DRUGS AND ALCOHOL
WONDER DRUGS

ACKNOWLEDGMENTS

I am especially grateful to my patients for repeatedly proving that excessive fear can be overcome, and to my collaborators and colleagues at Fair Oaks Hospital and the Yale University School of Medicine.

For their contributions to the project, my sincerest thanks go to A. Carter Pottash, M.D., Dan Montopoli, Lawrence Chilnick, Barbara Capone, Mary Hallock, Vince Rause, Michael Boyette, and Bonny Redlich.

CONTENTS

THE GOOD NEWS ABOUT PANIC, ANXIETY, & PHOBIAS

CHAPTER ONE

WHOSE
FAULT
IS
IT?

*T*HE FIRST TIME I met James, he looked as if he'd been living with a ghost. His hands trembled as he chain-smoked cigarette after cigarette, nervously crushing each one out when it was only half finished. He tugged absentmindedly at the sleeves of his expensive suit. His eyes darted around my office, only occasionally making contact with my own.

"These last two weeks have been a nightmare," he told me. "I can't eat, I can't sleep. I feel as if I'd be better off dead."

James is forty-five years old. He's a stockbroker—a good one—who's prospered through all the ups and downs of the market. He made his fortune years ago by founding and managing a mutual fund. When I met him, he was at the pinnacle of success.

But his life was a living hell.

"Two weeks ago," he told me, "I was watching television, and the most terrible feeling I've ever had came over me. My heart felt as if it would jump out of my chest. I felt as if I were choking.

"Then the chills came over me out of nowhere, and the room started spinning. When I tried to get up, I fainted."

James knew—or thought he knew—what was happening to him. "It was a panic attack—the worst one I've ever had," he said to me. "I can't stand it anymore. Suppose it happens to me at the office—or while I'm driving, God forbid?

"Dr. Gold, I simply cannot live like this!"

James had had his first attack some ten years before. Like this most recent episode, it struck without warning while he was sitting at home alone. Somehow he managed to walk from his house in an exclusive Connecticut community to his neighbor's house—nearly a quarter of a mile down the road.

His neighbors found him screaming on the patio. "I'm dying! I'm having a heart attack!" They called an ambulance, which took him to the nearest hospital.

There he was told that he had suffered a panic attack. The emergency-room doctor suggested he "calm down—learn to relax," and he referred James to a local psychoanalyst.

For four long years, James and his therapist peeled back his life like the layers of an onion. James learned that his extreme anxiety stemmed from the time he'd been lost at the beach when he was five years old. By age ten he was "petrified" of being left alone and afraid of free, idle vacation time. He was afraid of all the strangers in malls and dreaded going to one and being lost.

In spite of these fears, he managed to get accepted at a prestigious prep school and then at Princeton. He went on to the Wharton School, and after he graduated started working at a prestigious New York bank. He had a desire to succeed, which, his analyst showed him, was rooted in the same childhood insecurities that caused his panic attacks.

James had plenty to talk about and plenty to think about at these once-a-week sessions. His therapist described him as a good analytic patient. He himself felt that he understood himself as he never had before.

Unfortunately, however, the panic attacks continued. At forty-three he was having trouble leaving the house to go to the office. As his world crumbled, James felt increasingly more depressed. Not willing to give up completely, James traded his therapist for a psychiatrist. Almost immediately—in fact, at the conclusion of their first session—the psychiatrist knew what was bothering James: depression. Accordingly, the psychiatrist prescribed a popular antidepressant, a medication that, according to the psychiatrist, would help James "get back on track again." That night James was ecstatic. Finally he would be able to lead a normal life again.

There was only one problem: The panic attacks didn't stop. They made James feel even worse, and each day he grew more depressed. At first the psychiatrist said not to worry—the medication just needed time to work. Weeks, then months went by and James still felt depressed. The psychiatrist tried other medications, but they didn't work either. James tried other psychiatrists, and still his problems did not end. Finally he was referred for a course of electroconvulsive therapy (ECT)—that is, shock treatment.

Before he could be hospitalized for ECT, he had had that final attack. A mutual friend suggested he come see me at Fair Oaks Hospital. He'd agreed, but he doubted I could help. He had nothing against me personally, he explained, but he'd already spent tens of thousands of dollars on some of the best psychiatrists in the country. How could I help him if they'd failed?

After we talked, I examined him from head to toe and scheduled a complete course of medical, neurological, and endocrinological testing. James looked at me curiously. "Doc," he said, "I don't need a physical. The problem's up here, in my head."

"Humor me," I said, smiling. "The hospital spent a lot of money on this expensive equipment, and if we don't use it we'll have to give it back."

That week, while I was waiting for the test results, I reread all of his records. I talked to his sister and wife about him. His sister described herself as very nervous, like her mother. James's maternal grandmother had once been hospitalized for a "nervous breakdown."

During the examination, I'd found nothing that might be causing James's symptoms. Now I flipped through the test results. His electroencephalogram showed normal brain waves. His thyroid was normal. The other tests were normal, too—with one important exception.

Two hours into his glucose-tolerance test, James had a severe panic attack.

James hadn't known it, but he suffered from non-insulin-dependent diabetes—and his panic attacks were almost certainly triggered by wild fluctuations in his blood sugar levels.

So the ending of this story is not all rosy. James wasn't thrilled to find out that he had diabetes—it's a serious condition that requires proper attention. But today his diabetes is well controlled by medication. If it had continued to go undiagnosed, he would have suffered needlessly and his health would have dangerously deteriorated.

And though James still has occasional urges to panic when

he's under a lot of stress, they've been brought under control by his medication and behavior therapy. The behavioral therapy has helped him finally leave the house and go to work and be active again. He's able to live as normal a life as someone who, say, has recovered from a minor heart attack. And he's happier than at any time he can remember.

There must have been times during those long years of despair when James felt like the loneliest person on earth. Actually, he is joined in his misery by more company than he would ever guess.

Recent research conducted by the National Institute of Mental Health shows that in America anxiety disorders are the *number one* mental health problem among women and are second only to drug and alcohol abuse among men. Another very large NIMH-sponsored study, called the Epidemiologic Catchment Area (ECA) Survey, evaluated the incidence of anxiety disorders by surveying over 18,000 people in five different communities. The following tables illustrated just how widespread panic and anxiety disorders can be. Overall, 9.3 percent admitted feeling "frightened, anxious, or very uneasy in situations when most people wouldn't be afraid." And over 25 percent considered themselves to be a nervous person.

All in all, researchers believe that between 20 and 30 million Americans have their lives interrupted, their productivity sapped, and their happiness shattered by panic, anxiety, and abnormal fear.

Sadly, the torment caused by panic attacks lead many people to try suicide. A recent study found that when compared to the general public, people suffering from panic attacks were *18 times* more likely to try suicide. According to this study, a staggering 20 percent of all people with panic disorder had attempted suicide. These statistics testify not only to the emotional and physical pain caused by panic attacks, but also to the strength and determination of the overwhelming majority of panic attack victims who do *not* try suicide.

"Ever had a spell when all of sudden you felt frightened, anxious, or very uneasy in situations when most people wouldn't be afraid?" *

ECA Site	Percent "Yes"
New Haven	11.6
Baltimore	8.3
St. Louis	8.9
Durham	7.6
Los Angeles	9.9
Mean of 5 Sites	9.3
Munich	9.3

"Have you ever considered yourself a nervous person?" *

ECA Site	Percent "Yes"
New Haven	27.4
Baltimore	22.4
St. Louis	22.7
Durham	27.1
Los Angeles	27.6
Mean of 5 Sites	25.4

* Reprinted with permission from Weissman, MM, "Anxiety Disorders in the Community and the Family," Cross National Perspective on Treatment of Anxiety Disorders: Scientific Foundation for Clinical Practice. Presented at the Annual Meeting of the American Psychiatric Association, Montreal, May 8, 1988.

Like James, many of these people have struggled for years with a variety of anxiety disorders, seeking therapy that doesn't work, seeing their careers and personal lives fall apart, feeling their happiness fade. On top of the misery caused by these disorders, they've had to struggle with the awful feeling that their problems are somehow their own fault. If only I were stronger, they say to themselves, I could pull myself together and get on with my life. And often the people closest to them feel the same way. After all, they reason, people face anxieties every day without letting them ruin their lives. Some people suffering from panic attacks become so ashamed that they're too embarrassed to admit they have a problem or to seek treatment.

It's not surprising that they'd feel this way. Until recently, anxiety disorders, such as panic attacks and phobias, were almost always considered a purely psychological problem. Some psychiatrists and psychologists said they were an affliction of people who couldn't bear the stresses of life—in other words, *they were a failing on the part of the patient.* For decades, the diagnosis and treatment of phobias and anxiety disorders revolved around the deeply entrenched belief that abnormal anxiety resulted from an "intrapsyche conflict" and could be treated only by delving into the patient's mind.

Bull.

If you suffer from phobias and panic attacks, I want to tell you something that will change your life: *It's not your fault.* It doesn't mean you have a weak personality, or that your mother didn't love you enough, or that you simply lack the inner strength to deal with the stresses of normal life. *In reality, it's not the patient who fails the treatment; it's the treatment that fails the patient.*

The good news is that your problems may not be "all in your head." If you have panic attacks, you suffer from a physical condition just as surely as if you had the flu or high blood pressure. And here's the best news of all: Your condition can be treated—and in many cases, cured.

Exciting new research stemming from my Yale University colleagues and my research in the 1970s has uncovered evidence that crippling anxiety—and the disorders it eventually causes—can be triggered by discrete, *biochemical* abnormalities in the brain. This is staggering news, carrying the riveting implication that abnormal anxiety may not be simply the product of a disordered mind, generated by the stresses of living daily life. And since it can be a real physical condition, it requires an appropriate *medical* response.

At the same time, we are uncovering what we call "mimickers"—biological problems whose symptoms imitate the symptoms of mental illness. Dozens of purely physical conditions—from brain tumors to heart problems to vitamin deficiencies—produce symptoms identical to those involved in a

DO YOU SUFFER FROM THE CONSEQUENCES OF ANXIETY?

If you suffer one or more of the following symptoms, you may be suffering from the consequences of anxiety:

Chest pain or discomfort
Diarrhea
Difficulty concentrating
Dizziness
Eyelid or facial twitch
Faintness
Fatigue (always tired)
Fear of dying
Fear of going crazy
Fear of losing control
Feeling that things are unreal
Headaches
Hot and cold sensations
Impatience
Impotence
Inability to relax
Insomnia (or sleep problems)
Irritability
Muscle aches (back aches)
Palpitations (heart pounding)
Shortness of breath
Smothering or choking feelings
Tingling sensations
Trembling or shaking
Unsteady legs
Unwanted thoughts
Upset stomach

LIFE IMITATES ART

Author John Cheever described his overriding fear of bridges in autobiographical stories such as "The Angel of the Bridge." Cheever wrote passionately of his anxiety approaching the George Washington Bridge over the Hudson River: "I could see no signs of collapse, and yet I was convinced that in another minute the bridge would split in two and hurl the long lines of Sunday traffic into the dark water below us." Embarrassed, Cheever rarely admitted his fear except in fiction.

In her biography of her father, *Home Before Dark* (Houghton Mifflin, 1984), Susan Cheever described one of her father's methods of hiding his phobia.

> Once, when I was about fourteen, as we were coming back across the Tappan Zee Bridge from a particularly jolly morning at the Ettlinger's, I noticed that the car seemed to be stalling. As we approached the curving superstructure at the center of the bridge, the stalling seemed to get worse. I looked over at my father and saw that his foot was shaking against the accelerator. He was very pale.
>
> "Talk to me," he said.
>
> "About what?" I noticed that his hands were trembling, too. The car bucked along, edging toward the guardrail at the side of the bridge.
>
> "It doesn't matter, just talk."

By the time Susan Cheever had finished describing a novel she was reading, the car had reached the other side of the bridge, and her father had recovered from his panic attack.

panic attack. Sadly, huge numbers of these patients—having been diagnosed only on the basis of their symptoms—have undergone years of fruitless and expensive psychotherapy for a mental condition that didn't exist. And they have had other dangerous illnesses left untreated.

The implications are clear: If your symptoms are due to the presence of an undiagnosed physical illness—a mimicker—psychotherapy will do you little good. You may as well seek psychoanalysis for a broken leg—you may understand your childhood better, but your leg will still be broken.

Similarly, psychotherapy will have little impact on most panic attacks, since these attacks can be caused by malfunctions in the brain. In certain cases it may help reduce the anxiety symptoms associated with the attacks, but it will never get to the problem's core. For that, you need a comprehensive treatment regime that addresses first the body and then, if appropriate, the mind.

To illustrate what I'm talking about, let me give you an analogy. Imagine someone—let's call him Mr. Jones—has a heart attack and is taken to the emergency room of a big medical center. Now, instead of being rushed to the cardiac care unit, he's sent to a regular hospital room. There's no special life-support equipment around—in fact, no medical equipment of any kind. Nobody runs an electrocardiograph or any blood tests to assess the damage to his heart. Nobody hooks him up to a heart monitor. A nurse comes in, gives him some pain pills, and leaves. She doesn't ask about his symptoms or even check his pulse. She doesn't take any blood for laboratory tests.

Finally a doctor saunters in, glances at the chart—after all, there's not much there to read—and pulls a chair up close to the bed. "Well, Mr. Jones," he says, "let's talk about why you're having these heart attacks."

If that happened to a real heart patient, they'd call it malpractice. But sadly, that's exactly what happens to many people who suffer from anxiety disorders.

Now, I'm not saying that because anxiety disorders can be physical in nature, the more traditional psychological therapies for anxiety disorders are all wrong. They're useful tools—but they must be used properly. And to use them properly, doctors must understand what the real problems are.

Again, let's return to our hypothetical Mr. Jones. Nobody would suggest that his heart attack is "all in his head." But that doesn't mean that doctors should simply treat the heart and ignore the rest of him. He'll need counseling about his life-style and eating habits. He may have to change his job. He'll need help in learning how to deal with stress in new ways.

Similarly, counseling is important to people with phobias and anxiety disorders. But traditional therapy for these disorders is like counseling the heart-attack patient without bothering to treat his heart.

At the very least, psychiatrists should perform a thorough physical exam to rule out any physical causes for your symptoms. Psychiatrists are M.D.s—at least that's what it says on their license plates. Any decent psychiatrist should have been fully trained in doctoring the body. But when was the last time you heard of a psychiatrist performing an exam? Their province, after all, is the mind. If your problem isn't purely mental, it's really none of their business, is it? Astoundingly, despite all the new evidence to the contrary, most traditional psychiatrists still ignore—or pay only lip service to—the biological causes and components of anxiety disorders.

How do most psychiatrists diagnose their patients? They talk to them. They ask the patient to tell them what's wrong— and if the patient says "I'm depressed," chances are that's how he or she will be diagnosed. They gather symptoms and impressions. And then, using the clinical judgment they've formed over years of experience, they make the call. Sometimes they're right, sometimes they're wrong. Most times there's no way to tell.

Well, to my mind that's not medicine at all. No matter how many diplomas are hanging on the wall, it's nothing more than faith healing. And the diagnosis you get will depend on which psychiatric faith your doctor tithes to. If you've stumbled into the Church of Cognitive Therapy, you'll learn that your anxiety is a learned behavior and can be unlearned. The deacon at the First Reformed Family Therapists, on the other hand, will suspect the cause is some family dysfunction. The ministers of the Congregation of the Almighty Freud will probe your childhood.

The Evangelical Temple of Feminist Therapy will blame your fears on the stress of living in a male-dominated world.

To make matters worse, these disparate faiths of psychiatry aren't very ecumenical. Rather than exchanging knowledge and ideas, psychiatrists of different theoretical approaches tend to feud, each group arguing to establish its own approach as the one true path to effective psychiatry.

Obviously, this isn't an atmosphere in which new ideas and treatment approaches can flourish, and it also goes a long way toward explaining why so many psychiatrists are hostile to the growing body of information about brain science coming out of the research labs. To them, the notion that mental illness can be a genetic disease or at least have a significant biological component borders on heresy.

So, too many psychiatrists continue to ignore new discoveries and go on diagnosing patients on symptoms alone, according to their own theoretical predisposition. The sad but predictable result is that in an alarming number of cases, they get things wrong.

In my book *The Good News About Depression* I cited a research study that looked at one hundred consecutive patients at a psychiatric center who had been examined by staff psychiatrists and diagnosed as suffering from mental problems. The study found that 46 percent of these patients were suffering from medical problems—missed by the examination—which either caused or contributed to their psychiatric symptoms. When these patients were properly diagnosed and treated, 61 percent of them showed a dramatic clearing of psychiatric symptoms. And the remaining 39 percent showed a significant improvement.

According to the authors of the study, had these misdiagnoses not been caught, all of these patients would have been committed to state mental institutions.

In an earlier study, the same researchers found that 10 percent of six hundred psychiatric outpatients had biological problems which caused their "psychiatric" symptoms.

As the Research Director of Fair Oaks Hospital, I see similar signs of rampant misdiagnosis. We studied one hundred patients who had been diagnosed by their psychiatrists as suffering from depression. In 35 percent of those cases, we found a physical cause for their apparently mental disorders.

And psychiatrists are not even the worst offenders! The "real doctors"—the family practitioners, internists, cardiologists, emergency-room physicians—are the ones who see most of the patients with panic and anxiety disorders. In the overwhelming majority of cases, these patients *never* have their

VISITS IN PAST 6 MONTHS FOR PERSONS WITH RECENT ANXIETY DISORDER*

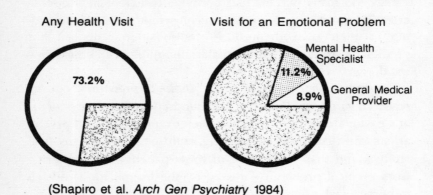

Any Health Visit

73.2%

Visit for an Emotional Problem

Mental Health Specialist

11.2%

8.9%

General Medical Provider

(Shapiro et al. *Arch Gen Psychiatry* 1984)

* Reprinted with permission from Weissman, MM, "Anxiety Disorders in the Community and the Family," Cross National Perspective on Treatment of Anxiety Disorders: Scientific Foundation for Clinical Practice. Presented at the Annual Meeting of the American Psychiatric Association, Montreal, May 8, 1988.

disorder diagnosed correctly. Instead, they may be treated for headaches, backaches, stomach disorders, and the great catch-all category "anxiety and tension." The following charts graphically illustrate how many anxiety disorder patients are not receiving treatment for their anxiety disorders.

And to make matters even worse, there are also the myriad *non*medical mental health professionals—psychotherapists, clinical psychologists, social workers—who encounter and treat anxiety and panic-disorder patients without having the medical background necessary for proper diagnosis and treatment.

MYTH VS. REALITY: DID YOU DO THIS TO YOURSELF?

I see it over and over again: victims of panic, anxiety, and phobia, after years of seeking help, give up hope because deep down inside they believe their symptoms are their own fault, a product of some lack of will or weakness of character. After all, if the problem is entirely in the mind, doesn't it imply some sort of weakness on the victim's part—a lack of character or moral strength?

Of course, the patient hasn't always reached this conclusion on his or her own. Often when the course of therapy prescribed for a patient by psychiatrists and psychotherapists fails to resolve their problem, the patient is labeled a "nonresponder." Never mind that the treatment may have been miles off target; help was offered and the patient failed to respond. The implication is clear: There's nothing wrong with the treatment—it's the patient who isn't coming around, who isn't trying hard enough.

Imagine that our poor Mr. Jones has left the hospital and now is back, barely hanging on to life, after suffering another heart attack. In the hallway, the doctor looks at the chart and sadly shakes his head. "I don't know why he did it. For some reason he wasn't able to accept the help that we offered. Obviously there's a self-destructive aspect to his personality—probably rooted in poor self-esteem as a child."

To add to the confusion, some very misinformed "experts" are claiming that the reason anxiety, phobias, and panic attacks are on the rise today is that we live in a world that could be destroyed at any moment by nuclear war. Since safety is so tenuous, these pundits suggest, people who aren't riddled with devastating fears are the *abnormal* ones.

This point of view just doesn't hold water. The threat of nuclear destruction is certainly a legitimate concern, but I doubt that's what causes a person's heart to pound, lungs to gasp, and legs to turn to jelly at the thought of riding an elevator or crossing a bridge. What really makes that notion objectionable is that it's loaded with the same old blame-the-victim sentiment: If you're suffering from phobias, anxiety, or panic attacks, it's all because you can't cope with the day-to-day stresses of modern life. Good treatment has been offered, and you still aren't well. It's no surprise that after a while, patients begin to believe all this, to believe that maybe they really *are* going crazy. Of course, this kind of thinking only leads to more psychological problems, a worsening of the anxiety condition, and a gradual loss of hope—results that have dramatic implications for our national health. In fact, a recent follow-up study, re-examining people thirty-five years after the intital study, found that severe anxiety was the best marker for developing future disease. In this study, over 52 percent developed cardiovascular disease, hypertension, ulcers, migraines, and other illnesses over a thirty-five-year period. Another recent study of panic patients with no history of heart disease, found that 20 percent of these patients showed signs of developing a very serious heart condition called cardiomyopathy (the most common indication for receiving a heart transplant). These studies suggest that the presence of panic attacks—especially if they are not treated—may someday be considered a significant health risk, similar to high blood pressure, smoking, or obesity.

WHERE DID WE GO WRONG?

Since its birth, psychiatry has been influenced by the centuries-old notion that the mind is divided into the world of matter and the world of spirit. In psychiatric terms, this would parallel the difference between the brain and the mind. The mind was a real and sovereign entity, existing independently from the flesh. Medieval scholars thought it hovered a few inches above the forehead. Leonardo da Vinci placed it inside the skull. Descartes said he had discovered it in the pineal gland. Wherever these thinkers looked for the mind, they held one concept constant—there was a sharp, unbridgeable gap between the body and the mind.

This way of thinking—philosophers call it dualism—naturally leads to the conclusion that the mind is not scientifically measurable. While we can physically study the brain, the mind eludes such a coarse grasp. The brain is an organ—we can see it—but the mind is ethereal, the core of our personality, the seat of the soul. This notion has driven modern psychiatric thought.

If the mind is the seat of the soul, and the soul is our identity, then mental illness can never be thought of as an innocent thing. We can pity the sufferer, but at the same time we suspect that the condition is due to some spiritual or moral weakness. This is the thinking that led to the notorious Bedlam asylum in Great Britain, where people with mental disorders were chained to the walls. Today the restraints aren't physical, but they still shackle our thinking about mental illness.

SIGMUND AND EMIL

For the last century, psychiatry has marched along two trails —one investigating the biological components of mental disease, the other preoccupying itself with the problems of pure mind. At the head of each procession stands a giant of medical science.

Sigmund Freud, of course, was a pioneer in unraveling some of the workings of the human mind. His discovery (or invention, depending on how you look at it) of the unconscious mind laid the foundation for the modern techniques of psychotherapy. As we shall see, Freud never intended his theories to distract psychiatrists from the study of the biological aspects of mental health, but unfortunately, that's what came to pass.

Emil Kraepelin, on the other hand, built a scientific framework of psychiatry and gave it a sound medical base. By studying large numbers of mentally ill patients over a period of years, Kraepelin began to identify certain similarities in their symptoms and behavior, which led him to identify certain syndromes, including what he called manic-depressive psychosis (now known as bipolar disorder) and schizophrenia.

This was earth-shattering work. Before, psychiatrists had treated mental patients as if each suffered from a unique and individual madness. By identifying specific sets of symptoms and showing that they occurred again and again—in different patients, in different places—Kraepelin proved that distinct mental disorders could be defined and diagnosed. In those days, psychiatrists could offer their patients little in the way of treatment, but at least the groundwork had been laid for the scientific and systematic study of mental disorders.

Poised at the beginning of the twentieth century with a strong medical orientation, psychiatry was ready to incorporate emerging medical technologies. It was an ambitious period for psychiatry; there was a spirit of cooperation and openness that would be rare today.

For example, practitioners of the new science of bacteriology discovered tiny disease-causing agents known as microbes. Psychiatrists borrowed from the bacteriologists and soon discovered that many mental disorders, once flatly written off as madness, were due to infections by these microscopic bugs.

First, bacterial illnesses were found in large numbers of supposedly schizophrenic patients. Actually, these patients were in an advanced state of syphilis, which we now know mimics the symptoms of schizophrenia.

Later, through laboratory examinations, doctors learned that thousands of mental patients who had been institutionalized for madness were in reality suffering from pellagra, a disease caused by a deficiency of niacin. In these cases, the only thing needed to cure their "insanity" was a balanced diet.

Now, you'd think that these successes would have laid to rest the old bugaboo of dualism once and for all. At the time, the future of psychiatry as a hard-edged, rigorous science looked bright. Psychiatrists expected that discoveries just around the corner would reveal how body chemistry, brain structure, and biological agents contributed to mental illness.

Unfortunately, medical psychiatry fell victim to its own heightened expectations.

Progress in science isn't straightforward; it tends to go in fits and starts. A few breakthrough discoveries will lead to a great deal of progress very quickly. Then, almost inevitably, the pace slows. It's sort of like mining for gold—after someone makes the first strike, it's pretty easy to find more gold nearby. Eventually, though, all the easy finds are mined out. You have to start digging deeper, and the going gets slower. That doesn't mean that there isn't more gold there, or that it isn't worth going after. But you have to be willing to take the long view.

When the pace of discovery slowed in medical psychiatry, unfortunately, many people took it as a sign that they'd reached a dead end.

But that wasn't the only problem the medical psychiatrists of that time faced. They created one of their biggest problems for themselves. Some of those who continued to count on technology to solve the problems of the mind overindulged in the questionable use of treatments such as shock therapy, psychosurgery, even teeth-pulling. Medical psychiatry suffered from an epidemic of faddism—and the rest of the medical community wasn't buying it.

Neither was the public. Before long, exposés of some of the most flagrant abuses began appearing in books, magazines, and movies. Medically oriented psychiatrists were portrayed— sometimes with considerable justification—as the worst kind of "mad scientists," performing ill-considered experiments on mental patients that left them little more than zombies.

PSYCHOANALYSIS TAKES OVER

Compared with these scenes, the psychoanalysts started to look like a pretty appealing bunch. They didn't use a lot of drugs or perform bizarre operations on the brain. Mostly they simply talked to their patients. And if they didn't always help, at least they didn't seem to do any harm.

And they *did* seem to know what they were talking about —even if nobody else understood them. They based their approach to therapy on Sigmund Freud's theories of the unconscious mind. They used erudite terms such as "id" and "ego" and seemed to understand just how the things those terms represented caused their patients' mental suffering. They painted a dramatic picture of a cosmic struggle being played out deep in the unconscious, a sort of internal Greek play that, with enough insight, we could train ourselves to see. Freudian psychoanalysis was mystical and poetic—just the sort of approach that seemed to suit the often bizarre and seemingly unexplainable symptoms of mental illness.

Freud theorized that neurosis, or personality disorder, was caused by the psychological impact of certain experiences in childhood, which occur as the child moves from one distinct stage of development to the next. These key experiences, he said, must be identified and reconstructed so that their negative impact on the life of the adult can be recognized and resolved. The method for uncovering these key experiences came to be called psychoanalysis, and it led the way for today's mind-only brand of psychiatry.

Surprisingly, though, Freud began his career as a neurologist, and he believed that biological causes of mental illness would one day be discovered. He devised his theories because he lacked the necessary diagnostic tools to investigate those causes. He never intended to abandon the biological aspects of mental health. In fact, he predicted that science would one day confirm the link between mind and body. "In view of the intimate connection between things physical and mental," he said, "we may look forward to a day when paths of knowledge will be opened up leading from organic biology and chemistry to the field of neurotic phenomena."

PSYCHOTHERAPY TAKES CENTER STAGE

Freudian psychiatry didn't overtake medical psychiatry all at once. In fact, the fertile atmosphere of scientific inquiry and medical exploration lasted through the 1940s and 1950s, but by 1963 it had lost much of its steam. That was the year Karl Menninger published *The Vital Balance,* an influential book which argued that all mental illnesses should be treated with the same approach—psychotherapy.

With this watershed book, hopes for a medically based psychiatry were dashed. The talking cure became the only game in town. Now, since medical skills were seen to be virtually irrelevant to psychiatric practice, the distinction between psychiatrists, who were physicians, and non-medical psychotherapists became indistinct.

All during this time the role of psychotherapy itself was changing. First intended as a tool with which psychiatrists could treat the mentally ill, it was now becoming a mass-market item. Soon it was being offered by psychologists, public mental health workers, and any "therapist" who wanted to hang out a shingle as a cure-all for life's problems, large and small, and as a boon to anyone who thought therapy might lead to a richer life. Uncertain about your career goals? Unlucky in love? Stuck in a dead-end career? Don't blame yourself; blame your mother. Psychotherapy was the answer. Of course, if you were suffering from a serious mental illness, you were likely to get lost in the shuffle.

THE TROUBLE WITH PSYCHOTHERAPY

From the start, there were drawbacks to using psychotherapy as the only type of therapy. For one thing, it's expensive. For another, it takes forever.

Just as important are the demands it places upon the patient. The talking cure requires lots of talk—good talk. Insights and intelligent observations are crucial to an effective course of treatment. That's why it became so fashionable among the educated—it's really not all that different from a graduate seminar. That's also why it left all those patients whose illnesses had robbed them of any grasp on reality out in the cold. Those patients, no matter what the causes of their psychiatric problems, wound up in institutions where they lived out their lives in varying degrees of misery and madness.

OVERRELIANCE ON DRUG THERAPY

But even as psychotherapy was approaching its heyday, the seeds were being sown for the current renaissance of medically based psychiatry. Many of those unfortunate people who were beyond the reach of psychotherapy were helped by the discovery of new antipsychotic drugs. These drugs—first Thorazine, then the tricyclic antidepressants, then an array of tranquilizers, and later lithium—freed millions of patients from the bizarre symptoms of their illnesses and let them lead relatively normal lives.

The drugs were a boon to psychiatrists, too. For one thing, the ability to prescribe the medication gave them an immediate advantage over the ever-increasing ranks of nonmedical psychotherapists. For another, after drawing fire for their inability to prove the effectiveness of psychotherapy, they enjoyed having this new and obviously effective weapon on their side.

But soon the sunny prospects of the new drug therapies blew up in the psychiatrists' faces. Once again swept away by hopeful enthusiasm, many began to dispense prescriptions too freely. The backfire was almost immediate.

Given in large amounts, certain antipsychotic medications cause severe and sometime irreversible side effects, such as an illness called tardive dyskinesia, in which the tongue and muscles of the face twitch involuntarily.

Word of these ill effects spread, and the stature of modern psychiatry tumbled even lower. People spoke derisively of psychiatrists as pill pushers and charlatans. Scalded by the criticism, many psychiatrists began pulling back on the dosages they prescribed, often to the point of rendering the drug useless. And that's how psychiatry got into the state it is today: in low regard, ignored by the best new medical talent, often ineffective.

Now it's time for us to heal the rift between mind and body, to begin treating patients first as doctors of the body, then as doctors of the mind. It's time to take the best from all we've learned in the past century—not to discard either traditional psychotherapy or medically based psychiatry, but to use them effectively as tools. Above all, it's time for psychiatrists to begin to act like doctors to become what I call "biopsychiatrists." That's why we're here.

BIOPSYCHIATRY AND WHERE IT CAME FROM

Biopsychiatry traces its roots to the emergence of psychiatric drugs, and for a very good reason. Though many didn't realize it at the time, the effectiveness of these drugs introduced a whole new set of questions for psychiatry and the nature of mental illness. If psychotics respond to a specific drug and depressives do not, is there an organic difference between those two conditions? Is brain chemistry being altered? Does the brain play a role in mental illness? Can chemical imbalances in the brain be the cause of mental illness?

Meanwhile, scientists studying the chemistry of the brain were asking questions about normal and abnormal brain function and the way it affected mood.

A group of psychiatrists—those who took note of new research and were not so deeply buried in their own theoretical framework that they were closed to new ideas—began to take all this seriously. Their colleagues in psychiatry had little love for them, but the more scientifically oriented neuroscientists began to cooperate with them.

Serendipitously, just as interest in the study of brain science was gaining momentum, new technologies began to emerge, giving these researchers the ability to peer into the brain, to track the activity of normal and abnormal brain cells in the mentally ill. We began to paint a picture of the biological basis of mental illness. As we watched how psychiatric drugs altered the chemistry of the brain, we began to open up new vistas of inquiry into the mechanics of mental illness. The fascinating promise of biopsychiatry is the same one that Freud identified a hundred years ago: As we understand the working of mental illness caused by brain disease, we can find a way to fix it.

WHAT BIOPSYCHIATRY CAN MEAN TO YOU

There are psychiatrists—myself included—who know your anxieties and fears *aren't* all in your head and *can't* simply be blamed on your failure to cope. I want this book to convince you that no matter how bizarre and distressing your panic attacks or phobias may be, they don't mean you're going crazy. I want to show that it's not your fault that your treatments haven't worked. Most important, I want you to see that we know what's happening to you; that there are ways we can help you get well, and reclaim your life from the devastating fears and apprehensions that have robbed you of joy.

This book will explain why the traditional routes of psychotherapy have never given you complete relief, and why psychiatrists have stubbornly and foolishly resisted the new methods of diagnosis and treatment that may help you. It will show how your problems can be accurately diagnosed and resolved. And it will introduce you to the biopsychiatrist, a new kind of doctor who understands that patients have minds *and* bodies, a fully trained psychiatrist who hasn't abandoned his medical skills.

As I've already said, psychiatrists are supposed to be full-fledged medical doctors, having gone through medical school, internships, and residencies. They've been taught all the basics that form the foundation of any medical doctor's practice; they can take temperatures, they can give shots, they can do blood tests and urine tests and all the other things any general practitioner can do. But commonly, when a young doctor decides to specialize in psychiatry, it's with the understanding that he or she will soon leave all that behind.

Imagine a heart surgeon or an obstetrician or any other medical specialist proudly and consciously abandoning his or her basic medical skills. It's unthinkable.

But still, we see nothing unusual about a psychiatrist who doesn't own a stethoscope, or a lab coat, or blood-drawing equipment, or a well-equipped doctor's bag. Those are the tools of physical health, we might say in defense; my shrink is working on my *mind.*

Well, that's no longer good enough.

Because on every new front, new scientific discoveries are giving biopsychiatrists a fresh perspective of mental illness. Emerging technologies are giving us new windows into the workings of the brain and mind. And new approaches to treatment are enabling us to hold out new hope to all victims of mental illness. If you're suffering from anxiety disorders, or something that seems very similar, biopsychiatry offers you real hope for a swift and effective cure. If you're seeing a psychotherapist and your treatment isn't working, a biopsychiatrist may be able to show you what's going wrong. If you aren't being treated but are considering seeking help, a biopsychiatrist will make sure you're properly diagnosed and treated from the beginning.

Happily, the world of psychiatry is beginning to hear our message. Surveys of psychiatric students stress the student's desire for a more scientific, medically based curriculum. Educators are once again insisting that psychiatrists receive a solid grounding in all the aspects of basic medical diagnosis and treatment.

All psychiatrists should be biopsychiatrists. We owe our patients nothing less. It's inevitable that psychiatry return to its medical roots. When that happens, psychiatry wins. We all do.

CHAPTER TWO

BIOPSYCHIATRY
AND
ANXIETY
DISORDERS

HOW BIOPSYCHIATRY DIAGNOSES ANXIETY DISORDERS

As medical psychiatrists, we begin our evaluation of a patient the way any other medical specialist would. We take an exhaustive medical history of the patient and his or her family, including information on the patient's past and present use of medication, alcohol, and illegal drugs.

The next step is a series of thorough medical, neurological, and endocrinological exams, followed by a battery of state-of-the-art diagnostic tests—probably the best work-up the patient has ever had.

If we find a physical problem related to the anxiety symptoms—a mimicker—we respond with appropriate medical treatment, saving the patient the needless frustration and expense of psychotherapy.

Once I got a desperate call from a college classmate I hadn't heard from in years. She was a very successful advertising executive and had traveled to Atlanta to make a presentation to an important client. In her hotel room she was suddenly overwhelmed by a wave of panic—her pulse hammered, her head spun, she could hardly catch her breath. She'd never felt anything like this before, and for a while she thought she might be dying.

The next morning she had a second attack. This time, she called a friend in New York who put her in touch with a therapist. The therapist listened to the woman's symptoms and asked her a little about her life. Finally, he came to the conclusion that the symptoms were due to the stresses of her rapid rise in the advertising business, a fear of failure, and conflicts about being more competitive and more successful than her male coworkers. In other words, he was saying, it was all in her head.

Fortunately, the woman called me for a second opinion. I referred her to an Atlanta biopsychiatrist. In the course of the routine physical examination, he discovered the woman had a minor heart condition called mitral valve prolapse. It is a very common and classic mimicker that produces symptoms so similar to those of a panic attack that even physicians are commonly fooled. Mitral valve prolapse will be discussed, along with other mimickers, in Chapter 6.

The Atlanta biopsychiatrist prescribed the proper medication, and the problem disappeared.

Her story had a happy ending, but imagine what her life would have been like if she hadn't gotten the proper diagnosis. She might have suffered for years, she might have lost her confidence and her job, and she might have had years of psychotherapy aimed at *correcting a mental problem that didn't exist.* It seems incredible, but it happens every day. If psychiatrists would act like doctors and acknowledge the need to base their diagnoses on facts gathered from a sound medical exam, most of these cases could be caught. Patients would be spared time, money, and anguish. Some would even be spared their lives.

Once I examined a young woman named Jennie who was suffering from a nearly textbook case of panic attacks, plus paranoid suspicions that people she worked with were spying on her and following her around. Her symptoms seemed so obviously psychiatric that all the psychiatrists and physicians she'd seen had quickly decided that Jennie was mentally ill.

"I don't want you to waste a lot of Jennie's money on testing," said the neurologist who referred her. "She's fine, except for her mental problems."

We tested her anyway, and our testing may have saved her life. An NMR scan—a sophisticated imaging technique that shows the inner structure of the brain—revealed the source of her behavioral problems: an operable brain tumor which triggered both her false panic and her paranoid suspicions. Luckily for Jennie, she traded her psychiatrist for a biopsychiatrist.

Jennie underwent a successful operation, and today she's fine. Without the testing, Jennie would have been diagnosed as a psychiatric case and probably put on a course of medication intended to control her symptoms, giving psychotherapists the chance to work on the illness in her mind. Meanwhile, Jennie would have been dying in front of their eyes.

PSYCHOLOGICAL EVALUATION

Of course, we don't always find underlying physical mimickers in patients complaining of anxiety symptoms. If our thorough physical exam, patient history, and battery of tests fail to turn up a biological abnormality, we move on to a similarly exhaustive psychiatric evaluation. We consider all the psychiatric conditions that could be causing the symptoms. Could the patient be suffering from manic-depression? How about an agitated depression, or schizophrenia? Here, of course, we must rely on our experience and clinical judgment as well as on laboratory tests, but the solid data we gather from interviewing family members help us make more informed decisions.

If, finally, we have ruled out all other physical and/or psychiatric alternatives, we can safely diagnose an anxiety disorder. But our work is just beginning. Now we have to discover which type of anxiety disorder is present (there are dozens of variations), why it exists, and what should be done about it.

Much of the rest of this book will describe how we answer those questions. But for now, here's a capsulized look at what the new research has taught us about treating anxiety disorders:

1. Panic attacks, anxiety disorders, and phobias are real conditions that can bring as much pain and anguish as cancer, heart disease, or any other physical disorder.

2. An accurate diagnosis is crucial. Many diseases cause symptoms identical to the physical manifestations of a panic attack. A thorough physical exam, along with state-of-the-art lab testing, can flush out most of these imitators. If you suffer from anxiety, when was the last time your psychiatrist—or anyone —gave you a physical exam looking for medical causes of your "mental" problems?

3. The reason nonmedical psychotherapists and most psychiatrists can't help you is that they ignore the biological component of your disease. They've decided, before even seeing

you, that anxiety problems are solely the province of the mind. Your symptoms, then, are shoehorned into this preexisting diagnosis. Obviously, if your anxiety is biologically based, your treatment is going nowhere. Psychotherapy alone can't cure biologically based anxiety.

4. We have learned that anxiety, phobias, and panic attacks are related disorders. Many patients we see are suffering from a combination of these conditions. It's important to remember that no matter how complicated your own condition, you can be helped. It's true that evidence shows that the longer you are ill, the more difficult treatment is, *but,* in general, the more severe your symptoms, the more likely your condition is a physical disease that can be treated successfully. Therefore early medical treatment is important.

5. More and more new research is finding a causative link between anxiety and various common diseases. Anxiety is thought to play a role in the development of alcoholism, depression, sexual dysfunction, heart disease, and a wide array of other illnesses.

6. Finally, and perhaps most importantly, I want you to understand that no matter how long you've suffered or how serious your condition seems to be, no matter how many doctors you've seen or how many treatment plans have failed, there's hope. A correct diagnosis and a solid treatment plan can work wonders. I've seen it time and again—and as you read this book, you will too.

PANIC, ANXIETY, PHOBIA: WHICH IS WHICH?

Everyone gets nervous. Who hasn't felt the familiar but unpleasant rush of stomach flutters, the clammy palms and the trembling chills just before a big date, a dentist appointment, or a job interview? It's an everyday part of life, and it has very little to do with the kind of anxiety disorders we're talking about. For one thing, normal anxiety has an external and obvious trigger: the date, the dentist, paying your bills, or whatever. A little anxiety may actually be good—it can improve your motivation and performance.

Sometimes, however, the amount of anxiety or fear is inappropriately high given the present situation. This overreaction constitutes an abnormal anxiety response. Later in the book we will examine all of the various abnormal anxiety responses, including those that can result in spontaneous panic attacks.

Victims may be riding a bus, driving a car, talking to a friend, or quietly reading a book at home when the terror, seemingly unrelated to surrounding events, begins.

The first panic attack starts a ripple effect of physical and psychological associations that may eventually cause phobias to develop. In some individuals it may even lead to obsessive-compulsive disorders, or perhaps a generalized state of abnormal, ongoing anxiety, conditions that are defined below. We'll take a more detailed look at each of these other conditions in later chapters, but for now, let's define a few essential terms that we will use throughout the book.

Panic Attack. The panic attack (PA) is a sudden, rapid onset of disabling terror, characterized by shortness of breath, dizziness, palpitations, trembling, shaking, sweating, choking and other severe and frightening symptoms. PAs come out of nowhere and disappear just as suddenly, leaving their victims physically exhausted and emotionally wrung out. Victims often report feelings of dread and impending doom, for no apparent reasons. Some panic attack sufferers claim feelings of disorientation or separation from reality, as though they're watching the attack happen from a distance or through a thick fog. Often they believe they are dying, going crazy, or losing complete control of themselves. Almost all describe an almost overwhelming urge to flee.

Many panic attack victims who experience chest discomfort and breathing difficulties rush to emergency rooms, convinced they're having a heart attack. One patient of mine, an influential real estate developer, went to three different emergency rooms during one three-week period, each time complaining of a heart attack. He had all the outward signs of a heart attack, even crushing pain radiating down his left arm, but no physiological changes to indicate that a heart attack had occurred—no ECG changes, no cardiac enzymes, nothing. Each time he stayed in the ER for hours, never making it into the coronary care unit, but always being told he needed to calm down. Nobody wanted to tell this powerful developer that he should see a psychiatrist. Finally, the man's longtime administrative assistant first suggested, then insisted that he see a psychiatrist—she even called my office to make an appointment. It seems she had read that panic attacks sometimes appeared to be heart attacks. Today he's doing fine, all because his assistant knew more than those emergency-room physicians.

Nor was my patient alone. One study suggests that one third of all cardiology patients seeking consultation are actually reporting the symptoms of a panic disorder.

Since the onset of panic attacks can't be predicted, the anxiety-ridden dread of the next attack is, as we'll see, an important factor in the worsening of the anxiety disorder.

Phobias. A phobia is a deep, persistent, abnormal fear or dread of a certain object or situation. Phobia sufferers are often so incapacitated by their fears that they are unable to lead normal lives.

The most common type of phobia is the simple phobia, in which the victim develops a fear of a specific object or situation: heights, closed spaces, or, as we'll see in the next chapter, birds. Simple phobias range from A to Z, from aerophobia (fear of the air) to zoophobia (fear of animals).

In the more complex social phobias, fears are associated with social situations in which the victim may be the focus of attention, such as giving a speech, dancing, dining in public, or meeting new people. The fear of public humiliation is a common component of these phobias.

Common, garden-variety "stage fright"—the kind that gives an actor the jitters before he goes on stage—is something most of us have experienced; it is similar to the social phobias but is technically known as performance anxiety. Usually, when we experience this mild but troubling fear, we can take a deep breath and then go on with our lives. But if the fear becomes extremely intense and is incapacitating—to the point, for instance, that it prevents the actor from performing at all—then it's labeled a phobia. One ex-patient of mine, a very famous rock star, had such severe stage fright that he consumed several bottles of cough syrup before performing. The codeine in the cough syrup, when taken in massive dosages, would calm his nerves enough for the star to face his adoring audience. He consumed so much cough syrup that he actually became addicted—I had to detoxify him before I could begin treatment for his stage fright. Ten years after treatment, he is a successful (if somewhat aging) rock star who has overcome his fear of performing with the aid of low dosages of propranolol, a common, non-addicting blood-pressure medication.

But what looks like stage fright can sometimes be a full-fledged panic attack. In 1981, while performing for thousands of her loyal fans, singer Carly Simon experienced a panic attack onstage.

"I had two choices," Carly told a *New York Times* reporter. "I could either leave the stage and say I was sick or tell the audience the truth. I decided to tell them I was having an anxiety attack and they were incredibly supportive. They said 'Go with it—we'll be with you.' "

But even the audience's support didn't help. Two songs later, her heart was still pounding. Desperate, Carly invited people on the stage.

"About fifty people came up, and it was like an encounter group. They rubbed my arms and my legs and said 'We love you,' and I was able to finish the first show."

But her panic attacks led to a fear of performing—Carly didn't appear for her next show and for the next eight years she avoided live performances. Fortunately, successful treatment has allowed her to return to the stage.

As in Carly Simon's case, it's thought that phobias are born when the victim of a panic attack associates the attack with a specific object or situation. For example, if you're in a car when your first panic attack strikes, you may develop a phobia of driving, of bridges or highways, or even of automobiles in general.

As more panic attacks strike in different places, phobias multiply and become more pervasive. Finally, the patient may develop *agoraphobia*. This is the most crippling phobia, since its victims develop a fear of so many objects and situations they often become totally housebound. And in some cases, agoraphobia may even occur without the agoraphobic associating a panic attack with a specific phobia. For these agoraphobics, even the fear of a potential panic attack occurring in an uncontrollable environment (called a "fear of fear") may lead to agoraphobia.

In some severe cases of agoraphobia, victims even confine themselves to their bed, or a particular chair, leaving the safe perch only when absolutely necessary, and returning as soon as possible.

Generalized Anxiety Disorder (GAD). For many years, GAD and panic attacks were lumped together under the term "anxiety neurosis." Recently psychiatry has realized that these two conditions differ: GAD lacks the specific, spontaneous panic attacks that characterize panic disorder. GAD now is defined as the chronic anxiety that occurs over "a period of six months or longer, during which the individual has been bothered more days than not by unrealistic or excessive worry ... about two or more life circumstances." This vague description is a good example of the type of subjective diagnosis favored by the diagnostic "bible" of traditional psychiatrists, the *Diagnostic and Statistical Manual of Mental Disorders,* third edition, revised, or DSM-III-R for short. (I'll have much more to say about this book later.)

Although it lacks the knockout punch of a full-blown panic attack, the wearying, relentless tension of this chronic condition can often, in the mind of the patient, become more troubling than even a panic attack would be.

The symptoms of GAD attacks develop more slowly, last much longer, and fade away more gradually than the blitzkrieg symptoms of panic attacks. Also, patients with acute GAD rarely report the feelings of doom and impending death that are quite common in PAs. And GAD appears to occur earlier in life, perhaps even in childhood, while panic attacks usually begin in the early to mid-twenties.

We usually determine that someone is suffering from GAD when he or she has unrealistic or excessive worries about at least two life circumstances. For example, if you are continually concerned about the health of your child when he hasn't been sick in months, and at the same time worried about money

---

DO PHOBIAS MEAN YOU'RE WEAK?

If you think that only people with a "weak personality" suffer from phobias or other anxiety disorders, consider this Who's Who of famous phobics:

- Frederick the Great, King of Prussia, was so afraid of water that he wouldn't wash. His servants were forced to wipe his face clean with a dry towel.
- Napoleon Bonaparte nearly conquered the world, but he couldn't conquer the obsession that forced him to stop in front of tall buildings and count the windows one by one.
- Edgar Allan Poe, a famous claustrophobic, used his real-life fear of closed spaces to illuminate such classic tales of confinement as "The Premature Burial" and "The Black Cat."
- Harry Houdini, who built a legend out of his ability to escape from tight spaces, was perhaps the most unlikely claustrophobe of all time. In his act, he was perfectly comfortable with confinement and would happily crawl into steamer trunks which would be dunked in water, or safes which would be dangled high above the ground. But twice in his life he was accidentally trapped in close quarters—once in a phone booth and again in a bathroom stall. Both times, he panicked, becoming violent and hysterical. After that, he'd never leave home without a special set of lock picks that could free him from the inside.
- Sir Laurence Olivier recently revealed that he suffered from bouts of stage fright so severe that he'd actually lose his voice.

when you've just gotten a healthy raise, your anxiety is out of control and you may be suffering from GAD.

Theoretically, at least according to DSM-III-R, GAD can even exist in the presence of panic disorder. It's up to the psychiatrist to determine if the patient is really worrying about the panic attacks, or if the patient's worries are connected to other life circumstances.

Obsessive-Compulsive Disorder. By obsessions and compulsions I do not mean the attachments we all have to our favorite coffee mug or local sports team. Rather, obsessive-compulsive disorder is a more complicated condition, related to anxiety, in which a patient develops certain unwanted thoughts or some pattern of compulsive, ritualistic behavior that interferes with normal functioning. It is important to realize that victims of OCD do not receive pleasure from their actions.

Obsessions may take the shape of intrusive thoughts involving repugnant or socially unacceptable images. For instance, a victim may be plagued by the unwanted thought that he will kill his children or commit an obscene act.

Obsessions are often bizarre. For example, one patient reported that he could not eat in a restaurant without thinking he would vomit. This obsession would not occur when at home, even in the presence of others. However, when he was in a restaurant, the obsession would become so strong that he could not continue eating.

Compulsive behavior most commonly involves rituals such as hand washing, repetitive actions, or constant checking to see if doors are locked, lights are turned off, windows are closed, and so on. For example, a person may develop a compulsion which forces him to repeat all his actions four times: He'll enter a room four times, turn the light on and off four times, sit down and stand up four times, say hello four times in a row.

Obsessive-compulsives aren't crazy. Instead, their condition seems to be clearly related to a biochemical imbalance in the brain. These disorders can be effectively treated with medications just now being used by psychiatrists.

In addition, obsessions and compulsions are believed to be

related to relieving anxiety. Compulsions result when the victim of anxiety believes that a certain ritual produces relief. He turns to it again and again, until ultimately the behavior becomes automatic.

Obsessions are essentially the mental counterpart of compulsions, and they work much the same way—only they involve repetitious thoughts and ideas instead of actual behaviors. We believe that the mind returns to these images again and again as a way of trying to cope with anxiety.

Posttraumatic Stress Disorder. Commonly associated with veterans of war, this condition can strike anyone who has undergone a severely stressful situation, including police or firefighters, crime or accident victims and witnesses to catastrophe.

People with this disorder relive traumatic events through nightmares or terrifying flashbacks. In very rare cases, victims dislocate from reality and fall into extended flashbacks which can last minutes, hours, even days.

This syndrome also robs people of their emotional suppleness: They experience a kind of psychic numbing that drains their enjoyment of their friends, family, and activities—of life in general.

One symptom of this condition is a heightened alertness. These patients are so high-strung that a sudden loud noise may cause them to jump or take cover. Other symptoms include insomnia, impaired memory, depression, "flashbacks" and an inability to concentrate or focus on completing a task.

Adjustment Disorder. A period of adjustment following a divorce or job loss is to be expected—most of us are familiar with the difficulties of coping with an unexpected or upsetting event. However, when a reaction following a stressful event impairs our social activities, relationships, occupation, or school work, or results in excessive symptoms it is classified as an adjustment disorder (AD). Symptoms of AD can include nervousness, depressed mood, tearfulness, a feeling of hopelessness, and an inability to function well in school or work.

Those are the most common subtypes of anxiety disorders. I want to emphasize that most anxiety patients suffer from more than one of these conditions. It's important for you to know that the presence of overlapping symptoms in no way lessens your chances of getting well.

ROOTS IN BIOLOGY

Early indications that anxiety disorder could be a physical rather than strictly psychological problem came when family studies began to show a possible genetic link for anxiety disorders. Researchers began to notice that anxiety patients tended to have one or more close relatives who also suffered from anxiety disease. Through epidemiological studies, it was determined that close relatives of anxiety patients were more likely to develop the disorder themselves than were people from families with no history of the condition. Mathematical analysis hinted at a dominant-gene pattern, in which the genetic predisposition to anxiety could be passed on by one parent.

The case for a genetic component was strengthened by more recent studies involving anxiety in fraternal and identical twins raised separately since their birth. These studies showed that it was more likely for *both* twins to suffer from anxiety if they were identical. Since both the fraternal and the identical twins had been raised separately but in similar environments, the findings of the studies strongly implied that genetic factors, which each set of identical twins shared, played a more important role than environmental factors, which all the sets of twins had in common.

So if the traditional psychiatrists are right and abnormal anxiety is a product of an individual's inability to cope with the stresses of the environment, we should expect that people who grew up in the same environment would face an equal vulnerability to anxiety disease. But the twin studies show us that susceptibility to abnormal anxiety really seems to be an inheritable trait, a conclusion that drives us to look for important biological causes of the disorder.

We still don't know which gene or genes to blame, nor do we understand the exact nature of the biological abnormality that would predispose a patient toward anxiety disorders, but every day researchers are turning up promising new leads.

One exciting area of investigation involves a nerve cell body in the brain called the locus ceruleus that manufactures stimulating chemicals called catecholamines. It's believed that patients suffering from anxiety disorders have excessive catecholamine activity or too many of these nerve endings, or that the ones they have are hyperactive. Meanwhile, other nerve endings, whose job it is to balance the catecholamines by releasing self-tranquilizing chemicals, aren't performing effectively, because of either a scarcity of the nerve endings or a weakness in the tranquilizers. So, unchecked, the abundance of stimulants creates a biological reaction of anxiety, triggered by chemicals in the brain.

Another fascinating lead was first discovered back in the 1940s, when researchers at Harvard found that some anxiety sufferers who exercised experienced a distinct worsening of anxiety symptoms (although exercise may relieve anxiety for others, as we will discuss in a later chapter). Blood tests revealed an unusually elevated level of lactate—a by-product of exercise—in their bloodstreams.

Building on that information, other researchers found that injections of sodium lactate could spontaneously trigger symptoms of panic attack symptoms in subjects who had previously experienced abnormal panic. By interrupting the infusions, the researchers discovered they could stop the symptoms. Significantly, people who hadn't previously suffered panic attacks showed no reaction to the lactate whatsoever. This was strong evidence of a biological base for anxiety, since the attacks were being triggered not by any environmental factors, but by a specific chemical that occurred naturally in the body. If a chemical could trigger an attack in the lab, why not on the street, at church, on the golf course, or anywhere else?

More evidence appeared when certain drugs were found to interrupt the panic-inducing function of the lactate. Researchers discovered that by spiking the lactate injections with calcium ions, panic attacks could be blocked. More recently, it was found that other drugs—the MAO inhibitors, tricyclics, and triazolobenzodiazepine—could stop lactate from causing panic attacks in panic attack patients. The biological evidence was mounting.

Next, researchers using new lab technology bolstered the argument for a biological cause. For example, some investigators began using a sophisticated technique called positron emission tomography, or P.E.T. P.E.T. scans gave researchers the ability to peer into the actual physical workings of the brain—to study the brain function of anxiety patients.

P.E.T. scans on subjects undergoing lactate-induced panic attacks began to show an abnormal flow of blood in a small region of the brain, called the parahippocampal gyrus, which is associated with emotional expression and fear. Although researchers couldn't explain the precise link between this asymmetrical bloodflow and the panic state, they had accomplished an important achievement: Not only had they spotted a definite physical abnormality that could be related to the ongoing panic attack, they had taken its picture!

In the 1970s, I worked with Yale researcher Eugene Redmond, Jr., M.D., on a series of pioneering experiments which built upon all these findings. We produced even more tangible evidence of a biological root of abnormal anxiety.

Our studies involved stump-tailed monkeys and focused on a small region in the lower brain called the locus ceruleus (LC). By stimulating the LC with drugs or mild electrical shocks, we were able to elicit symptoms of anxiety: perspiration, pulse, and blood pressure would increase; the monkeys would fidget, bite their nails, even wring their hands, apparently in tremendous fear.

We also discovered that by damaging the LC or by administering certain drugs, we could interrupt the panic state. In fact, some monkeys with their LC function destroyed showed no fear at all, even in the most threatening situations.

As you can see, the evidence for a biological connection in

anxiety disorders is compelling. We still don't completely understand the mechanics of the biological abnormalities behind panic and anxiety disorders, but there are certainly some good leads that point toward the fact that your problem is *not* entirely in your mind.

THE ROAD TO AGORAPHOBIA: HOW PANIC PROGRESSES TO PHOBIA

So it seems that anxiety disorders may begin with biological or biochemical abnormalities in the brain. Now let's take a look at how the panic and anxiety triggered by these physical conditions combine with psychological factors to create the kind of incapacitating anxiety states that can ruin lives.

The first step is the panic attack. Because of some brain function gone awry, you are one day ambushed by a bolt of fear and dread so strong and so terrifying that your life is instantly changed. You wrack your brain trying to find a reason for the attack. Is it stress? Is it your heart? Are you losing your mind?

When you fail to identify a specific trigger, suddenly *everything* seems as if it could be a potential spark for a second attack. Just as a patient with an unstable heart condition, waiting for a bypass operation, lives in the minute-by-minute fear that some stress or startling noise will trigger a heart attack, you find yourself increasingly preoccupied with the possibility that a second attack, as unexpected and devastating as the first, will explode at any moment, and again, you won't know why.

Research tells us that unexpected traumatic situations have a more severe and lasting impact than traumas that happen to people who have some reason to expect a frightening experience. For example, a trained policeman who finds himself in a gun battle with criminals will probably endure fewer and milder emotional aftereffects than a civilian who is surprised in an alley by a robber with a gun.

The intense, unexpected pain of a panic attack strikes at the heart of the victim's sense of security and well-being. It becomes difficult for that person ever to feel completely safe, to put the memory of the first panic attack behind him.

The most troubling thought for these patients is that they have absolutely no warning that an attack is coming and no way to pinpoint its source. They figure that if they knew the cause of the panic, they could avoid it in the future. But since they have no clue, their minds begin to search for other ways to relieve the tension. Subtly, defense mechanisms take shape that may give the patient some short-term comfort, but in the long term just create more problems. Here's why:

Let's say you are at the ocean when your first panic attack strikes. You can't find any rational cause. But your mind may have already begun to associate the awful experience with the sea. The sea itself may begin to make you feel anxious. Avoiding the sea may bring relief, and even a sense that you can exert some control over your fears. The more you avoid the sea, the better you feel; at the same time, your feeling better reinforces your urges to avoid the sea. Very rapidly, a conditioned response develops, reinforcing the avoidance behavior. Soon your fear and dread of the sea become overwhelming, and before you realize it, a phobia is born.

If it stopped at this point, it would be bad enough. But things can get even worse. In time, even though you avoid the ocean, the mere thought of it triggers anxiety. And as the conditioning process continues, your phobic behavior generalizes and intensifies. You begin to fear swimming pools, then you dread taking a bath. Finally, your pulse pounds and your anxiety skyrockets whenever you see a glass of water.

As the anxiety disorder worsens, you suffer more panic attacks, causing more avoidance behavior, which, in turn, triggers additional phobias. These too can fan out and generalize, until your life becomes hopelessly entangled in an inescapable web of terrors.

Patients at this point in anxiety disorders face two different kinds of anxiety. One is biologically based, triggered by the underlying abnormalities in the brain; the other results from the mental tension caused by various phobias.

To complicate things even further, we've found that in some cases of advanced anxiety, normal body functioning may trigger panic. A person's heart may pound while climbing steps, for instance. Since this is a common symptom of panic, the increased heart rate may spark the attack, as if the body had learned to recognize that symptom as a cause for a panic response.

THE NEED FOR A NEW APPROACH TO TREATMENT

Having seen the complex nature of the cause and progress of the anxiety disorders, you should understand why any effective treatment must embrace the biological, psychological, and environmental aspects of anxiety.

It also becomes clear that behavioral or psychological therapies, applied with complete disregard for any possible body-based causes, are doomed to fail when treating panic attacks. Why, then, do millions of psychiatrists, psychologists, and mental health professionals ignore all the new information coming out of our research and continue to diagnose and treat anxiety as a purely psychological phenomenon?

I can't say for sure. Maybe it's simply human nature, but too many traditional psychiatrists have bought into the "conventional wisdom" that they first learned in school and their residency programs—wisdom that may be twenty, thirty, even fifty years out of date. In too many cases, it's as if they think all that needs to be said on the subject of psychiatry has already been said. It's as if the entire profession were frozen in time. While all other branches of medicine are energetically expanding their horizons, embracing new knowledge and technologies, and rewriting the textbooks every day, the vital job of exploring and understanding the problems of the brain and the mind is being neglected by the very people whose patients stand to benefit most from increased knowledge.

Psychiatry needs to reconnect with its medical origins. It needs to open up to lab research and biological testing and the interplay of new ideas. That's the basic message that biopsychiatry brings.

Nowhere is the message of the biopsychiatrist more urgent than it is in the case of anxiety disorders. In the past few years, my fellow biopsychiatrists and I have seen hundreds of seemingly hopeless anxiety cases referred to us by other mental health professionals as classic "nonresponders." Many of these patients had been suffering longer than I've been in practice. They came to us with little hope. Many had been told simply to learn to live with their problems. Most doubted we could help them, since nobody else seemed to be able to.

But, with proper diagnosis and an appropriate medical and psychological treatment plan, the good news became apparent: These patients have shed their fears and today are living happier, more productive lives.

Biopsychiatry is not magic, and it's not a miracle cure. It's rigorous medical science. It's what *all* psychiatry should be. I believe that the future of psychiatry and the quality of psychiatric care depend upon a widespread acceptance of biopsychiatry's principles. Instead, for more than fifty years, psychiatrists have been steering the profession, at breakneck speed, in the opposite direction. As we'll see, that poor judgment is primarily to blame for the sad state in which psychiatry finds itself today.

CHAPTER THREE

ALL THAT'S ANXIETY ISN'T PANIC... ALL THAT'S FEAR ISN'T PHOBIA

*I*magine a time in our distant evolutionary past when clans of our earliest ancestors roamed open savannas in search of food. Life was a struggle, and danger lurked everywhere in the tall grass. But the alert, uncomplicated minds of those hunters and gatherers weren't cluttered by anticipatory fears. They were wary of other predators, but not fearful of them. Fear was a tool; it helped them survive. When the cheetah approaches, that's the time for fear. When there is no cheetah, there is no fear, and the search for food and water continues.

But then one of the clan steps into a small clearing and finds himself eye to eye with a hungry leopard. Now the man feels fear, as real as hunger or thirst or pain. His heart pounds, his muscles tense, and his breath comes in gasps as his entire body automatically prepares itself to flee or do battle.

But in seconds, other members of the clan appear, and the leopard, spooked by their arrival, runs away. As the big cat slips through the tall grass, the frightened hunter relaxes. In minutes, his system is back to normal and thoughts of the leopard have vanished, replaced by the more pressing preoccupation with finding food and water.

The "fight or flight" response, which vastly improved the evolutionary odds of those early humans, is the basis of anxiety, a primal warning instinct which we share with many animals. Strictly speaking, it is not really a fear, but the body's instinctual response to fear, an alarm bell rung by the perception of imminent danger.

In more intelligent creatures, this response becomes more complex. Let's jump ahead a few hundred generations, when more intellectually complex humans, capable of foresight, crouched in their cavern homes and worried about the future: Would the winter be hard? Would the hunting improve? And didn't I see a cave bear out on those ledges this afternoon?

Today, we don't spend much time worrying about cave bears and confrontations with hungry leopards, but we do have plenty to worry about. On the grand scale there's the state of the economy, the nuclear threat, the depletion of the ozone layer, and the rising rate of crime, for starters. In our personal lives we face stresses from careers, relationships, illnesses, and financial problems. On any given day, the average human being faces conflicts and tensions capable of sending anxiety levels through the roof. But unlike the cave man, we cannot choose between fighting or fleeing for the majority of our stressful situations. Oh, we may think about running away to Tahiti or even nailing our boss with a good right cross, but we never (or almost never) do it. Instead we may allow the anxiety to build within us. Sometimes our worries nag us for days, or even weeks: we become preoccupied with a problem at work, for example, or a marital conflict, or our inability to pay the bills. These worries may cause an unpleasant level of tension in our lives, but they may also spur us on to seek that job promotion, to go back to school to get our degree, to make our lives more rewarding. This level of tension is certainly anxiety, but—unless it intensifies—it is *not* an anxiety disorder.

There is a sharp distinction between normal anxiety and the pathological conditions psychiatrists call anxiety disorders. Think of normal anxiety as the body's alarm system. In the presence of danger, this alarm system, triggered by the central nervous system, revs up the cardiac and respiratory systems and dumps adrenaline and other stimulating hormones into the bloodstream. In a matter of seconds, we're pushed to our physical peak, ready for a burst of furious physical activity that will either help us confront the threat or carry us away to safety. The survival benefits of this response are obvious at every level of the evolutionary chain.

But what about human beings, with our ability to think ahead, anticipate and imagine? For us, the anxiety alarm is set off not only by the presence of actual physical danger, but also by potential or intangible "threats" which, in reality, threaten no danger at all: giving a speech, asking for a date, and so on.

Simply put, normal anxiety is a reasonable response to a specific, identifiable, external stimulus, whether the source of your anxiety is an armed robber confronting you with a gun, or the fact that your report card is on its way in the mail.

What happens, though, when the amount of anxiety we experience is inappropriately high, given the danger? This type of anxiety is called *exogenous anxiety,* because it results from anxiety sources generated outside *(exo-)* the individual. The student who finds answering questions so difficult that he begins to miss important classes and the businesswoman who finds flying so traumatic that she refuses a job promotion requiring frequent travel are victims of exogenous anxiety.

A second form of anxiety, called *chronic anxiety,* occurs when anxiety levels remain above normal for an extended period of time. A state of chronic anxiety will often develop into generalized anxiety disorder (see page 74 for more information on generalized anxiety disorder).

The third type of anxiety is known as *endogenous anxiety.* "Endogenous" means "born from within." This type of anxiety occurs when no threat can be identified. Instead of responding to a real external threat, the anxiety alarm system is tripped from within; a switch is thrown and the body reacts with all the severe physiological stresses of a full-blown fear response.

As we'll see, exciting research efforts are showing us that endogenous anxiety is most likely a genetic trait that plays a key role in the genesis of panic disorder and combines with the process of conditioning to foster the development of other anxiety disorders.

PANIC DISORDER

For years, panic disorder and generalized anxiety disorders were lumped together in a single classification known as "anxiety neurosis." It was believed that the difference between chronic generalized anxiety and panic anxiety was simply one of degree. In other words, as chronic anxiety persisted over a period of time, it gradually intensified until it reached the flash point and erupted into an explosion of panic.

But more recently, the spontaneous attacks associated with panic disorder have separated this condition from the chronic anxiety typical of generalized anxiety disorder.

The severity of panic attacks can vary. In a full-scale attack the victim experiences not only the intense physiological responses, but also psychologic symptoms, including depersonalization, an overwhelming sense of dread, and the terrifying certainty that death is only moments away. On the other hand, milder attacks may be experienced mainly as physical discomfort, with none of the attendant psychological responses.

In some cases, the panic victim experiences only one attack. More often, attacks occur several times a week, and in severe cases even daily. Between attacks, most patients experience some degree of anticipatory anxiety related to the fear of the next attack.

Sometimes, after a period of weeks or months, the attacks will cease spontaneously, but it's more likely that the condition will persist for years, with panic-free periods of remission followed by a return of the full-blown attacks.

To its victims, a panic attack is an unprovoked, inexplicable ambush of terror. It's the unpredictable nature of the attacks which gives panic disorder its devastating effect. Panic patients quickly realize that their attacks can strike anywhere, at any time, with no warning and no chance for escape.

It is this unpredictability of panic attacks that differentiates them from the experiences of those who willingly choose anxiety-provoking situations. Racecar drivers, mountain climbers, amusement-park devotees, and even sports fans love the rush of adrenaline that causes our hearts to beat faster, our mouths to dry, and our blood pressure to rise. Our reactions to these anxiety-provoking situations may vary, but the majority of willing participants find these events satisfying and enjoyable. To our bodies, however, there is little physiological difference between a ride down Space Mountain and a full-blown panic attack. What is different is the feeling of control—we *choose* to go on an amusement-park ride, but we do *not* choose when to have a panic attack. This lack of control, the very randomness of panic attacks, is what makes these attacks so terrifying. A panic attack victim often feels like a prisoner on a roller-coaster ride that won't end.

THE FEAR INVENTORY

People ask me all the time how they can tell whether their fears are normal or constitute phobias. A conversation I had recently with a few of my associates at Fair Oaks reminded me how odd and disturbing a phobia can be for a person experiencing it, particularly if the phobia seems to materialize suddenly, with no previous panic attacks or unpleasant associations.

"Is there anything, anything at all, no matter how absurd, that really terrifies you?" I asked one day over lunch. As usual, I received some of the standard replies:

"I'm scared of walking through Central Park at night."

"I can't stand snakes; they make me sick."

But on that day, a hospital administrator named Janet responded with a more unusual fear. After hesitating briefly, she said, "I know this sounds crazy, but I have this real fear of birds. I'm not talking about eagles, hawks, or condors, but your average, everyday bird. The funny thing, though, is that I never knew I was afraid of them until a couple of weeks ago, when we gave in to my five-year-old's desperate desire for a pet. Well, my husband's allergic to cats, and a dog seemed like too much trouble, so we thought we'd get a parakeet. At first, I didn't think twice about it.

"But one Saturday, when my husband was cleaning the cage, the bird escaped and started flying around the house. I freaked out, started screaming—somehow I thought that little bird was going to attack me. I finally hid myself in a closet, but I couldn't stop screaming. This sounds so stupid. I know that little bird would never attack me, but I couldn't stop myself. Finally, after a few minutes, my husband caged the bird again, but it took me a half hour to calm down. From that moment on, I was terrified that the bird would escape again. No question about it, that bird had to go—my husband returned it the next day to the pet shop. I can laugh about it now, but if there's a hell, I know what mine would be . . . "

Janet then added as an afterthought, "I hope this doesn't

mean I'm crazy, but for years I've been fascinated by pictures of birds. Walk into my office and you'll see several photographs of them. I'm sort of a collector. The pictures don't bother me —fact is, I just bought another one yesterday."

I assured Janet that she sure wasn't crazy, that a fear of birds is a common fear—even her collection of bird photographs could be seen as an overcompensation for her fear. Some people respond to their fears with a challenge to themselves, a *counterphobia*, in effect: A man with a fear of flying may become an expert pilot, a woman with a fear of public speaking may become a powerful orator. Janet's collection of photographs was such a counterphobia.

Now, would I consider Janet's fear of birds to be a phobia? Yes. Is it a problem? No. Not unless her fear worsened to the point where any bird—even on a distant telephone wire—terrified her, or if she suddenly decided to become an ornithologist. As it now stands, her fear isn't likely to interfere with her life.

Other fears that people admit to, such as being afraid of walking through Central Park alone at night, or of flying through a hurricane, aren't phobias, they're simply common sense. In some cases, a fear may be a little excessive—for example, neighbors of mine may be a little too protective of their child. But since their somewhat excessive precautions don't really interfere with their lives, their worries are essentially harmless.

Clearly not every fear is a phobia. The first criterion I use in evaluating whether any fear constitutes a phobia is: Does the individual actively strive to avoid the fear? If the answer is yes, the next question is: Does this avoidance negatively interfere with the individual's life. As a psychiatrist evaluating a prospective phobia patient's case, I consider these two questions the most important that I must ask.

Of course, the circumstances of your life may prevent a fear from ever developing into a phobia. You may have a fear of walking through Central Park at night, but unless you are a police officer assigned to that beat, you'll never have to confront this fear. Hence there is no need to indulge in avoidance behavior and your fear will not develop into a phobia.

However, some individuals' fears cannot conveniently be avoided. For these people, even understandable fears can sometimes develop into full-blown phobias.

For example, a colleague of mine recently told me of a

CHILDHOOD FEARS

Just as some levels of anxiety and fear are normal responses to actual threats, some fears are normal at different stages of development. Most parents are very aware of their children's unusual fears. My own son, Kyle, went through a period of fearing "slimers," his term for those creepy, ghost-like characters in *Ghostbusters*. Other childhood fears, such as a fear of loud noises, animals, darkness, and school, are also very common. Parents often mistakenly try to minimize them, using logic to help overcome their child's fear. Telling a five-year-old that "there's no reason to be afraid of the dark, there's no such thing as a ghost, monsters or bogeymen" really does not help. In the child's mind, ghosts and monsters are real.

A far better strategy involves giving the child some control over the situation. A child's control can be enhanced by giving rewards for perseverance through a situation, or a "magic word" that will make the monster disappear. As a physician and a father, I know that a child's fear of doctors can be greatly reduced if the doctor gives the child some control over the examination—merely asking the child to select which finger to be pricked will greatly help the child feel more comfortable.

While most children pass unscathed through their fears, others with severe or prolonged fears require professional treatment. A recent survey in Ontario, Canada found that 6 percent of children four to eleven years old had fears worthy of treatment. Unfortunately, only 20 percent of these children ever received professional help.

---

patient, named Wilson, who quit his job as a medical technician because he had developed an extreme AIDS phobia. Wilson's job as a medical technician required that he handle many substances containing serious and potentially communicable diseases, including AIDS. However, proper precautions, such as double-gloving and frequent washing, virtually eliminate even the most remote possibility of acquiring any of these diseases. Although Wilson had a long-standing fear of contracting a number of communicable diseases, from hepatitis to tuberculosis, he had lived with his fear by steadfastly following the safety precautions. But the threat of AIDS pushed Wilson "over the edge." Even the most stringent safety practices couldn't allay his fears, and he soon quit his job.

Unfortunately, quitting his job and avoiding any contaminated blood didn't help. His phobia deteriorated into obsessive-compulsive disorder. Wilson began washing his hands several times each hour; he felt compelled to wash his clothes six times, using several gallons of bleach, before he felt they were "safe" to wear. (He had destroyed every article of clothing he had worn in the laboratory, including his shoes.) He refused to touch a doorknob unless he was wearing rubber gloves. Every facet of his life was affected by his phobia. Fortunately, Wilson realized the desperate nature of his situation. Recently he entered a treatment program, and all preliminary indications point to a subsequent return to a normal and productive life.

Is the fear of AIDS normal for a medical technician? Yes, and the normal response to this fear is to observe established safety procedures. An AIDS fear like Wilson's, which interfered with his lifelong career and livelihood, is definitely not normal.

Why do phobias exist? In subsequent chapters we'll explore in detail the possible physiological and genetic causes. But for now, if I had to give a "capsule" explanation of why phobias exist, it would be: *Most phobias exist because a "survival center" has gone haywire.*

Our survival centers are responsible for keeping us alive—if we cannot breathe because a piece of plastic covers our nose and mouth, our "suffocation survival center" forces us to tear the plastic away while we gasp for air. Similarly, other survival centers in susceptible individuals may be affected by exposure to heights, snakes, insects, birds, or other potential—if remote —threats to life. These fears can be classified as evolutionary; they represent a response to factors that were undoubtedly a greater threat to our ancestors. Survival centers in phobia-prone individuals may be overly sensitive to these external "threats."

Even many extremely obscure and unusual phobias, such as the fear of peanut butter sticking to the roof of the mouth, can be viewed as a means of avoiding a "threat." Breathing and swallowing would both be very difficult with a gob of peanut butter lodged in the throat, so for susceptible individuals, peanut butter may represent a threat to their suffocation or choking survival centers.

The threats posed by some phobias, such as the fear of strangers or the fear of open places, are very subtle and may reflect our ancestors' worries about being attacked by human predators. Other phobias, such as the fear of public speaking, or the fear of sex, may conjure up atavistic fears of being ostracized from human communities—a fate that could have been fatal for early humans.

Obviously, there are many fears that can afflict us. To assess your own susceptibility to fears, I recommend you complete the following inventory my colleagues and I used at Fair Oaks Hospital:

THE FAIR OAKS FEAR INVENTORY

Do you have a fear of:	NO FEAR	SOME FEAR	FAIRLY FEARFUL	VERY FEARFUL	EXTREMELY FEARFUL
Airplanes	___	___	___	___	___
Angry people	___	___	___	___	___
Automobiles	___	___	___	___	___
Bats	___	___	___	___	___
Being alone	___	___	___	___	___
Being criticized	___	___	___	___	___
Being hurt	___	___	___	___	___
Being ignored	___	___	___	___	___
Being in an elevator	___	___	___	___	___
Being in strange places	___	___	___	___	___
Being robbed	___	___	___	___	___
Being teased	___	___	___	___	___
Being unable to cope without assistance	___	___	___	___	___
Being watched while working	___	___	___	___	___
Birds	___	___	___	___	___
Blood—animal	___	___	___	___	___
Blood—human	___	___	___	___	___
Blushing	___	___	___	___	___
Cats	___	___	___	___	___
Cemeteries	___	___	___	___	___
Closed places	___	___	___	___	___
Crawling insects	___	___	___	___	___
Crossing streets	___	___	___	___	___
Crowds	___	___	___	___	___
Darkness	___	___	___	___	___
Dead animals	___	___	___	___	___
Dead people	___	___	___	___	___

THE FAIR OAKS FEAR INVENTORY (continued)

Do you have a fear of:	NO FEAR	SOME FEAR	FAIRLY FEARFUL	VERY FEARFUL	EXTREMELY FEARFUL
Dentists	___	___	___	___	___
Dirt	___	___	___	___	___
Doctors	___	___	___	___	___
Dogs	___	___	___	___	___
Driving	___	___	___	___	___
Dull weather	___	___	___	___	___
Dying	___	___	___	___	___
Entering a room where other people are already seated	___	___	___	___	___
Failure	___	___	___	___	___
Falling	___	___	___	___	___
Fast driving	___	___	___	___	___
Feeling angry	___	___	___	___	___
Feeling disapproved of	___	___	___	___	___
Feeling rejected by others	___	___	___	___	___
Fighting	___	___	___	___	___
Fire	___	___	___	___	___
Flying insects	___	___	___	___	___
Germs	___	___	___	___	___
High places on land	___	___	___	___	___
Imaginary creatures	___	___	___	___	___
Irregular heartbeats	___	___	___	___	___
Journeys by car	___	___	___	___	___
Journeys by train	___	___	___	___	___
Large open spaces	___	___	___	___	___
Lightning	___	___	___	___	___
Looking down from high buildings	___	___	___	___	___

THE FAIR OAKS FEAR INVENTORY (*continued*)

Do you have a fear of:	NO FEAR	SOME FEAR	FAIRLY FEARFUL	VERY FEARFUL	EXTREMELY FEARFUL
Looking foolish	____	____	____	____	____
Losing control	____	____	____	____	____
Losing your job or failing in school	____	____	____	____	____
Losing your mind	____	____	____	____	____
Loss of memory	____	____	____	____	____
Loud voices	____	____	____	____	____
Making mistakes	____	____	____	____	____
Mice	____	____	____	____	____
Not accomplishing what you would like to do	____	____	____	____	____
Not being able to sleep	____	____	____	____	____
Nude men	____	____	____	____	____
Nude women	____	____	____	____	____
One person bullying another	____	____	____	____	____
Open wounds	____	____	____	____	____
Pain	____	____	____	____	____
Parting from friends	____	____	____	____	____
People in authority	____	____	____	____	____
People who seem insane	____	____	____	____	____
People with deformities	____	____	____	____	____
Prospect of a surgical operation	____	____	____	____	____
Receiving injections	____	____	____	____	____
Seeing other people receive injections	____	____	____	____	____
Sexual relations	____	____	____	____	____
Sick people	____	____	____	____	____

THE FAIR OAKS FEAR INVENTORY (*continued*)

Do you have a fear of:	NO FEAR	SOME FEAR	FAIRLY FEARFUL	VERY FEARFUL	EXTREMELY FEARFUL
Sight of deep water	____	____	____	____	____
Sight of fighting	____	____	____	____	____
Sirens	____	____	____	____	____
Snakes	____	____	____	____	____
Speaking in public	____	____	____	____	____
Standing in line	____	____	____	____	____
Strangers	____	____	____	____	____
Strange shapes	____	____	____	____	____
Sudden noises	____	____	____	____	____
Suicide	____	____	____	____	____
The opposite sex	____	____	____	____	____
Thunder	____	____	____	____	____
Tough-looking people	____	____	____	____	____
Ugly people	____	____	____	____	____
Guns or other weapons	____	____	____	____	____
Witnessing surgical operations	____	____	____	____	____
Worms	____	____	____	____	____

If you've responded to any of the above fears by checking off columns 3, 4, or 5 (fairly fearful, very fearful, or extremely fearful), you may be a candidate for developing avoidance behavior. Or you may find yourself already practicing elaborate behaviors to avoid confronting your fears. In either case, this book will provide valuable information that can help you overcome your fears and anxieties.

In the next section I'll describe how fears can turn into phobias, and how the other anxiety disorders can affect your life.

THE FEAR-PHOBIA-AGORAPHOBIA CONNECTION

Here are some real-life examples of phobia situations:

• A young woman, Carol, happily married and the mother of three, is morbidly afraid of thunderstorms. She can't really express why she's so afraid of storms—she doesn't really think she'll be harmed in any way. Still, during storms she hides in a part of the house far from any windows so that if lightning flashes she won't have to see it.

But Carol's fear doesn't start only with the storms. It begins whenever the weather report even forecasts stormy weather. If a storm approaches and her husband isn't at home, she'll often arrange to visit a friend, since companionship seems to diminish the fear.

Carol realizes that her fears are irrational, but that realization brings no comfort or lessening of the terror. In fact, she has noticed that her condition has been growing steadily worse.

• A twenty-year-old college student, Bill, has a fear of public speaking. He finds himself in a history class requiring lots of verbal interaction. Until now he has manipulated his schedule to avoid small discussion-type classes. If he couldn't manage to avoid a discussion class, he'd find a seat at the rear of the room and sit silently for an entire semester. Naturally his grades suffered, but it was better than the searing anxiety he felt whenever he was called on to answer a question or share an opinion in front of twenty or thirty strangers.

But this required history class is an exception. The professor insists that students take part in class discussions on a regular basis.

The first time Bill was called on he froze. Blood surged to his temples, his pulse pounded, and sweat beaded on his forehead. The other students turned to look at him, waiting for his reply, but Bill could get nothing out. His head swam, his thoughts scattered, and his throat clenched. Even if he could have thought of something to say, he wouldn't have been able to get it out.

Bill's anxiety continued to mount until he could no longer stand it. He slipped from his seat and fled the classroom. A sense of humiliation dogged him for days. He never returned to the class.

When asked to describe their symptoms, phobia victims don't call it mere fear; they're more likely to speak of dread, terror, and panic, and an irresistible urge to flee.

The word "phobia," as a matter of fact, comes from the Greek *phobos,* which means, among other things, flight.

The overpowering urge to flee an object or situation which holds no real threat of danger is a hallmark of a phobic disorder. In phobia victims like Bill and Carol and the millions of Americans whose lives are plagued by phobias, the phobic stimulus produces a flight response that is almost impossible to resist. Unfortunately, by fleeing the phobic situation, phobia sufferers only nourish their fears and allow them to grow stronger.

To see more clearly how the fear/avoidance cycle works, let's consider the case of a golfer with snake phobia who suddenly encounters a harmless garter snake in the rough. Instantly, he feels terror, and his body responds with extreme physiological reactions of phobic attack that grow deeper and more unbearable the longer he stays near the snake. Although the golfer knows the snake won't hurt him, he can't control his fears. It's as if every cell in his body were screaming at him to get out of there, and that's exactly what he does.

As he puts distance between himself and the snake, he feels his anxiety nosedive—his heartbeat stabilizes, the hard breathing slows to normal, and the weird sense of impending doom evaporates. He feels an almost euphoric wave of relief. But by fleeing the snake, the golfer has only made his problem worse. He has conditioned himself to associate his flight with relief. The next time he encounters a snake, he'll flee more quickly.

As his condition progresses, it takes less and less to trigger the golfer's fear. Soon a photograph of a snake or even seeing the word "snake" in print can trigger a phobic reaction. This happens because the golfer is afraid not so much of the snake, but of the way the snake makes him feel. By continually fleeing encounters with that feeling, he has taught himself the fear of fear.

Also, it's not uncommon for the phobic person to generalize fears to other objects or situations, so that a snake phobic may eventually experience a phobic reaction attached to garden hoses or coils of rope, or even to the game of golf itself.

Phobias are classified into two groups. *Simple phobias,* such as the golfer's fear of snakes or Carol's fear of thunderstorms, focus upon a specific object of dread. The most common simple phobias include fear of heights, enclosed spaces, animals, and water. But virtually any object, place, or situation can become the focal point of a phobia. In many cases, the simple phobias may be a remnant of our evolutionary past. A fear of snakes or heights may have actually kept our ancestors alive. Psychiatric journals record cases of people with phobic fears of rainbows, flowers, balloons, chins, various colors, and anything French.

The other category of phobic disorder is *social phobias.* Social phobics dread social situations in which they can be scrutinized and evaluated by others. The underlying fear is an abnormal terror of humiliation.

Bill, the college student who panicked when asked to respond to a classroom question, was a social phobic. When pinned down to particulars, he made it clear that his fears had less to do with the actual task of speaking in public than with the way it made him feel: on the spot, under scrutiny, inadequate, disgraced.

Intense fear of public speaking is the most common social phobia. Other frequently occurring social phobias include eating or drinking in public, using the telephone, standing in line, being introduced to a stranger, and speaking to a member of the opposite sex. Some social phobics are even horrified by the simple task of signing their name in front of others.

A few years ago, while attending the sixth game of the 1986 World Series, I had to call upon my professional expertise in the most unusual of circumstances: the public restroom at Shea Stadium. While waiting in line, it became apparent that the young gentleman ahead of me was suffering from one of the most embarrassing and frustrating social phobias: *the fear of urinating in a public restroom.* Imagine this nightmare scene: a long line of unruly fans growing more abusive while the guy ahead of me stands frozen at the urinal. Now the Shea fans aren't known for their patience or gentlemanly behavior, and the longer the man took, the worse the situation became. Clearly, I had to intervene quickly or risk being an inadvertent participant in a very nasty scene. I went up to the poor fellow and quietly told him to take a deep breath (not an easy thing to do in the urinals at Shea), while concentrating on letting the tension flow out of his body. Within seconds, the man had become sufficiently relaxed to urinate, proving that behavior therapy can work even under these difficult circumstances.

The avoidance behavior caused by social phobia can place devastating limits on a person's life. Careers, education, and romantic and social relationships have all been destroyed by the constricting effects of these fears, which blocked their victims from enjoying full, rich lives.

Another common and potentially embarrassing social phobia involves a *fear of sex.* Some individuals are so fearful that merely being in the same room with a member of the opposite sex will cause extreme anxiety, others find that they can't make eye contact or speak with the opposite sex. In some instances, married couples will go years without consummating their marriage. In cases where a fear of sex arises from a sense of shame or humiliation, cognitive and behavioral therapies will usually provide the best relief.

However for some individuals, the fear of sex actually develops from sexual orgasm. In these individuals, the physical symptoms of sexual arousal—rapid heart beats, increased breathing and perspiration—may precipitate a panic attack. Sex, especially the lack of physical control brought on by orgasm, may be associated with panic attacks. Often, these people either avoid sex entirely, or never let themselves fully enjoy the sex act.

Psychiatrists have identified hundreds of simple and social phobias; magazines and talk-show hosts are fond of digging up bizarre phobias. But the simple fact that a phobia has been described and given a long Greek name doesn't mean anything more than that at least one person has suffered from it. Though it's interesting to list different phobias, it's important to know that the phobic object is, in a way, arbitrary and insignificant. The important thing to remember is that while phobic objects may differ, the underlying phobic process is the same.

The phobia sufferer in a phobic situation experiences the same fight-or-flight response that normal people feel only when faced by a real and present danger. The difference is that in the case of phobic fear, no real danger exists. Since a tangible threat can't be identified, rational attempts to control the situation and master the fear is impossible. Instead, the phobic's sense of helplessness keeps compounding until the terror becomes too much to take and the victim flees.

It's important to remember that phobic individuals may not actually fear harm from the things they fear. People with an abnormal dread of cats, for instance, aren't necessarily afraid of being clawed or bitten; they simply dread the panic and emotional distress they feel when a feline draws near. In the same way, social phobics don't so much fear exposure to public activities as they fear the feelings of embarrassment and humiliation such exposure causes them.

When a phobic attack begins it seems to follow a predictable course, no matter what the source of fear.

First, as the phobic victim enters the feared situation, he or she conjures up vivid images of catastrophe: a cat phobic encounters a cat and imagines the cat jumping on his lap; a snake phobic imagines hissing reptiles slithering across her skin; the social phobic having dinner with strangers imagines humiliating himself by vomiting at the table.

Next come the riveting physiological manifestations of phobic fear: the rapid pulse, the dizziness, and so on. Feelings of dread and doom surface, growing darker and more terrifying with each passing moment. Finally, the terror boils over; the victim can't stand it any more and is forced to flee.

The first phobic episode is especially traumatic. After it's over, the victim is left in a state of complete confusion. Often, victims fear they're losing their minds. Frequently, they're so ashamed of their behavior that they keep the attack secret. Still, they continue to be puzzled and concerned by their experience, agonizing over the cause of the reaction, fearing for their sanity, and imagining all the ways this new fear will interrupt and interfere with their lives.

As these worries persist, the phobic victim finds himself in a vicious circle. The phobic situation is encountered and the body reacts with the physiological reactions of anxiety. These body reactions trigger the images of catastrophe, which intensify the bodily reactions, which in turn trigger more frightening images. The process builds rapidly, stoking the fires of anxiety and pushing the phobic victim to the point where the level of fear simply can't be tolerated and emotional composure collapses. The phobic victim is completely incapacitated by the terror and left with only one option: flight. Often, these phobias multiply into agoraphobia.

AGORAPHOBIA

On a warm spring day, Patricia was gardening in her backyard when her first panic attack struck. It lasted about ten minutes and then passed, leaving her exhausted, confused, terrified.

For the next few days she could think of nothing else. What had happened to her? What had triggered the attack? Would it happen again? Was she sick? Was she crazy?

She remembered how helpless she had felt during the attack, and thanked God that it had happened in the privacy of her backyard. Suppose it had happened in public where others could have watched! The thought chilled her. She had always been a self-conscious person, and the idea of public humiliation was unendurable. How terrible if strangers could see her in that awful state: gasping, cowering, her eyes wide with terror. It was too terrible a thought to endure, but it was the beginning of a pattern of thinking that would eventually ruin her life.

A few days after the attack, Patricia was waiting for a department-store elevator with two other shoppers. As she waited for the elevator to arrive, Patricia realized that the tiny space of the elevator, which she shared with two total strangers, would be a horrible place to have an attack. Immediately, her heart began to race. She remembered that the first thing she had noticed about her attack in the garden was the sudden rapid heartbeat. Fear shot through her, and she was certain that another attack was beginning. She was also certain that the two strangers could see her sweating, that they were beginning to notice her panic. Patricia knew that she had to leave the department store before a panic attack embarrassed her—she fled the store even before the elevator had opened its doors.

Patricia avoided the panic attack that day, but she had allowed her anticipatory anxiety—the fears that she would soon be having an attack—to change her behavior, to force her to leave the store.

The episode left its mark, and Patricia soon began to avoid any store with elevators. In fact, just thinking about elevators pushed her anxieties to uncomfortable levels.

But this avoidant behavior didn't help. As weeks passed, Patricia suffered more panic attacks. As the attacks became more frequent, her dread of panicking in public grew more powerful. She was especially concerned about places from which escape would be difficult or embarrassing. What if she was trapped in a checkout line when an attack struck? What if she was in a crowded pew at church, or driving through a tunnel or across a bridge? She visualized herself panicking in all these situations, and the images made her blood run cold. She began grocery shopping at odd hours in small twenty-four-hour stores, never approaching the cash register until she was certain to be the only person in line. Unfortunately, even this wasn't enough. She began to avoid these places. Soon she began to avoid even thinking about them.

As her condition progressed, Patricia's dread of panicking in public became the dominant influence in her life. She stopped driving, stopped shopping, gave up eating out and visiting friends. Her world was rapidly shrinking. Finally, she couldn't leave her home at all without feeling unbearable levels of anxiety. Patricia had become an agoraphobic.

If you made a list of all the things Patricia seemed to be afraid of, it would be as long as your arm. She was afraid, apparently, of everything. So it would be easy to guess that she was actually suffering from dozens of overlapping, intertwined phobias. But in fact, Patricia had only one fear—the fear of panicking in humiliating situations—which formed a central core of anxiety that triggered all her fears.

In the vast majority of cases, agoraphobia begins with a panic attack. Agoraphobics experience the attack, and the loss of control it causes, as a catastrophic event. The agoraphobic's worst nightmare is that an attack will happen in a situation from which escape to a safe place would be impossible or humiliating. Agoraphobics are not afraid of the situation itself, but of losing control there.

Like Patricia, they begin a process of "what if" thinking: What if an attack strikes while I'm at a business meeting, or in a busy restaurant, or on a moving bus? They conjure vivid images of these scenarios, and see themselves in the throes of panic, completely out of control, and completely unable to escape the mortifying scrutiny of the people around them. These horrifying images, along with the sharp anticipatory anxiety they provoke, are enough to convince the agoraphobic that these situations should never be allowed to happen. The only way to be certain of that, they conclude, is to avoid them. Avoidance reduces the anxiety. Rapidly, the victim is conditioned to associate avoidance with relief. Predictably, the avoidance behavior spreads until the victim's life becomes dominated by an elaborate strategy of avoidance.

Unfortunately, the fear/avoidance behavior only hastens the agoraphobic process. Eventually, agoraphobics learn to avoid so many places and situations and their "safe zones"—the places they can visit in relative comfort—are so restricted that they become effectively housebound.

So agoraphobia is not, as commonly thought, simply a fear of open places. It's a complex, progressive disorder usually triggered by a spontaneous panic attack—an attack that is, as we will see later, biologically based. These panic attacks feed on a cycle of fear and avoidance which eventually robs the victim of any comfortable freedom of movement. The underlying fear in agoraphobia is of suffering a panic attack in a place from which escape is either difficult or extremely embarrassing.

The mechanism by which agoraphobia progresses from the first panic attack to the widespread avoidance of almost everything involves a devastating one-two punch—first the anticipatory anxiety, then the avoidant behavior.

In Patricia's case we saw her anticipatory anxiety while she waited for the elevator in the department store. A learning process, called conditioning, is at work here: Patricia anticipated a possible panic attack in the enclosed elevator and felt her anxiety rising. By fleeing from the elevator, she avoided her anxiety, and she felt a great sense of relief. Her anticipatory anxiety was so great that she didn't have to experience an actual panic attack—so great that it resulted in avoidant behavior. As this happened over and over, Patricia's avoidant behavior was strongly reinforced, and her agoraphobia took a tighter and tighter stranglehold on her life.

The agoraphobic spends so much time fretting about the possibility of having a panic attack that he or she becomes hyperalert to physiological symptoms which are inappropriately associated with panic. For example, one of the most frightening symptoms of Patricia's real panic attacks was the hard racing beat of her heart. When she felt her heartbeat race at the restaurant, she interpreted it as the beginning of an attack. When no attack appeared, she attributed that to the fact that she had fled the frightening situation.

So Patricia finds herself in a difficult and discouraging dilemma. If she gives in to her anticipatory fears and avoids frightening situations, her agoraphobia will continue to progress. But if she fights off the avoidant behavior, her anxiety will continue to rise.

In some cases, a single panic attack is enough to trigger agoraphobia. Sometimes the progress of the disorder is swift, moving from the first panic episode to full-blown avoidance and withdrawal in a matter of months. More often, its course fluctuates through periods of lessened anxiety. During these milder periods, the victim's area of movement increases, especially if a trusted companion is along.

The trusted companion would be someone safe and dependable, preferably someone who was aware of the agoraphobic's problem and who could intervene if a panic attack occurred. Accompanied by such a companion during periods of lessened anxiety, an agoraphobic can even venture into some of the most feared situations without unendurable anxiety. Interestingly, the companion function can sometimes be performed by a favorite pet or even a comforting token, such as a familiar article of clothing or a photograph.

Researchers still haven't drawn a definitive portrait of the agoraphobic personality, but some personality characteristics can be identified as predisposing factors which allow the biologically based anxiety introduced by the panic attack to blossom into a wide-ranging phobic avoidance.

People afflicted by this disorder tend to be highly imaginative, a trait which enables them to visualize their fears vividly, making the effects of anticipatory anxiety much more potent. Clinical observations have identified other traits which also seem to make an individual more susceptible to agoraphobia.

Agoraphobics tend to underrate their own value and abilities. They set unreasonably high goals for themselves and then worry about failing. They are highly concerned with accommodating others and avoiding conflict. And they are intensely afraid of being embarrassed.

Some research indicates that agoraphobic patients tend to show a history of anxiousness as kids, and that they are likely to be the children of fearful parents. One study found that 25 percent of close relatives of panic attack sufferers could be diagnosed as also having panic disorder, while another 30 percent experienced infrequent panic attacks. The significance of these familial ties is controversial; some experts (including me) point to a biological connection that is inherited, while others believe the panic attack patients *learn* their behavior from relatives. In this view, the parents or relatives show their fears openly—for example, they react excessively when an insect or stray animal draws near. Kids who see this openly fearful behavior may model their own behavior after it.

I must stress that not every phobia is connected to a panic attack. Simple phobias, such as the golfer's fear of snakes or Carol's fear of thunderstorms, can exist without preceding panic attacks. The distinction between phobias with panic attacks and those without, while sometimes difficult to discern, is absolutely crucial to the treatment process, a process that I'll explain in Chapter 7.

The absence of panic attacks is equally important in the classification of another condition called generalized anxiety disorder.

GENERALIZED ANXIETY DISORDER

David is a thirty-three-year-old schoolteacher who has been suffering from chronic "edginess" for about twenty-one months. "I'm always keyed up," he says. "Can't relax, can't concentrate." David reports trembling hands, sweaty palms, fatigue, and frequent heart palpitations. "I feel that I'm always on guard," he says. "As if something bad is about to happen. Exactly what, I don't know."

For months, David's vague misgivings have taken on two focuses. He worries about his job constantly, fearing that he'll be fired and his family will face financial ruin. At the same time, he has been incessantly nagged by worries over the health of his three-year-old son. Both of these worries have become an overwhelming preoccupation for David, filling his life with gnawing, insidious anxieties that have robbed him of his peace of mind.

The fact is that David is a popular and respected teacher whose job is in no jeopardy at all, and his young son is in perfect health and has never suffered any serious illnesses. It would be clear to anyone that David's fears are exaggerated and unrealistic. At times, David would even say so himself. But still, the fears exist, they are real, and they are ruining David's life.

David's case is a classic example of generalized anxiety disorder (GAD), in which the body's natural anxiety response goes out of kilter, sending out messages of danger that far outstrip the normal reaction.

In many ways, GAD is a difficult disorder to pin down, since it has no clear and easily observed symptoms. By contrast, panic disorders are marked by recognizable panic attacks, and phobic disorders are distinguished by the extreme anxiety that occurs when a phobic stimulus is encountered. Theoretically, at least according to DSM-III-R, GAD can coexist with panic disorder—I am quite skeptical that these two conditions can coexist simultaneously, but I suppose almost anything is possible theoretically. In my experience, I have found that if GAD did exist with panic disorder, the GAD was never a primary disorder, but always secondary to the panic disorders. Treat the primary panic disorder and the GAD would disappear.

GAD is a relatively new diagnostic classification. Its most essential symptom is the presence of irrational, inappropriate worries, concerning at least two life circumstances, which have lasted at least six months. Other symptoms include motor tension (trembling, muscle tension, restlessness, and fatigue), autonomic hyperactivity (heart palpitations, shortness of breath, sweaty palms, clammy skin), and signs of vigilance (edginess, insomnia, lack of concentration).

It's possible for all the symptoms of GAD to exist in other anxiety disorders, so it's important to understand that a diagnosis of GAD can't be made if anxiety is related to the fear of having a panic attack (as in panic disorder), or of being publicly humiliated (as in social phobia), or of being contaminated (as in obsessive-compulsive disorder). Also, chronic anxiety that

occurs as a by-product of physical or mental disorders cannot
be classified as GAD.

OBSESSIVE-COMPULSIVE DISORDER

• A teenage boy, bothered by disturbing, intrusive thoughts
that he may kill his brother with an ax, feels compelled to
perform bizarre ritual behavior to "keep anything bad from
happening." First, his compulsions drive him to avoid sharp
objects, then to avoid members of his family. If he comes across
the word "ax" or any of the letters contained in his brother's
name in print, he is forced to mentally repeat certain phrases to
"defuse" the horrible mental images which obsess him.

• A traveling salesman must stop every time his car hits a
bump in the road to make sure he hasn't run over a human
body. Even after checking under the car, he is compelled to
check the area to be certain that the body hasn't been thrown
into the nearby brush by the impact.

• A young woman spends hours each day showering and
washing her hands. She refuses to shake hands, touch door-
knobs, or use public phones for fear of germs and contamination, and although she knows that lethal diseases can't be
transmitted by touch, she still continues her avoidance behavior and ritual washing, because if she doesn't something terrible
will happen.

At first glance, it seems obvious that these people are suffering from some severe mental illness. Surprisingly, though, not
one of these individuals can accurately be called insane. Instead,
they are victims of a bizarre and incapacitating condition
known as obsessive-compulsive disorder (OCD). In most cases,
it appears to have a biological cause.

Victims of OCD are plagued by recurrent, persistent, and
disturbing thoughts (obsessions) and the repetitive, ritualistic
behavior patterns they provoke. OCD sufferers realize that their
obsessions and compulsions are irrational and hate the way
these unwanted impulses dominate their lives. Though they

struggle to overcome their urges, the tug of OCD is simply too strong to resist. The conflict between the OCD patient's wishes to be free of the despised impulses and the deep, irresistible drive to obey them is the source of intense shame, despair, and anxiety.

OCD has traditionally been thought to affect about 0.05 percent of the general population, although more recent surveys have reported prevalency rates as high as 2 percent. Most recently, NIMH sponsored studies that suggest a rate of OCD twenty-five to sixty times greater than what had previously been thought. Obsessive-compulsive disorder is equally common among men and women; it is more common among those who are young, divorced or separated; and it is less common among black than non-Hispanic white respondents. These figures are compromised, however, by the fact that many OCD patients don't report their symptoms. That's not surprising. OCD sufferers are typically so ashamed of their behavior that many of them, even those with the most bizarre, elaborate, and time-consuming rituals, manage to keep their conditions secret, even from close friends and family members.

Considering the oddness of OCD symptoms, it's fascinating that the disorder seems to assume several distinct and predictable forms.

Washing. These people are preoccupied with avoiding contamination and may spend hours each day washing themselves. They avoid shaking hands, using public restrooms, and other situations which they regard as possible opportunities for the transfer of germs or filth. If the washer's symptoms become extreme—if the patient can't use public restrooms, for example—this condition can severely restrict freedom of movement. About half of all OCD cases fall into the washer category.

Checking. In this form of the disorder, patients are driven to perform constant, repetitive checking. For example, a checker plagued by thoughts that he'll cause a catastrophic fire may repeatedly check stove burners and gas lines to make sure no gas is leaking. But no matter how carefully and frequently the checking is done, the checker's doubts are not assuaged, and the checking behavior continues. In extreme cases, checkers are unable to leave their homes.

Counting. This category of symptoms is closely related to checking behavior, but instead of ritual inspection of locks, gas jets, and so on, the counter responds to obsessions by compulsively counting objects, or by compulsive repetitive behavior. One OCD patient repeated everything four times. In the morning, for example, he snapped the bathroom light on and off four times, brushed his teeth four times, showered four times, and so on.

Pure Obsessions. About 25 percent of all OCD victims fall into this category, which is marked by intrusive, reprehensible thoughts, usually sexual or aggressive in nature and often centering on the victim's fear that he or she will cause harm to a loved one.

Victims of pure obsessions are compelled to perform mental rituals, such as counting or repeating "charmed" phrases to ward off the terrible images and intrusive thoughts that plague them. The pure obsessionals' fear is that if the ritual is not performed, the worst of their reprehensible obsessions will come true and someone they love will be harmed. One OCD patient described the mental ritual as a way to "cross out" the disturbing thought and block anything bad from happening.

For example, a young woman was bothered by intrusive thoughts that something she might do—she couldn't say what —would cause her beloved grandfather to die. To ward off the thought, she repeated multiples of the number three, sometimes for hours at a time. And whenever her grandfather's name was mentioned, she would repeat it three times silently to herself. While she was aware that her actions were meaningless, she was unable to overcome the deep fear that if she neglected any of these compulsions, something terrible would happen to her grandfather and she would be at fault.

Primary Obsessional Slowness. In all types of OCD cases, the elaborate ritual behavior devours hours of the patient's time each day. Some washers, for example, will rise at dawn to begin showering for a luncheon appointment.

But in rare cases, this deliberate slowness becomes the prime symptom of the disorder. In primary obsessional slowness, patients slow the pace of their activity to make sure whatever they're doing is done perfectly. They may take hours to brush their teeth or comb their hair, paying obsessional attention to each detail. One patient, for example, took so long to wash her hands that she had to be treated for bruiselike sores on both ankles which resulted from the lack of circulation caused by her standing at the bathroom sink for eight to ten hours a day.

EVIDENCE THAT OCD IS A BIOLOGICAL DISEASE

It is becoming increasingly clear that the roots of OCD are not buried in the unconscious psyche, but in the biological workings of the brain.

The first hints that OCD was a biological disease came in the early 1900s when Europe was struck by an epidemic of viral sleeping sickness. After the epidemic passed, many previously normal survivors experienced OCD symptoms. That led researchers to investigate the possibility that biological changes, brought on by the virus, could be the underlying cause of obsessive-compulsive behavior.

More recent experiments, using advanced brain-scan techniques to monitor energy use in the brain, have shown that OCD patients exhibit abnormal patterns of energy flow in the caudate nucleus, the part of the human brain corresponding to the section of the animal brain which controls instinctive, repetitive behavior such as grooming and nesting. The fascinating implication here is that the caudate nucleus may trigger repetitive thoughts in humans, just as its counterpart in animal brains triggers repetitive, ritualistic behavior.

A recent news story reported that one distraught victim of OCD tried to kill himself with a bullet to the brain after repeated failures to overcome his condition. Fortunately, the suicide attempt failed—the patient lived even though the bullet became lodged in his head. Amazingly, the suicide attempt did cure his OCD! Somehow the bullet disrupted the abnormal activity that resulted in his obsessive-compulsive behavior. (This, by the way, is *not* a treatment that I recommend. There are far simpler and safer methods of treating OCD.)

The most convincing evidence that OCD is a physical disease comes from clinical use of an antidepressant drug known as clomipramine. In tests since 1980, OCD patients have shown a marked improvement after clomipramine treatment. In just a few weeks, the drug allows patients to reduce the time they spend in ritual behavior by 80 percent.

POSTTRAUMATIC STRESS DISORDER (PTSD)

This disruptive, disabling disorder, which was first studied in soldiers suffering from the extreme stresses of war, has been known by many names, including shell shock and battle fatigue. The war in Vietnam brought PTSD into public focus, as stories of Vietnam vets plagued by terrifying flashbacks and nightmares of combat were widely reported. In reality, war vets have no monopoly on this disorder. PTSD can strike anyone.

PTSD is seen in people who have suffered a traumatic episode of violence, horror, or intense fear. Military combat, of course, provides a multitude of traumatic situations, but PTSD is also a risk in people who have survived or witnessed earthquakes, hurricanes, and other natural disasters, air or auto crashes, fires, violent crime, torture, and so on. Interestingly, traumas of human design—rape, torture, assault, and so on—produce more intense and longer-lasting symptoms. Recent refugees to the United States are particularly prone to PTSD—often they are fleeing cruel conditions in their native lands, conditions that may have included torture and starvation.

Such terrible events would leave a mark on anyone, but in some individuals, a syndrome of pathological behavior occurs that results in the development of PTSD.

There are three main characteristic symptoms of this disorder. First, the PTSD victim relives the traumatic situation in a variety of ways. He or she may have persistent and highly distressing thoughts about the experience, or may recreate the traumatic moment in vivid, recurring dreams of the event. In rare cases, flashbacks occur, in which the patient dissociates with reality and behaves as though the trauma were happening again—the war veteran takes cover in his backyard and watches in horror as his company is shot to pieces once again; the rape victim, safe in her own home, suddenly slips into a hallucinatory state in which she once again faces her attacker. Sometimes these flashbacks are triggered by events which resemble or symbolize the trauma. The Vietnam vet, for example, may have been watching a movie about the war before his flashback occurred; the rape victim may have been approaching the anniversary of the attack.

A second characteristic of PTSD concerns the victim's attempts to avoid thoughts or feelings related to the trauma. The victim may be unable to recall key aspects of the experience, and may refuse to be involved in situations or activities that are reminiscent of the trauma.

It's also common for PTSD sufferers to experience a sense of emotional numbness. They feel detached and estranged from other people, and lose interest in activities which once gave them pleasure. Many PTSD victims undergo a kind of "emotional anesthesia," in which feelings, especially those of intimacy, tenderness, and sex, are smothered with a pessimistic view of the future.

PTSD patients also experience persistent symptoms of increased anxiety: They may have difficulty falling asleep, lose their ability to concentrate, and startle easily. Aggressive behavior is also commonly seen in these patients. It may come in the form of mild irritability, but in more severe cases can express itself in unpredictable outbursts of anger and belligerence.

Symptoms usually occur soon after the traumatic event, although the reexperiencing symptoms may be delayed by months or years. PTSD can strike in two forms. In the acute form, symptoms begin and end within six months of the trauma. In chronic or delayed PTSD, symptoms occur six months or more after the trauma.

PTSD can strike at any age. In young children, it may begin

with realistic dreams of the trauma. Within weeks, the dreams become nightmares involving monsters, bogeymen, and other terrifying threats. Children with PTSD don't mentally relive the traumatic event, but repeatedly reenact it in their play. Since children may be unable to describe their symptoms clearly, they should be watched for significant signs—for example, loss of interest in favorite games or toys, or pessimistic feelings about their future.

PTSD victims are also likely to suffer anxiety and depression symptoms severe enough to be diagnosed as anxiety or depressive disorders. Impulsive actions are frequent: Patients may abruptly change residence or otherwise alter their lifestyles, may take a hastily planned trip or simply disappear without warning. Patients who are survivors of events in which others were killed may suffer bitter pangs of guilt, focused either on the things they had to do to survive (such as killing in combat) or on the simple fact that they survived while others didn't.

The emotional turmoil caused by PTSD interferes with its victims' lives on practically every level, shattering confidence, self-esteem, and peace of mind. Marriages, friendships, family relationships, and careers all may suffer. The combination of guilt, depression, and emotional numbness could lead to self-defeating, suicidal behavior, or other physical disorders.

Follow-up studies of the Iranian hostages, taken one year after their release, found that 40 percent were still experiencing excessive anxiety. Five years later, 71 percent of these anxiety-suffering hostages were still suffering from poor overall health. Conversely, of the hostages who did not suffer from anxiety, only 33 percent reported poor health after 5 years.

Some researchers have drawn attention to possible similarities between PTSD victims and adult children of alcoholics (ACOAs). The experience of being a child raised by alcoholic parents has been compared to the trauma of PTSD. Researchers have noted that ACOAs may experience psychic numbing, feelings of emptiness, difficulty with separation, antisocial behavior, substance abuse, and suicidal tendencies, symptoms similar to those of PTSD sufferers. A recent study of ACOAs and PTSD sufferers found that while there may be similarities between the groups, the differences were greater than expected. The researchers suggested that these differences may result from the fact that all of the PTSD victims in their study were adults at the time of their traumatic event. I believe that is a good possibility and that a strong similarity between ACOA and PTSD patients who experience their trauma as children will be established, as our knowledge and understanding of both of these conditions grow.

APPROACHES TO TREATMENT

In the first part of this chapter, I've described in detail the most common panic and anxiety disorders and just how devastating they can be to the individual sufferers. The rest of the chapter will explain the most prominent psychological theories used in diagnosis and treatment of these conditions.

While there are almost as many different psychological methods of treating panic as there are neurons in the brain, I have found that grouping these approaches into three broad-based classes helps to clarify a very confusing field. Briefly, the major areas of psychotherapy involved in treating anxiety and panic are the *psychodynamic,* the *humanistic-existential,* and the *behavior* therapies. These treatment modalities, or variations of these treatments, may be practiced by a number of mental health professionals, ranging from psychiatrists to therapists to social workers. However, each of these approaches, as we will see, has serious flaws that preclude its effectiveness in both explaining and treating panic and anxiety disorders.

PSYCHODYNAMIC PSYCHOTHERAPY

Best known among the psychodynamic therapies are the teachings of Sigmund Freud and his disciples. Freudians argue that anxiety stems not just from external forces, but also from the internal struggle between the unconscious mind (the id) and the conscious mind. According to Freudians, the chronic anxiety typical of generalized anxiety disorder (GAD) results from the ongoing battle between the id and our conscious defenses that struggle to repress the hidden desires of the id. Many Freudians believe panic attacks occur because the id moves even closer to the conscious mind, and that phobias arise when the patient displaces the emotions and fears caused by hidden urges onto another object. This definition of phobia is still current today: The most recent edition (1988) of the *American Psychiatric Glossary* defines phobia as "an obsessive, persistent, unrealistic, intense fear of an object or situation. The fear is believed to arise through a process of displacing an internal (unconscious) conflict to an external conflict symbolically related to the conflict." Notice that this definition ignores the possibility of biological basis for a phobia.

The following cases are excellent examples of how Freud would approach panic and anxiety disorders.

Freud once treated a woman with an intense dread of touching anything made of rubber. She couldn't explain the fear, but said she had felt it for as long as she could remember. Under analysis, Freud uncovered an intense, traumatic childhood memory.

As a girl, she adored her father and resented that she had to share his affections with a younger sister. In her young mind that resentment was often so strong that she wished her sister were dead.

One day, the father brought home a balloon for each child. In a fit of temper, the patient burst her younger sister's balloon. She was immediately and severely punished by her father and forced to give her own balloon to the younger child.

Freud interpreted the bursting of the balloon as a symbolic act of violence against the younger sister. The swift punishment exacerbated the guilt she was already feeling for wishing her sister dead and drove those feelings deep into the unconscious, where they were associated with the rubber balloon and emerged later as a phobic dread of rubber objects.

In a more famous case, Freud's patient was Hans, a five-year-old boy with a phobic dread of horses. His fears developed shortly after he saw a horse fall violently in the street. A few days later he became agitated and frantic, clinging to his mother and expressing a fear that a white horse would bite him. His fears quickly progressed until he couldn't go on short trips outside the house without intense fear.

Freud quickly determined that the child seemed excessively close to his mother, insisting that they "cuddle" constantly, especially when his anxieties were high. Significantly, Hans's fears mounted whenever he was separated from his mother.

Under analysis, Hans explained that he sometimes worried that his father would take his mother away and he'd be left alone. Freud surmised that the boy's phobic behavior stemmed from his conflicting feelings about his father. On one hand, Hans wanted his father gone so he could have his mother all to himself; on the other hand, Hans loved his father and did not want him to leave.

According to Freud, the solution to the dilemma came on an unconscious level. The boy's disturbing and unacceptable resentment of his father was repressed and stored in the unconscious mind. But the distressing thoughts didn't die there. Instead, they associated themselves with an external symbol—the frightening image of a white horse.

When the boy's fears and hatred were directed toward the father, Hans was powerless to do anything about them. But after they were externalized and directed toward the image of horses, he had some degree of control. He could fear and hate the horses with no sense of remorse. More important, he could avoid the horses, while he could not avoid his father.

Freud's theory of phobic development has influenced the psychoanalytical treatment of phobia patients for several decades.

Ironically, Freud himself saw the limitations of traditional psychotherapy when treating agoraphobia and other phobias, stating that "one can hardly master a phobia if one waits till the patient lets the analyst influence him to give it up." While many Freudian therapists recognize the limitations of the psychodynamic approach, others continue to use it as the treatment of choice. One former patient of mine initially experienced this "treatment of choice."

This patient, a professional actor whom I'll call Jason suffered from a fear of dogs (cynophobia). He explained it to me during his first visit:

"I've been afraid of dogs for a long time now, but since I've always lived in New York I could pretty much limit my exposure. I made sure that I stayed out of Central Park and other places where dogs run wild.

"But about three years ago my agent called me with a chance to star in a TV pilot. I was all set to give up the New York stage and fly to the coast. But then I read the script. My worst nightmare—the entire script revolved around a dog. In fact, the dog was the real star of the show.

"I figured this was the excuse I was waiting for, the excuse I needed to finally get over this ridiculous fear of dogs. In the past I never would have auditioned for a role in a dog show, but this time I was determined to overcome my weakness. So I went to see a therapist, one that an actor friend of mine had recommended. I started seeing this guy, a Freudian, four times a week.

"Well, as luck would have it, my big audition called for a nice 'warm-fuzzy' scene with the golden retriever star, a scene guaranteed to warm the hearts of millions and enough to make me crazy. Well, I blew it, I panicked, forgot all my lines. I didn't even wait for the rejection, I just flew back to New York immediately.

"I was pretty depressed, but I decided to stick with my therapist and give him a chance. Besides, I felt that some introspection might help my acting. Well, four years later, my acting hasn't improved and my fear of dogs has gotten worse. I was turning down any work, even one-day commercial shoots, that called for me to be near a dog.

"Enough is enough. I can't have my career threatened by this crazy fear."

Jason explained that his Freudian therapist "diagnosed" him as suffering from unresolved oedipal conflict—supposedly still harboring hidden desires for his mother, Jason also had hostility for his father. This hostility, the Freudian theorized, was combined with anxiety over fears that the father would castrate Jason. According to the Freudian therapist, Jason's fear of castration was displaced onto dogs. The therapist told Jason that by avoiding dogs, he was able to relieve his anxiety over castration.

After Jason gave his history, I didn't know whether to laugh at the absurdity of this explanation or to cry at the needless—and expensive—suffering Jason had endured. After a few months of biopsychiatric treatment—a treatment that I'll describe shortly—Jason was cured. That's right, *cured.* And "cured" is a term that physicians use very, very sparingly.

As Jason discovered, the goal of psychodynamic therapy—unlike that of biopsychiatry—is to expose and neutralize the hidden urges and desires of the unconscious mind that cause anxiety. Once these terrors are unmasked, the theory goes, they lose their power over us. Frequently, a therapist may use the techniques of free association, dream interpretation, or hypnosis to help unlock these hidden desires. These therapists usually do not consider the symptoms or characteristics of a panic attack. Rather, they emphasize the thoughts or feelings the patient may have experienced just prior to the attack.

Other leaders in psychodynamic therapy, who have expanded, modified, and in some cases rejected the teachings of Freud, have been Carl Gustav Jung, Alfred Adler, Harry Stack Sullivan, and Erik Erikson.

WHY THE PSYCHODYNAMIC APPROACH FAILS

As I pointed out in Chapter 1, the single greatest drawback of the psychodynamic approach is the failure to acknowledge the physical causes of a panic attack. What little benefit this therapy might bring in seeming to alleviate anxiety crumbles when the unchecked panic attack resurfaces. And by ignoring the symptoms of anxiety, the psychodynamic therapists not only miss the physical causes of panic but miss diagnosing the dangerous mimickers of anxiety described in Chapter 6.

THE HUMANISTIC-EXISTENTIALIST THERAPY

Like the Freudians, the humanistic-existentialist (H-E) therapists see anxiety as arising from intrapsychic conflicts. However, according to the H-E therapists, the conflict is not between the unconscious and conscious minds, but rather between the person's lofty view of what he would like to be (the ideal self) and his negative view of who he really is (the self-concept). An individual with a negative self-concept is anxious about his inability to reach the ideal self. A *humanist* therapist blames a person's upbringing for causing this dichotomy: A child may be told that he must always be the best, while anything he does accomplish is never good enough. The anxiety that arises from this split prevents an individual from growing and blossoming as a human.

A popular variation of the humanistic approach, called *client-centered therapy,* was developed by Carl Rodgers. According to Rodgers, an anxiety-troubled individual, like any other troubled soul, needs only to be respected and understood by another person (i.e., the therapist). The goal of client-centered therapy is to "hear" what the individual is actually thinking and feeling, and then to show that the therapist understands and accepts these feelings by restating the individual's thoughts. According to this theory, the unconditional acceptance that the therapist gives improves the patient's self-concept.

Like the psychodynamic and humanistic therapists, *existentialists* are not very concerned with the symptoms of anxiety, but focus on the intrapsychic conflict. While very similar to humanistic therapists, existentialists see the intrapsychic conflict arising not from the struggle between the self-concept and the ideal self, but rather from the struggle between the values of the individual and the forces of society that act against these values. The goal of existentialist therapy is to help the patient live "authentically," according to his or her own values, in today's society.

An existentialist therapist may practice a technique called "paradoxical intention" when treating phobias and obsessive-compulsive disorders. In this therapy, compulsive individuals will be told to indulge their condition. For example, a person who compulsively and repeatedly checks every door to see if it is locked may be told to spend all day checking the locks. By overindulging an activity a person may learn control—if you can deliberately overdo an action, you can deliberately not do the same action.

WHAT'S WRONG WITH THE HUMANISTIC-EXISTENTIALIST APPROACH?

While individual humanistic or existential therapists may differ, they all agree on one central tenet: *Responsibility for change lies with the client.* To them, the goal of therapy is to create an emotional environment in which change can occur.

The H-E theories all sound very nice. They all appeal to our most noble nature as we strive to be the best possible person we can be. But there are problems with these H-E therapies: They require a great deal of time; the strengths of the individual therapist's ability weighs heavily in the treatment's outcome; they benefit primarily a very select group (sometimes called the YAVIS group—Young, Attractive, Verbal, Intelligent, Successful); and the health you have at the beginning of therapy usually determines how well you'll be at the finish (one expert called it psychotherapy's version of "the rich get richer").

In reality, there's only one truly significant problem with these theories—they don't work. Like the psychodynamic approaches described earlier, the H-E therapies don't work in the treatment of panic because they neither confront nor treat the basic physiological reasons why panic attacks occur. In the end, these will almost always result in the patient's being blamed for not benefiting from the therapy. In fact, it is the theory behind this treatment that fails, not the patient who fails at treatment.

THE PSYCHOTHERAPEUTIC APPROACH: BETTER THAN NOTHING?

The overall ineptitude of unaided psychotherapy—especially the psychodynamic and humanistic-existentialist therapies—in the treatment of anxiety disorders becomes apparent when comparing psychotherapy to no treatment at all. For example, one study rating the efficacy of psychotherapy in anxiety disorders over a two-year period found a recovery rate of only 42 percent, while another study of *untreated* persons over a two-to-eight-year period found a spontaneous recovery rate of 51 percent! Other studies have supported the relatively equal efficacy of psychotherapy and no treatment, which has led many experts to give up trying to prove the superiority of psychotherapy. Instead, they grasp at straws by claiming the *possibility* that psychotherapy might hasten recovery when compared to no treatment. As one review of anxiety in the medical literature found:

> To summarize the vast literature on psychotherapeutic treatment, we are left with the uneasy but modestly affirmative judgment that although no one method of treatment appears to be indisputably better than another, most evidence at least suggests that treatment of some sort is preferable to no treatment at all —despite the absence of a rock on which to establish that tenet. (From Friedman, AM, "Psychopharmacology and Psychotherapy in the Treatment of Anxiety." *Current Psychiatric Therapies:* 1986. Grune & Stratton, pp. 107–8.)

Clearly psychotherapy is on very shaky ground in the treatment of anxiety disorders.

And when psychotherapy is compared to the psychopharmacologic approach favored by biopsychiatrists . . . well, it's no contest. Psychopharmacology wins hands down. The same review of medical literature quoted above reached the conclusion that "the effectiveness of pharmacotherapy alone in the treatment of anxiety is unequivocally established" and that "combined therapy of pharmacologic agents and psychotherapy would appear to be superior to either therapy alone."

It is this combination of medication and psychotherapy, especially the behavior therapy outlined below, that forms the cornerstone of the highly successful biopsychiatric approach.

GETTING CLOSER TO THE GOOD NEWS: THE BEHAVIORIST APPROACH

Unlike the psychodynamic therapists, behaviorists focus on the concrete evidence that constitutes a panic attack or phobia. Behavior therapy is considered by many experts to be the most successful nonpharmacologic therapy. I, too, feel that for many disorders behavior therapy is the treatment of first choice. But understanding the limitations of behavior therapy, especially when applied to panic attacks, is a very significant—and contro-versial—part of my treatment plan. In order to understand both the pluses and minuses of behavior therapy, we need to under-stand how it works.

Behaviorism arose as a reaction against the introspection that dominated the theories of Freud and other nineteenth-century psychologists. Behaviorists thought that the causes of our actions need not be plumbed from the depths of the uncon-scious mind but could be found in the immediate environment. In this environment, certain agents or stimuli provoke, rein-force, and punish our responses which result in *learning,* and our behavior changes in response to our environment. In fact, behaviorists view learning as the most important part of both normal and abnormal behavior.

While the early behaviorists focused mainly on observable behavior and the external environment, later theorists have ac-knowledged the importance of the mental processes, such as thought, emotion, expectation, and interpretation, in coloring our response to our environment. These mental processes, taken collectively, are known a *cognition.* Cognition has as-sumed an important role in the evolution of behaviorism.

A major proponent of a behavior approach, Dr. Aaron Beck, has developed an interesting cognitive approach. Beck views anxiety disorders as a vulnerability stemming from an individ-ual's tendency to underestimate his or her problem-solving abil-ities while overestimating the threat in a situation. For example, a good student may do poorly on exams because of excessive anxiety caused by her exaggerating the difficulty of a test, while denigrating her intellectual abilities.

A more classic behaviorist theory views anxiety as arising from a person's associating a neutral object or action with another negative stimulus. For example, a child whose parents always fought when they drove would associate the act of driving with the anxiety caused by her parents fighting. Every time the child avoids driving with her parents, her anxiety is relieved. Gradually she associates the anxiety caused by driving with her parents with driving in general. Over the years, she learns to avoid this anxiety by never learning to drive.

A behaviorist would treat a phobia by having the person concentrate on recognizing and removing the symptoms of anxiety. A classic behaviorist technique involves *systematic desensitization.* Patients draw up a list of their increasingly worst fears (for example, from seeing a photograph of a mouse to having a mouse crawl on them). Under the guidance of a therapist, the patient imagines these situations, progressing from the least to the most traumatic. Patients are also taught simple relaxation techniques that help them to remain calm. Cognitive methods may also be used to help patients control anxiety. For example, patients may be told to count out loud or to converse with themselves when they feel an attack imminent. Or they may be taught to repeat statements that reaffirm their need to stay in the anxiety-provoking situation, acknowledging their anxiety while reducing their fears of death, being trapped, etc. Ideally, by using these cognitive and relaxation techniques, the patient will eventually be able to imagine even the most upsetting scenario while not getting upset.

A variation of this office-based treatment is called *in vivo desensitization.* It involves actually exposing patients to their real-life phobias. This exposure may be sudden (called *flooding*) or gradual. I prefer a gradual desensitization, since the patient usually finds the treatment more tolerable.

How does a biopsychiatrist like me use in vivo desensitization? Remember Jason, the actor with the fear of dogs? After hearing the details of his Freudian "treatment," and after a thorough physical that ruled out any other possible cause for his disorder, I recommended beginning treatment with in vivo desensitization. First, I introduced Jason to some simple relaxation strategies. He picked these techniques up quickly, since he used similar strategies while performing onstage. Also, I discussed using cognitive techniques involving mental dialogue. In this dialogue, Jason would first confront his fear while repeating that no harm would come to him and that he was capable of overcoming his fear (see Chapter 9 for more information on cognitive strategies). Next, I showed him pictures of nonthreatening dogs in everyday situations, while he practiced his relaxation and cognitive techniques. During the next session, I had Jason walk into a room backward and stop fifteen feet away from a very friendly, obedient, and leashed collie. Why backward? Because that is actually the safest way to approach an unknown dog, since the dog has no inviting target to bite. During the next sessions, Jason would gradually turn around and approach the dog, all the while practicing his relaxation techniques. Eventually, he was able to tolerate the presence of different dogs, even briefly petting the more friendly ones.

Was the treatment a success? Yes and no. No question that Jason had almost completely overcome his fear of dogs—most doctors would have considered him an unqualified success. But six months later, on a follow-up visit with Jason, I could sense that there was something wrong. When I asked him what the problem was, he hesitated, then replied:

"You know, I should be grateful for all the progress I've made. I can actually go into Central Park and not be afraid—during the day, that is—of an unleashed dog. But I still find it difficult to act with a dog present. I haven't had to turn down any TV commercial work—after all, there's hardly any acting involved there. But when I have to act, really act, and a dog is there, well, I tighten up. I mean, I don't go running kicking and screaming from the set anymore, but my performance is definitely off. I thought it might improve, but I seem to have reached the point where I can't get any better."

When Jason said that, I looked at him and said, "What makes you think the treatment has stopped? I'm not ready to give in." By Jason's standards, admittedly very high ones, his behavior therapy was a failure. No matter how hard we tried, behavior therapy alone wouldn't give him the freedom he needed to perform successfully. Clearly, another tack was needed. Accordingly, I prescribed a very low dose of a beta-blocker medication (see page 238 for more information on beta blockers). Within weeks, Jason was able to handle even the most difficult roles with aplomb. As he put it, "I could do Macbeth with a Doberman dancing on my chest—well, maybe a Chihuahua." Later, Jason called to invite me to a local dog show—he had purchased a prize Kerry blue terrier and was dying to show him off. As he put it, "Now he's my kind of dog: loves me and hates all other dogs!"

Now that's what I call a successful treatment.

Jason's case illustrates the importance of a physician's treating each case as an individual challenge, and of tailoring both the treatment and the treatment resolution to meet the personal and professional requirements of the individual patient. While other doctors might have settled for the improvements brought on by behavior therapy, I kept striving for the best possible solution for Jason, not only a solution that he could live with, but one that would allow his career to flourish.

THE LIMITS OF BEHAVIORISM

Many proponents of behaviorism argue that this approach, by itself, is an effective means of treating agoraphobia and panic attacks. I disagree. To understand *why* I disagree requires an understanding of agoraphobia and panic attacks. As I explained earlier, the essential component of almost all agoraphobia is panic. And an important component of panic is the anticipatory anxiety that frequently precedes an attack. Following a panic attack, or even as a result of the fear that a panic attack might occur, an agoraphobic person will frequently avoid situations that might provoke an attack; this is called avoidant behavior. A panic attack can be so devastating that the slightest expectation that a situation might trigger a panic attack can produce anticipatory anxiety and avoidant behavior. Often the anticipatory anxiety can be so intense that it fools the patient and the doctor into believing a panic attack has occurred. In reality, the actual panic attack differs significantly from the anticipatory anxiety.

In my view, behavior therapy alone relieves the anticipatory anxiety and diminishes the avoidant behavior, but leaves the actual cause of the panic attack untreated. This view is supported by studies:

> ... the data reflect that 30–40 percent of all agoraphobics who complete [behavioral] treatment fail to benefit, and of the remaining 60 to 70 percent, a substantial proportion may not attain clinically meaningful levels of functioning. Marks (1971), for example, reported that only 3 of 65 patients were symptom-free at follow-up. McPherson and colleagues (1980) reported that only 18 percent of improvers were symptom-free at posttreatment. (From Craske, MG, "Cognitive-Behavioral Treatment of Panic." *Review of Psychiatry,* Volume 7, American Psychiatric Press, 1988.)

Left untreated, the panic attacks eventually return. Thus patients who once thought that they had defeated their problem now will often reexperience the panic, with an even greater sense of failure.

In addition, many patients cannot face the desensitization treatments of behaviorism. The median dropout rate for desensitization in general is 12 percent, with 25 to 40 percent dropping out of intensive exposure or desensitization. And some of the few patients who appear to have benefited from the behavioral treatment may actually be stoically accepting a panic attack without admitting an attack has occurred. These two factors diminish the already weak success rate cited above for unaided behavior therapy.

Unfortunately, in an attempt to understand a difficult subject like panic, we—both the professional and the layman—tend to divide the subject into easily digestible labels. Those who promote the behavioral approach are in one camp, while those who feel medication is effective are in the other. Unfortunately, this divisiveness fosters debates that—instead of moving the two camps closer—result in a therapeutic stalemate. While the debates prosper, the patients suffer.

Conversely, biopsychiatry breaks down these polarities and uses strategies that combine the best of both approaches. Many patients are surprised to learn that biopsychiatrists recommend behavior therapy as an integral part of a successful treatment plan. A common misconception about biopsychiatrists—and one that infuriates me—views biopsychiatrists as pill-pushing fanatics who view medication as the panacea for all of their patients' problems. Nothing could be further from the truth. Actually, if any group could be labeled as medication fanatics, it might be the traditional psychiatrists and physicians who blindly treat each case the same, with the same drug and the same dosage they gave their last patient. As we'll see, this traditional pill-pushing or blind-pharmacology approach can have as many pitfalls as the psychotherapeutic approach.

In this chapter we have seen not only the many faces of anxiety disorders, but also the many theories that have been proposed to account for their existence and that have served as the basis for many years of ineffectual treatment. In the next chapter, we'll examine why many psychiatrists today continue to misdiagnose and mistreat the various anxiety disorders.

CHAPTER FOUR

THE MISDIAGNOSIS OF ANXIETY DISORDERS

TRIP'S CASE

It was the first day of kindergarten and five-year-old Trip was terrified. He stood in the middle of the classroom with tears streaming down his face as he screamed in fear. His teacher couldn't calm him down, and none of his fellow students could distract him. Finally, Trip's mother, who was watching from the doorway, had to fetch her son and take him home.

That scene was repeated every day for the first two weeks of school. Finally, Trip's worried parents sought the help of a psychiatrist who had been highly recommended by the school psychologist.

In their first meeting, Trip's mother described her son's reaction when she tried to leave him at school. "It was a nightmare," she said. "I never saw him so afraid. He was almost hysterical. It was as if he thought his life was in danger."

Trip's problems had started about a month before classes began. Trip, usually a cheerful, cooperative boy, had grown restless and timid. He seemed afraid of being alone and wouldn't let his mother out of his sight. When she asked him what was wrong, Trip began to cry and begged her not to send him to school.

"The idea scared him to death," said Trip's mother. "He thought the people there would hurt him, or that we'd leave him there and never come to get him, or that something bad would happen to me while he was gone. I tried to reassure him, but it did no good.

"He's always been a friendly, well-adjusted boy," she continued. "I just can't imagine where this came from."

The child psychiatrist nodded as he listened, and then asked a few questions, from which he learned that Trip was very dependent upon his mother and that in his short life the boy hadn't been separated from his parents for any significant length of time. He seemed to expect to hear that, and after a little more discussion he delivered his diagnosis.

"Trip has a classic case of 'school phobia,' " he said. "We'll treat it with psychotherapy to try to get to the root of the problem, and I'll also refer him to a psychologist in my office to use some behavioral techniques. He'll introduce Trip step by step to the classroom, showing him that nothing bad is going to happen. That way, he'll gradually become desensitized to his fears, and the phobia should disappear."

In the eyes of most psychiatrists, it was a responsible and appropriate treatment plan. But six weeks after treatment, Trip was still mortally afraid of school.

LINDA'S CASE

Linda, a twenty-six-year-old woman, had recently moved from her small Midwestern hometown to take a challenging new job in a large city on the East Coast. The move was a stressful one. She had broken off an engagement with a man back home and had left behind a secure but boring job at a local bank. She'd never lived so far from her family, and was, at first, a little intimidated by the pace of metropolitan life. But at the same time, she was excited and optimistic about the new life she was just beginning.

One evening, about six months after her arrival, Linda was at a play when suddenly, out of nowhere, she was jolted by a wave of fear and dread so intense that she had to struggle to keep from screaming in the quiet theater. Her pulse skyrocketed, pounding far more furiously than she'd ever felt during her brisk morning jogs. She felt her throat constrict and had to gasp for breath. There was numbness and tingling in her arms and legs and a suffocating tightness in her chest.

Unable to fight off the terror, Linda bolted from her seat and took refuge in the ladies' room. Slumped in a stall, she tried to calm herself, but it did no good. The terror grew worse and worse. She was sure she was going to die. The attack lasted about ten minutes, and then passed. That had been three weeks ago. Since then, she'd had four more attacks. Fearing that she was losing her mind, Linda consulted a psychiatrist.

The psychiatrist asked questions about the onset and duration of Linda's attacks and the nature and severity of the symptoms. He noted her recent life-style changes and the anxiety they'd caused. And then he made his diagnosis: panic attack.

Accordingly, he prescribed treatment with a common antidepressant medication, generally acknowledged by most psychiatrists to be the treatment of first choice for panic attacks.

ANDY'S CASE

Andy, a production worker in a plant that makes industrial lighting fixtures, went to his psychiatrist complaining of a bizarre fear of strangers. "It happens every time I'm alone with people I don't know," he said. "The first time I noticed, I was on an elevator with two other people. All of a sudden, my heart's pounding, my lungs are aching, I'm scared to death, and all I want to do is get out of there.

"Now I feel it on buses, in restaurants, stores. I see myself surrounded by strangers, I get jittery, scared. The closer they get, the worse I feel."

Andy explained that his odd fear was beginning to interrupt his life. "I like people," he said, "but I find myself avoiding situations where I might be surrounded by strangers. It's even getting hard to go to work. My plant employs hundreds of people, and while I'm working I'm thinking about where I can eat lunch to avoid the ones I don't know. I'm nervous all day," he said. "I know this isn't normal. I know there's nothing to be afraid of. So I thought I'd better get some help."

It didn't take Andy's psychiatrist long to come up with what seemed to him to be an obvious diagnosis: Andy was suffering from xenophobia, an abnormal fear of strangers. The treatment plan based on that diagnosis resembled the one that Trip's psychiatrist had designed—psychotherapy to unravel the psychological core of the xenophobia, and exposure therapy, in which Andy would become deconditioned to his fear by tolerating the presence of strangers for increasingly longer periods of time. As in Trip's case, the plan made sense, and few psychiatrists would have argued with it. But months after his treatment had begun, Andy's fears were only getting worse.

ANOTHER LOOK AT TRIP, LINDA, AND ANDY

Three cases of people in trouble. Three diagnoses reached with speed and confidence by successful, esteemed psychiatrists using interviews and checklists. Three treatment plans prescribed by the end of the first appointment—and doomed to failure from the start.

Let's take another look at these three patients. Trip certainly *was* afraid of school. No doubt about that. His symptoms of extreme dread certainly fit the diagnostic description of a phobia. Also, there's evidence to show that children who develop school phobia tend to feel very close to their mothers and have spent little time away from their parents. Trip fit these criteria as well. The diagnosis met the criteria used by other psychiatrists. The DSM-III criteria are solid, and the treatment plan his psychiatrist suggested has been highly successful in treating real school phobias. Why, then, wasn't Trip getting better?

The fact is that Trip's child psychiatrist—a trained physician, who had even finished a pediatric internship and psychiatric residency—never performed even a routine physical examination. That's why he missed the tiny gold-green rings around the corneas of the young boy's eyes. These rings are a distinctive symptom of a rare metabolic disorder known as Wilson's disease, in which copper accumulates in the body, eventually causing damage to the nervous system.

Wilson's disease usually strikes young people between the ages of five and twenty. It triggers a range of psychiatric symptoms, including anxiety and, remarkably, school phobia. The exact mechanism by which this disorder causes such specific phobic behavior isn't completely understood, but the connection has been firmly established by research.

Trip's fears weren't all in his mind. They were symptoms of a distinct, medically treatable physical disease. Trip needed medical care. And with that care he got better. Obviously, any treatment plan based on psychiatric therapy had no chance but to fail.

Now, let's reconsider Linda's case. Clearly, there were

enough stress factors—the move, the new job, the end of a relationship—to produce a significant amount of anxiety in anyone's life. It's only normal.

But Linda's anxiety wasn't normal. It was incapacitating and overwhelming. The attacks themselves were devastating, and Linda also had to deal with the constant day-to-day anxiety she felt as she wondered when the next attack would come.

All of Linda's symptoms fit the textbook definition of panic disorder to a T. Her doctor could follow the official diagnostic criteria like a Chinese menu: One symptom from column A, two from column B—no doubt about it, she had panic disorder. Given the details of Linda's case, nine out of ten psychiatrists would probably have rendered that same diagnosis. Of course, it's not likely that any of those ten would have given Linda a detailed, exhaustive physical evaluation before making their diagnosis.

But physical diagnostic testing was just what Linda needed. She had pheochromocytoma, an endocrine disorder which secretes hormones that may spontaneously trigger an anxiety response. Early symptoms of this disease are indistinguishable from the classic description of panic attack, making it a common cause of psychiatric misdiagnosis.

Like Trip, Linda was suffering from a distinct disease. Psychiatric treatment couldn't cure it, but in more than 90 percent of cases, surgery can.

What about Andy? There's no way his bizarre dread of strangers could be caused by a physical condition, right? Wrong.

Andy was a production worker in a plant that manufactured industrial lighting. Weeks before his symptoms began, his department had received a big order for mercury-vapor lamps. If Andy's psychiatrist had been more aware of the possible physical causes of his patient's condition, he might have known that two symptoms of mercury poisoning are heightened anxiety and xenophobia. Andy was being exposed to mercury vapor in the workplace and was being slowly poisoned. He didn't need psychiatric help, he needed to end his exposure to the toxic metal. But, like Trip's and Linda's, Andy's psychiatrist began with the assumption that his patient's symptoms were clearly signs of a psychiatric disease, so he swiftly dismissed the possibility that a hidden physical condition could be at fault.

And then, quite literally adding insult to injury, he accused Andy of being "uncooperative" and labeled him a nonresponder when the treatment plan based on this bad diagnosis failed!

In each of these three cases, a misdiagnosis was made because the psychiatrist involved accepted the most obvious diagnosis and saw no need to investigate alternative causes. For each patient, a series of comprehensive, sophisticated physical, neurological, and endocrinological exams by an expert would have uncovered the biological causes of the problem and suggested an appropriate and effective course of treatment.

But if you consider the way these diagnoses were reached, you'll see that none of the psychiatrists here seemed to be very concerned about *causes.* Instead, their diagnoses were based entirely upon their patient's *symptoms,* and how closely those symptoms matched predetermined, officially sanctioned descriptions of psychiatric disorders.

Trip's symptoms were almost a perfect match with the official diagnostic criteria for school phobia, so school phobia it was! The same goes for Linda's panic attacks and Andy's fear of strangers. They *looked* like the mental or emotional conditions described in the diagnostic manuals, so their doctors assumed that's what they had to be.

With the exception of psychiatrists, most modern physicians believe that diagnosing by symptoms alone is a bad idea. It's unscientific and imprecise, and too often it leads to misdiagnosis and unsuccessful treatment. The subjective symptoms of a hiatal hernia, for example, are very similar to those of a heart attack. But heart medication won't cure a hiatal hernia, and in fact, it will just introduce a whole new set of problems.

As with any kind of medicine, successful psychiatric treatment depends upon a correct diagnosis, and a correct diagnosis depends upon a scientific evaluation of the facts. Psychiatrists may not all agree, but if we compare the way modern physicians make a medically based diagnosis with the way psychiatric patients are assessed, we'll see how far many of today's psychiatrists are from that mark.

MEDICAL DIAGNOSIS—OR DIAGNOSIS THE RIGHT WAY

A patient appears in a hospital emergency room complaining of severe chest pains. The doctor on duty observes that the patient is sweating profusely and having difficulty breathing. The patient's blood pressure, respiratory rate, and pulse are measured immediately. The results indicate that a heart attack may have taken place, but the physician knows that a number of conditions may result in these findings. More specific information is needed, including the patient's health history and any medications or illegal drugs the patient may have taken.

Accordingly, while the patient is being questioned, the doctor orders an electrocardiogram (ECG), which will chart the electrical rhythms of the heart and detect any irregularities that would indicate a heart attack (called a myocardial infarction or simply an MI).

The ECG results indicate not only that an MI has occurred, but that it's a type of heart attack that will respond best to a specific form of treatment, called thrombolytic therapy. Most heart attacks occur when a blood clot (or thrombus) lodges itself in the blood vessels of the heart. If the clot is broken up (the breaking up is called lysis, or thrombolysis) in time, then very little damage occurs. But the longer the clot remains, the more heart muscle dies. Thrombolytic therapy works well only when administered within six hours of the MI; after six hours the medication may do more harm than good. But the patient cannot establish the time of the heart attack, since he can't remember exactly when the pain began.

Therefore the doctor requests a serum enzyme test both to confirm the MI and to indicate whether the MI has happened recently enough for thrombolytic therapy to work. When heart cells die, they release a distinctive enzyme. The serum enzyme test detects the enzyme's presence in the bloodstream—signaling the kind of heart damage typical of MI—and the amount of enzymes may be followed over time to indicate when the MI occurred.

The serum enzyme test confirms the patient had a *recent* MI. Thrombolytic therapy is administered. Afterward, a follow-up serum enzyme test and a repeat echocardiogram indicate that the therapy worked—the clot was destroyed and blood flow resumed. All indications point to the patient's complete recovery within months.

Now that's real, state-of-the-art medicine at work, medicine that will save thousands of lives this year.

The doctor's systematized, information-based approach combined objective data from tests with his own clinical experience, and resulted in a sound diagnosis upon which a good treatment plan can be based. In addition, cardiology is constantly improving diagnostic tests and procedures and uncovering new treatment approaches for myocardial infarction.

PSYCHIATRIC DIAGNOSIS—OR DIAGNOSIS THE WRONG WAY

Now let's see how Linda's psychiatrist reached his diagnosis of panic attacks. Linda arrived at his office and explained the attack she'd experienced at the theater. The psychiatrist asked her to describe all her symptoms and when they started. He asked about the severity of the symptoms and the duration and frequency of the attacks. Did she ever feel she was going crazy? Did she ever feel as if she was going to die?

The psychiatrist listened to Linda's responses. He suspected panic disorder from the start, and the more he heard, the more he was convinced. Midway through the first appointment, he diagnosed panic attack and began to map out Linda's treatment.

His diagnosis was entirely based on symptoms, and he felt confident in this approach.

Because despite its obvious shortcomings, this is the approach that's received psychiatry's official seal of approval.

Let me explain. The American Psychiatric Association—this country's largest professional body for psychiatrists—has a manual that's the bible of the field: the third edition of the *Diagnostic and Statistical Manual of Mental Disorders,* or DSM-III. The manual's 1987 revision is called DSM-III-R. It is a widely used, deeply influential reference book used by psychiatrists and mental health practitioners everywhere in the diagnostic process. It lists mental disorders and their symptoms in clear, menulike formats. The psychiatrist simply checks his patient's symptoms against the DSM-III-R criteria until he finds a match and a diagnosis can be made.

Here are the DSM-III-R criteria for panic attack:

A. At some time during the disturbance, one or more panic attacks (discrete periods of intense fear or discomfort) have occurred that were (1), unexpected, i.e. did not occur immediately before or on exposure to a situation that almost always caused anxiety, and (2) not triggered by situations in which the person was the focus of other's attention.
B. Either four attacks, as described in criterion A, have occurred within a four week period, or one or more attacks have been followed by a period of at least a month of persistent fear of having another attack.
C. At least four of the following symptoms developed during at least one of the attacks:
    (1) shortness of breath (dyspnea) or smothering sensations
    (2) dizziness, unsteady feelings, or faintness
    (3) palpitations or accelerated heart rate (tachycardia)
    (4) trembling or shaking
    (5) sweating
    (6) choking
    (7) nausea or abdominal stress
    (8) depersonalization or derealization
    (9) numbness or tingling sensations (paresthesias)
    (10) flushes (hot flashes) or chills
    (11) chest pain or discomfort
    (12) fear of dying
    (13) fear of going crazy or of doing something uncontrolled

NOTE: Attacks involving four or more symptoms are panic

attacks; attacks involving fewer than four symptoms are limited symptom attacks (see Agoraphobia without History of Panic Disorder).

D. During at least some of the attacks, at least four of the C symptoms developed suddenly and increased in intensity within ten minutes of the beginning of the first C symptom noticed in the attack.

E. It cannot be established that an organic factor initiated and maintained the disturbance, e.g., Amphetamine or Caffeine Intoxication, hyperthyroidism.

NOTE: Mitral valve prolapse may be an associated condition, but does not preclude a diagnosis of Panic Disorder.

Reprinted with permission from: *The Diagnostic and Statistical Manual of Mental Disorders, 3rd Edition, Revised.* American Psychiatric Association, 1987.

Unfortunately, any psychiatrist relying solely upon the diagnostic criteria for panic and anxiety disorders given in DSM-III-R could easily be confused, especially when you consider how much DSM-III-R has changed since the DSM-III of 1980. Psychiatrists had such difficulty following DSM-III criteria that a major revision in panic disorder diagnostic criteria was necessary only seven years after DSM-III's introduction.

While DSM-III called for at least three panic attacks in a three-week period before a panic disorder is indicated, DSM-III-R requires only one or more attacks in a four-week period, or one or more attacks followed by at least a month of fear over having another attack. In addition, the old criteria (used from 1980 to 1987) did not even mention such conditions as cocaine, marijuana, amphetamine or caffeine intoxication, hyperthyroidism, or mitral valve prolapse (MVP), and did not mention that panic attacks can occur suddenly and unexpectedly. Also, the old criteria required that at least four of twelve symptoms always be present before a panic diagnosis should be made. Under the old criteria, many people suffering from panic disorder would not have been diagnosed correctly.

However, DSM-III-R does mention sudden and unexpected attacks, and stipulates that in some attacks it is not necessary to meet the arbitrary requirement of four symptoms. And while the new criteria of DSM-III-R do allude to amphetamine and caffeine intoxication, hyperthyroidism, and mitral valve prolapse as possible causes, they do not demand that even these obvious possible causes be vigorously considered until proved not responsible, and that other diagnoses be ruled out. In fact, only three out of fifty possible or more conditions that can mimic an anxiety disorder are even mentioned.

Clearly, however, DSM-III-R is moving toward a broader view of panic disorder. But confusion still dominates the DSM-III-R diagnosis. According to the DSM-III-R's description of generalized anxiety disorder (GAD), it can coexist with panic if the patient does not focus on having another panic attack. Also according to DSM-III-R, social phobia can be diagnosed, theoretically, in the presence of panic attacks, if the fears of the phobia are unrelated to the fear of having another panic attack. Confusing? You bet it is.

With the DSM-III-R criteria, the traditional method of diagnosis still requires a psychiatrist to *judge* whether the occurrence of or preoccupation with a panic attack accounts for the anxiety. With the psychiatrist's judgment comes judgment errors—and *there will be many opportunities for errors, since panic attacks occur in almost all anxiety disorders.*

Amazingly, DSM-III-R does not mention any objective, diagnostic laboratory tests—not even the tests for substance abuse that have become standard medical procedure in all other branches of medicine. Lamentably, an inaccurate diagnosis often results in ineffective treatment, especially since different anxiety and panic disorders frequently require different treatment strategies.

Now, my colleagues in the APA will say I've given DSM-III-R a bad rap. Look at the bottom of the diagnostic criteria list for panic attack, they'll say. See item E? That clearly says that this is what doctors call a "rule out" diagnosis. You can only make it after you've ruled out all the other possibilities.

Theoretically, they're right. But it doesn't work out that way in practice. Linda's psychiatrist, for example, used DSM-III-R criteria to diagnose her problem. You can't say he was wrong. Her symptoms clearly met all the DSM-III-R standards.

And who can blame him if he didn't spend a lot of time

PANIC THEN...AND PANIC NOW

The following table illustrates how traditional psychiatry has struggled to establish diagnostic criteria for panic disorder. As you can see, what constitutes a panic then (1980—87) differs greatly from what constitutes one now.

Panic Disorder Criteria in *DSM-III* and *DSM-III-R*

DSM-III	*DSM-III-R*
A. At least three panic attacks within a three-week period in circumstances other than during marked physical exertion or in a life-threatening situation. The attacks are not precipitated only by exposure to a circumscribed phobic stimulus.	A. At some time during the disturbance, one or more panic attacks (discrete periods of intense discomfort or fear that were (1) unexpected, i.e., did not occur immediately before or on exposure to a situation that almost always caused anxiety, and (2) not triggered by situations in which the individual was the focus of others' attention) occurred within a four-week period, or one or more attacks were followed by a period of at least a month of persistent fear of having another attack.
B. Panic attacks are manifested by discrete periods of apprehension or fear and at least four of the following symptoms appear during each attack: (1) dyspnea (5) dizziness, vertigo, or unsteady feelings (2) palpitations (11) trembling or shaking (9) sweating (4) choking or smothering sensations . . .	C. At least four of the following symptoms developed during at least one of the attacks: (1) shortness of breath (dyspnea) or smothering sensations (2) dizziness, unsteady feelings, or faintness (3) palpitations or accelerated heart rate (tachycardia) (4) trembling or shaking (5) sweating

DSM-III (cont.)

(10) faintness

(6) feelings of unreality

(7) paresthesias (tingling in hands or feet)

(8) hot and cold flashes

(3) chest pain or discomfort

(12) fear of dying, going crazy, or doing something uncontrolled during an attack

C. Not due to a physical disorder or another mental disorder, such as Major Depression, Somatization Disorder, Schizophrenia

D. The disorder is not associated with Agoraphobia

DSM-III-R (cont.)

(5) sweating

(6) choking

(7) nausea or abdominal distress . . .

(8) depersonalization or derealization

(9) numbness or tingling sensations (paresthesias)

(10) flushes (hot flashes) or chills

(11) chest pain or discomfort

(12) fear of dying

(13) fear of going crazy or doing something uncontrolled

D. During at least some of the attacks, at least four of the C symptoms developed suddenly and increased in intensity within ten minutes of the beginning of the first C symptom in the attack.

E. It cannot be established that an organic factor initiated and maintained the disturbance, e.g., Amphetamine or Caffeine intoxication, hyperthyroidism. Note: Mitral valve prolapse may be an associated condition but does not rule out a diagnosis of Panic Disorder.

DSM-III Criteria for Agoraphobia
and DSM-III-R Criteria for Panic Disorder with Agoraphobia

DSM-III: Agoraphobia

A. The individual has marked fear of and thus avoids being alone or in public places from which escape

DSM-III-R: Panic Disorder with Agoraphobia

A. Meets criteria for Panic Disorder.

B. Agoraphobia: Fear of being in places or situations from which escape

PANIC THEN . . . AND PANIC NOW (*continued*)

DSM-III: Agoraphobia (*cont.*)	*DSM-III-R:* Panic Disorder with Agoraphobia (*cont.*)
might be difficult or help not available in case of sudden incapacitation, e.g., crowds, tunnels, bridges, public transportation.	might be difficult (or embarrassing) or in which help might not be available, in the event of panic attack. . . . As a result of this fear, there are either travel restrictions or need for a companion when away from home, or there is endurance of agoraphobic situations despite intense anxiety. Common agoraphobic situations include being outside of the home alone, being in a crowd or standing in a line, being on a bridge, traveling in a bus, train, or car.
B. There is increasing constriction of normal activities until the fears or avoidance behavior dominate the individual's life.	Mild agoraphobic avoidance: some avoidance (or endurance with distress), but relatively normal lifestyle, e.g., travels unaccompanied when necessary, such as to work or to shop; otherwise avoids traveling alone.
	Moderate: Avoidance results in constricted lifestyle, e.g., the person is able to leave house alone, but not go more than a few miles unaccompanied.
	Severe: Avoidance results in being nearly or completely housebound or unable to leave house unaccompanied.

PANIC THEN ... AND PANIC NOW (*continued*)

DSM-III: Agoraphobia (*cont.*)

DSM-III-R: Panic Disorder with Agoraphobia (*cont.*)

C. Not due to a major depressive episode, Obsessive Compulsive Disorder, Paranoid Personality Disorder, or Schizophrenia.

Reprinted by permission from: *The Diagnostic and Statistical Manual of Mental Disorders, 3rd Edition, Revised.* American Psychiatric Association, 1987.

---

considering item E? It's certainly a mild warning, almost an afterthought. And it doesn't give him a hint as to *how* these other problems might be uncovered. You'll notice it doesn't even mention pheochromocytoma.

Linda's psychiatrist did ask if she had been using amphetamines or was a heavy coffee drinker, but he didn't even begin to think about the kinds of examinations needed to rule out conditions like hyperthyroidism. The possibility of pheochromocytoma never entered his mind. He was satisfied with the symptom-based diagnosis that DSM-III-R had helped him reach.

Abnormal anxiety, panic disorders, and phobias can be caused by a wide range of biological conditions, but in an evaluation based on DSM-III-R criteria, that simply doesn't matter. DSM-III-R encourages *psychiatric* diagnoses. If your symptoms match up, you've got a *psychiatric* problem, no matter what may be wrong with your brain or body. Among mental health professionals, this is currently the predominant method of diagnosis.

This method of diagnosis overlooks one solid fact: There are no symptoms associated *only* with mental disorders. Even some of the most bizarre patterns of behavior and thinking can be traced to biological sources. Certain types of epilepsy, for example, can trigger auditory and visual hallucinations. Some toxic metals can actually trigger phobic behavior. In fact, bio-

psychiatrists know that dozens of conditions, including infections, metabolic disorders, and unbalanced hormones, as well
as decidedly physical agents such as drugs and toxins, can produce symptoms similar to various psychiatric conditions.

But you won't learn much about them by reading DSM-III-
R. The most alarming shortcoming of that book is that it says so
little about the possible organic causes of the symptoms in
question.

There are dozens of physical conditions that can mimic
panic attack, but in item E, DSM-III-R lists only four. (At least
that is an improvement over earlier versions. Maybe the message of biopsychiatry *is* starting to be heard.)

If biopsychiatrists had written the manual, the information
in item E would have come *first*—and it would have been expanded to included all the biological, chemical, and environmental agents capable of triggering paniclike symptoms. In fact,
each listing would begin with an exhaustive discussion of the
nonpsychiatric conditions which must be ruled out before a
psychiatric diagnosis can confidently be made.

Clearly, all three of these patients would have been better
served if their psychiatrists had looked beyond the symptoms
and paid appropriate attention to their patient's physical conditions—if, in other words, their psychiatrists had acted like
real doctors.

I'm convinced that the high rate of misdiagnosis in psychiatry today has a lot to do with this insistence upon symptom-
based diagnosis, a system that survives because of psychiatry's
stubborn resistance to medically based diagnostic testing. This
tendency toward diagnosis-by-number is simplistic and naive.
You know something's wrong when a radio-talk-show host or a
computer program can toss off a diagnosis just about as well as
people who have invested a decade or more in their medical
education—or when criminals, actors, and reporters can fool
psychiatrists so easily just by telling them what they expect to
hear.

Diagnosing by symptoms is more than ineffective. It's down-
right dangerous, since misdiagnosing a physical symptom as a

psychiatric sign often allows a serious organic condition to progress undetected.

But what I find most frustrating of all is that these days it's totally unnecessary. In later chapters, we'll take a close look at sophisticated new testing procedures that can help determine whether your symptoms are truly psychiatric or are the result of a hidden physical ailment. But first, it's important to understand why symptom-based diagnoses so often lead to false conclusions and ineffective treatment. Here are five reasons:

1. *Symptoms can be nonspecific.* In other words, no symptom, or group of symptoms, can be linked to a single disorder. Remember Linda? Her symptoms were identical with the recognized symptoms of panic attack. But this same group of symptoms could be caused by other conditions, and obviously in her case they were. To put it simply, her symptoms were not *specific* to panic attack. Clearly, more concrete, objective information was needed before a really sound diagnosis could be made. That kind of information comes only from thorough testing and physical evaluation.

2. *Emotional symptoms are often vague and hard to describe.* Physicians know that even when they are dealing with distinct physical symptoms, such as pain, it's hard to get reliable and objective information based on the patient's subjective experience of the symptom. People have different tolerances to pain, and they feel it differently. One person's "severe" pain is another's "moderate" pain. And a sensation which one patient may describe as "burning" pain may feel like a "stabbing" pain to another.

Now, if it's that hard to get objective information from a patient's experience of physical symptoms, imagine how that difficulty is magnified when the patient is asked to describe the intangible, interrelated, and sometimes bafflingly complex symptoms of a psychiatric disorder. In essence, the psychiatrist is relying upon the patient to diagnose himself or herself.

That, incidentally, is why psychiatrists who adhere to different philosophies always seem to end up with patients whose disorders are just the sort they're most familiar with. When you're relying on subjective symptoms, it's very easy for a psychiatrist to unintentionally steer patients toward the diagnosis you want or expect to hear. Thus, when the Freudian asks questions almost exclusively about the patient's childhood, is it any surprise that he eventually concludes that that's where the root of the problem lies? As the old saying goes, "To the man who has only a hammer, everything looks like a nail."

3. *Symptom-based diagnosis ignores racial, sexual, and cultural factors.* Women often express emotional symptoms quite easily, while men tend to bury those symptoms behind a facade of strength—or drown them in alcohol. Various ethnic groups differ in the ways they experience and express emotional disturbances. Some cultures frown on overt displays of feelings, others encourage emotional expressiveness. In a psychiatric evaluation, these differences can strongly influence the reliability and usefulness of the patient's description of symptoms.

4. *Symptom-based diagnosis overlooks alcohol and drug abuse.* Drug and alcohol abuse is one of the most prevalent mimickers of depression, anxiety, panic, even outright psychosis. But don't look for the patient's symptoms to differentiate the two. And don't expect the patient or the family to volunteer any information about the substance abuse—one of the hallmarks of these disorders is denial. A simple urine test, by contrast, can quickly identify a drug-abuse problem—and ensure that the patient receives the special treatment that is required.

5. *Diagnosing illness based on the presence of certain symptoms implies that the illness is cured when those symptoms disappear.* Biopsychiatrists know this isn't true. We've seen that in many cases, the biological aspects of a disorder can be present before psychiatric symptoms appear, or after the symptoms have abated. By pronouncing a symptom-free patient cured, the psychiatrist may be opening the door for an inevitable relapse.

THE TOOLS ARE HERE

In the past, before sophisticated diagnostic procedures were available, all medical professionals were forced to rely on symptom-based diagnoses. They simply didn't have the knowledge, or the technology, to be more specific.

At one time, countless individuals were hospitalized with symptoms of anxiety, depression, and dementia. Often these individuals were bothered by headaches, insomnia, and memory lapses—more proof that their problem was "all in their head." In reality, these poor individuals were suffering from pellagra—a condition caused by a vitamin (niacin) deficiency. For many years, pellagra was a very common problem in the United States, especially in the South, where a diet based on corn, fatback, and molasses often caused pellagra. Approximately 50 percent of some state mental institutions' hospitalized patients were really suffering from a niacin deficiency—an easily treatable condition! Since science discovered the niacin factor in 1937, the vitamin has been added to many cereal products, greatly reducing the number of pellagra's victims.

Physicians would have been irresponsible to ignore this new information about niacin, or to ignore any other advances, but that's exactly what many modern psychiatrists are doing: ignoring new information and technologies that could vastly improve the accuracy of their diagnoses. Why? Because they are philosophically convinced that blood testing, urine analysis, brain scans, and all the other messy poking and prodding that form the basis of medical diagnosis are, for them, irrelevant. They are, after all, doctors of the mind, and you can't put the mind under a microscope, can you?

We've already seen how that attitude has damaged the profession's credibility and sapped its vigor, and how it has caused countless thousands of patients to endure needless pain and hardship. And we keep coming back to the same point: *Successful psychiatric treatment depends first upon a correct diagnosis, and a correct diagnosis depends upon a scientific evaluation of the facts.*

MISDIAGNOSIS *AND* INEFFECTUAL TREATMENT

Besides the emphasis on symptom-based diagnosis, I have identified five other mistakes that contribute to misdiagnosis and/or ineffectual treatment for panic and anxiety disorders.

THE FIRST MISTAKE: THE FIFTY-MINUTE SOLUTION, OR NO TIME FOR A PHYSICAL

Today, a patient walking into any doctor's office, especially a psychiatrist's office, expects treatment, preferably the faster the better. When it comes to this "fast-food" approach, psychiatrists rarely lag behind the other medical specialists. In fact, the majority of psychiatric patients receive medication upon their first fifty-minute-long visit. While immediate service may rate four stars in a restaurant, in a psychiatrist's office it can lead to disaster.

One study conducted at Harvard's Massachusetts General Hospital found that 70 percent of panic attack patients had been to more than ten physicians each before they were properly diagnosed! Usually these treatment "failures" were labeled as neurotics suffering from hysteria, hypoglycemia, hypochondria, or cardiac neurosis—other conditions that reflect primarily the specialty or bias of the examining physicians.

The fifty-minute solution means, of course, that any physical cause for a patient's anxiety will probably be missed. And with less than 10 percent of all psychiatrists even attempting outpatient physical examinations (and—even more amazingly—less than 40 percent of psychiatrists perform physical examinations on *hospitalized* patients!), chances are the majority of any physical mimickers will be missed—particularly noteworthy when the high national incidence of alcoholism and drug abuse (conditions that may be mistaken for other psychiatric illnesses) is considered. The fifty-minute solution helps explain a study I already mentioned where forty-five out of a hundred consecutively studied psychiatric patients were found to have undiagnosed medical conditions that either accounted for or worsened their psychiatric symptoms!

THE SECOND MISTAKE: PATIENT, DIAGNOSE THYSELF

Psychiatrists err not only because of undetected physical mimickers, but often because they miss the correct psychiatric diagnosis. The symptoms of the anticipatory anxiety that accompany a panic attack are often mistaken for generalized anxiety disorder (GAD). A psychiatrist, expecting to see a large number of patients with anxiety, often ignores or fails to detect the signs of a panic attack. A colleague of mine, Dr. James C. Ballenger, tells of viewing a videotape about GAD that was made by a very prominent psychiatrist. The videotape demonstrated an interview session between this psychiatrist and a female patient. The woman began the session by claiming, "I've been anxious my entire life." After describing all the symptoms, such as irritability and sweating, that fit GAD, she added, "And when I go into crowds I get this suffocating feeling, my chest beats fast, and I know I'm going to die." Dr. Ballenger was shocked when the acclaimed psychiatrist ignored this obvious description of a panic attack and instead diagnosed the woman as suffering from GAD!

This famous psychiatrist duplicated the mistake made by countless other psychiatrists: He allowed the patient to diagnose herself. The patient's early statement that she had been anxious all her life predisposed the doctor to a diagnosis of anxiety; he heard only the symptoms that supported his initial predisposition, while ignoring the woman's near-textbook description of a panic attack. If the woman's first statement had been "...and I've been *depressed* all my life," would she then have been diagnosed as suffering from depression? Probably, since the anxiety symptoms she described frequently accompany depression. Is there another branch of medicine that places such an emphasis on patients' diagnoses of themselves? (Imagine if a hypertension specialist declined to record a patient's blood pressure and instead commenced therapy immediately, simply because the patient said, "I've been suffering from high blood pressure all my life." The action would probably result in a suspension of the doctor's medical license.)

THE THIRD MISTAKE: ONE DRUG FITS ALL

Following the truncated diagnostic procedures employed by most traditional psychiatrists, the doctor will usually move quickly to prescribing medication as the treatment of first choice. If the psychiatrist suspects anxiety (highly likely, since the traditional psychiatrist usually misses any physical mimickers of anxiety, as well as the panic disorders often mistaken for anxiety), the traditional treatment of choice has been the benzodiazepine class of medications. In the 1970s, a prescription for a benzodiazepine usually meant a prescription for Valium (chemical name: diazepam). The preponderance of the anxiety diagnosis, by psychiatrists and other medical practitioners, made Valium the most popular psychiatric drug of the 1970s, and one of the most profitable drugs of all time. Physicians prescribed Valium so frequently that it became a "one drug fits all" medication. Whether you had headaches, backaches, nervousness, insomnia, or panic attacks, the prescription would frequently be the same: Valium. Unfortunately, Valium and the other benzodiazepines have considerable potential for dependency and addiction, and the more they were prescribed unwisely, the more people became dependent and addicted to them. The value of Valium (as well as of other benzodiazepines) as an antipanic medication is controversial. My experience with panic patients and with the benzodiazepines' potential for drug dependency leads me to prefer the tricyclic antidepressants as the treatment of first choice in panic.

Today, Valium's role as the "one drug fits all" leader has been usurped by another benzodiazepine-like medication, Xanax (chemical name: alprazolam). Unlike the other benzodiazepines, Xanax has been established as having antipanic effects. There is no question that Xanax appears to be a major pharmaceutical development. Like any other new treatment, questions remain regarding the long-term efficacy and safety of Xanax, questions that only time and further study will answer. In addition, Xanax has not proved to be superior to the already well-established and successful treatment regimen, a regimen that will be explained in the next chapter. When the choice is between a new treatment and one of equal efficacy that is tried and true, I take the more established route.

Other psychiatrists have not shown the same restraint with this relatively new drug. Xanax's popularity continues to grow. In 1988, Xanax was the number-one prescribed medication in the U.S.A. with $400 million in worldwide sales (conversely, Valium had dropped to nineteenth). To me, the reasons for Xanax's increased prominence as an antipanic medication is *laziness.* That's right—the laziness of psychiatrists and other physicians. Why bother to diagnose a patient correctly, to differentiate between generalized anxiety disorders and panic disorders, if giving one drug treats both conditions?

Xanax's utility doubles when the drug's antidepressant abilities are considered. With 50 percent of all depressed patients exhibiting symptoms of anxiety, it doesn't matter if the patient is suffering from anxiety disorders or depression. After all, without working too hard—even without knowing exactly what they're treating—psychiatrists can achieve a success rate far better than they normally reach. So a few patients have underlying physical conditions that go undetected, and a few other patients fail to benefit from therapy—these psychiatrists can't be too concerned with a few failures. Xanax's popularity reminds me of the old days when no matter what the diagnosis, the treatment was always the same: psychotherapy. Today, the prescription pad has replaced the couch.

However, a biopsychiatrist like me cannot accept the slightly above-average success rate of a lazy psychiatrist, because I know that with a thorough examination, a proper diagnosis, and a proven treatment plan tailored to the individual patient, biopsychiatry can achieve a success rate that approaches 90 or even 95 percent for panic disorders.

THE FOURTH MISTAKE: FAILING TO USE BEHAVIOR THERAPY
The psychiatrists' tendency to rely upon the easy solution provided by medication frequently means they neglect other nonpharmacologic strategies. Foremost among these strategies are the behavioral treatments, especially desensitization, de-

scribed in Chapter 9. Desensitization provides effective relief of anxiety, particularly of the anticipatory anxiety that surrounds a panic attack. But behavior therapy takes time and effort—additional staff members or referral to panic and phobia treatment centers may be necessary. Because of this additional time and effort, as well as the overreliance upon medications and ignorance of behavior therapy, desensitization techniques are ignored by the majority of psychiatrists.

THE FIFTH MISTAKE: GIVING UP TOO SOON

Even if psychiatrists have managed to make the correct diagnosis and have recommended the proper medication, they often give up before the therapy has had a chance to work. Psychiatrists may abandon a medication before establishing its proper dosage and before it has the proper time to work. They may switch to another drug too soon, without testing to verify that the patient has actually taken the recommended dosage, and without providing sufficient time for the first drug to "wash out" of the patient's system. Or they may take a patient's complaints of recurring panic attacks during treatment at face value and conclude that the treatment is not working, even though the patient may actually be describing the symptoms of anticipatory anxiety and not a panic attack. Sadly, many patients are needlessly labeled as "treatment-refractory," meaning treatment failures. Fortunately, some of these failures end up in the care of biopsychiatrists.

NONPSYCHIATRIC PHYSICIANS

Being a psychiatrist, I tend to focus on the deficiencies among the psychiatric profession. But my fellow psychiatrists are not the main culprits for the misdiagnosing and ineffectual treatment of anxiety disorders. Nor are the psychologists or other nonmedical mental health professionals the primary offenders.

In actuality, the nonpsychiatrist physicians, the "real doctors," are statistically the worst offenders. Those who seek treatment for panic attacks are more likely to visit family doctors, internists, gynecologists, cardiologists, and other nonpsychiatric physicians than to see mental health professionals. Some surveys have found that at least one of every four patients treated in a primary care setting has a very real and important psychiatric disease and not simply psychiatric symptoms. Remarkably, 11 percent of all visits to primary-care physicians (internists and general and family practitioners) and almost 50 percent of all visits to cardiologists actually involve panic and anxiety disorders. Sadly, of the millions of people suffering from these disorders, less than one-quarter ever seek help—the other 77 percent remain untreated, or turn to alcohol and/or other drugs to help them cope. And of those few who do seek treatment, most receive care that is outdated and ineffectual, and often for the wrong condition.

Almost always these nonpsychiatric physicians will miss the underlying panic disorder. Most persons suffering from anxiety who visit their family physician are concerned primarily with the insomnia, exhaustion, digestive disorders, headaches, or muscle pain that may *accompany* an anxiety disorder. Most often, these doctors, after ruling out the obvious possible physical causes for the patient's symptoms, usually diagnose the patient as suffering from anxiety neurosis, hypochondria, or some other vague psychosomatic condition. They may mumble something about a patient being under a lot of stress lately and prescribe a benzodiazepine.

Other mental health conditions besides anxiety disorders are badly handled by nonpsychiatric physicians. One study stated that "60 percent of the estimated 32,000,000 sufferers of mental illness receive treatment with the primary care system exclusively." These physicians "manage most of these patients entirely within their practice and refer only 10 percent . . . to a psychiatrist. Unfortunately, despite extensive contact with psychosocial issues in the care of their patients, most physicians have had little formal training in the evaluation of these factors."

Not surprisingly, nonpsychiatric physicians—like people in general—have a tendency to identify and label as "most disliked" patients who exhibit psychiatric symptoms. Often a physician will pay less attention and follow less stringent examination and laboratory testing procedures when examining a patient with psychiatric symptoms. And when the examination and lab tests fail to identify a physical cause, the patient may be incorrectly declared "medically normal." The patient may then be told that the problem is in his or her head, and that the doctor cannot do anything.

Why, then, don't I focus more specifically on the errors of these nonpsychiatric physicians? While I certainly do not condone their mistakes, I can understand their errors more easily than the mistakes made by psychiatrists. It is difficult for even psychiatrists to stay abreast of developments in their specialty; it is nearly impossible for the nonpsychiatric physician to remain current in psychiatry. And if the majority of psychiatrists do not treat anxiety disorders correctly, how can we expect the nonpsychiatric physicians to do what the psychiatry profession cannot?

For the most part in this chapter I have described how *not* to diagnose or treat anxiety and panic disorders. Occasionally I have hinted at better methods to come. Well, later in the book I will present a very detailed account of how I, practicing as a biopsychiatrist, conduct a thorough diagnosis and implement effective treatment plans.

But first I should explain the fundamental tenet of biopsychiatry's approach to panic and anxiety disorders: that many of these conditions have a biological basis—a biological basis that will influence a biopsychiatrist's approach to treatment.

CHAPTER FIVE

THE BIOLOGICAL BASIS:

Why It's Not Your Fault

*T*HE SUBJECT OF this chapter—the biological basis of panic and anxiety disorders—may at first seem of interest only to researchers gathered around their test tubes.

In reality, this subject is far more than academic esoterica. Only through understanding these biological causes can patients truly stop blaming themselves for their panic disorders. Furthermore, comprehending the different theories concerning the biological basis of panic and anxiety disorders provides insight into the reasoning behind the treatment strategies designed by biopsychiatry.

The foundation for the theory of the biological basis of panic and anxiety was laid in the 1960s when a team led by my colleague Donald Klein, M.D., noted that certain tricyclic antidepressants reduced the symptoms of patients suffering from acute attacks of intense anxiety. These same medications had no beneficial effect on anxiety of a chronic, "nonattack" nature. This discrepancy led Dr. Klein to hypothesize a *qualitative* difference between the two anxiety states. In other words, the sudden burst of severe symptoms seen in the attack anxiety was not simply an extension and aggravation of the milder chronic form, but a completely different reaction. Klein described the attack anxiety as panic and the chronic form as anticipatory anxiety, and proposed that they probably had distinct and separate triggering mechanisms. Anticipatory anxiety, he said, was triggered by contact with or anticipation of specific external stimuli, while panic was internally triggered by biological forces.

In the late 1960s, the establishment of sodium-lactate-induced panic attacks only strengthened suspicions of a biological connection. The fact that one substance could induce attacks and another could block them fascinated researchers and led to the search for the neurochemical answer to the question: What causes panic attacks? I will lead up to the answers to that question by explaining something of the basis of neurobiology.

A CRASH COURSE IN NEUROBIOLOGY

Neurobiology is the science which seeks to understand the workings of the central nervous system (CNS) and the peripheral nervous system (PNS), which combine to form the body's elaborate, elegant, and tremendously efficient communications network. The CNS includes the brain and the spinal cord, and the PNS includes the remaining network of nerves.

The central nervous system, because it is the main center for control and coordination of the entire body, has been the primary focus of anxiety research. The intricacies of our central nervous system are breathtaking—billions of electrical impulses race along CNS pathways, carrying sensory input from the senses to the brain and relaying directions from the brain back to body systems. The activity of the CNS regulates a wide range of human behavior, from sleep/wake cycles and muscular coordination to memory, thought, and emotions. This wide-ranging activity has led panic disorder researchers to focus on the central nervous system.

The basic working unit of the central nervous system is the neuron, a specialized cell with the ability to generate and transmit electrical impulses. Chains of neurons form the pathways along which those impulses race on their way to the appropriate regions of the brain. Impulses triggered by input from the ear, for example, flash along the auditory nerve on the way to the superior temporal lobe of the brain, where they are processed into meaningful sounds, while impulses from the optic nerve reach the occipital lobe, where they are translated into visual images. How this translation works is unknown, but we do know that brain chemicals known as neurotransmitters are intimately involved.

Neurotransmitters, an essential part of CNS activity, regulate the transmission of impulses between neurons, which makes them tremendously influential in determining the flow of nerve impulses along the neural pathways.

Basically there are two types of neurotransmitters—those that say yes and those that say no. The yes neurotransmitters facilitate the transmission of the nervous impulse by acting as a chemical bridge between neurons. The no neurotransmitters act as a blockade, doing their best to stop an impulse in its tracks.

Since neurotransmitters are so influential in regulating the flow of sensory input to the brain, they play an important role in virtually every brain activity, from sleep, pain, and pleasure to thoughts, emotions, and anxieties. This has presented investigators with an intriguing question: Are there systems of neurotransmitters which specifically regulate the nervous impulses which trigger or block the anxiety reaction in the brain? If such a system could be found, we'd be well on our way to discovering the brain's biological mechanics of anxiety. In fact, neurotransmitters and the roles they play in mediating emotional responses have become an exciting focus of the scientific search for the biological underpinnings of anxiety.

Researchers are especially interested in the portions of the brain that are known to control anxiety responses. In an earlier chapter I mentioned research that involved stump-tailed monkeys that exhibited panic reactions when their brains were electrically stimulated. The electrical charges were directly on the *locus ceruleus,* a brain-cell region which contains an abundance of *noradrenergic* neurotransmitters—specifically the neurotransmitter norepinephrine—that stimulate the flow of nerve impulses.

We know that the locus ceruleus, or LC, is associated with the production of fear responses, so logically we'd expect that an increase of noradrenergic stimulation here would result in rising anxiety. And that's exactly what the study with the stump-tailed monkeys showed. A logical conclusion is that the electrical charges stimulated the norepinephrine neurotransmitters to overfire, which provoked the anxiety-producing capabilities of the LC to trip the biological alarm system that results in a panic response. That conclusion was bolstered by other studies that showed that drugs which increase the flow of these noradrenergic transmitters from the LC increase anxiety, while those that inhibit the flow decrease anxiety. The theory that panic attacks arise from central noradrenergic malfunctioning is sometimes called the central noradrenergic activation hypothesis.

One problem with validating this hypothesis is that it is still rather vague and nonspecific, involving a relatively large area of the brain. Many other areas besides the locus ceruleus may be involved in the genesis of a panic attack. These other areas of the brain—sometimes referred to as the brain's limbic system —that may be involved in the central noradrenergic malfunctioning include the *amygdala,* the *thalamus,* the *hypothalamus,* and the *hippocampus.* The amygdala, located deep within the brain, has direct connections with our olfactory nerves (responsible for our sense of smell) and with the hypothalamus. While its role is not definitely established, the amygdala appears to be concerned with mood, feelings, and memory. (Perhaps the amygdala's direct connection with our olfactory system accounts for the power of smell to evoke so many memories.) The amygdala may also be involved with our autonomic, behavioral, and endocrine responses of anxiety and other emotional expressions. The thalamus acts as a relay center for all the other senses (except smell), and it is believed to be where we first become consciously aware of pain, temperature, and touch. Above the thalamus sits the hypothalamus, the part of the brain thought to be responsible for regulating our basic desires of hunger, thirst, and sex, as well as our sleep and basic autonomic nervous system. It is believed that the hypothalamus affects changes in our respiratory and cardiovascular function during anxiety. Finally, the hippocampus receives information that has been processed by other parts of the brain. This highly processed information may be used to direct our sometimes complex responses, including our physical behavior based on our emotions, instinct, and memory.

BRAIN MAPPING AND PANIC ATTACKS

Until the advent of positron emission tomography scans (P.E.T. scans), the direct study of brain function had largely been limited to animal models. With sophisticated P.E.T. scans, science now has the ability to map cerebral function in humans, giving us valuable information about cerebral structures during the experiencing, evaluation, and expression of the various parts of anxiety.

P.E.T. scans have been used to map cerebral function of panic disorder patients to detect any abnormality in their cerebral function during normal, resting, *nonpanic* situations. These studies have indicated that there is abnormally high cerebral blood flow in an area of the brain called the *parahippocampal gyrus* in panic attack patients, but not in normal individuals. The parahippocampal gyrus is located near the hippocampus and appears to funnel sensory information into and out of the hippocampus. Furthermore, the parahippocampal gyrus receives information from a number of sources, including the locus ceruleus. The increased cerebral blood flow in the parahippocampal gyrus suggests abnormally high activity in panic attack patients during *normal nonpanic situations*. This information has led researchers to speculate that this increased activity indicates a biological *vulnerability* to panic in panic disorder patients.

While increased activity *into* the parahippocampal gyrus may mean a vulnerability to panic attacks, increased activity *out of* the parahippocampal gyrus may implicate this area in the *generation* of panic attacks. According to this theory, some triggering event (perhaps neurotransmitter activity in the locus ceruleus serves as the brain's "panic button") is processed through the parahippocampal gyrus into the hippocampus, where a panic attack response is then funneled out through the parahippocampal gyrus and into the various areas of the brain responsible for enacting the physiological, psychological, and behavioral effects we associate with a panic attack.

Clearly many questions remain. For example, does this increased blood flow in the parahippocampal gyrus reflect a genetic predisposition to panic or to anticipatory anxiety? And what about the triggering event—does the increased activity in the parahippocampal gyrus reflect a malfunction in the locus ceruleus or other areas of the brain that may be responsible for starting the panic attack reaction?

In addition, studies have found seemingly conflicting results concerning cerebral blood flow and anxiety. One very recent study found that lactate-infusions did increase cerebral blood flow in panic patients but not in other subjects. However, another study found no increase in cerebral blood flow when phobic individuals were exposed to their phobia. While a study of obsessive compulsive patients revealed that cerebral blood flow *decreased* when exposed to a phobic situation, but increased when the patients imagined their phobia. While the results of these studies appear conflicting, I believe that they reflect the complexity of our anxiety response combined with our improving but still relatively inexact methods of studying the brain.

Obviously the central noradrenergic system is quite complex, and unraveling which part or parts are directly involved in triggering the neurotransmitter abnormalities that cause the panic attack will take additional time and research. Perhaps the most important thing to understand is that a panic attack may not be triggered simply by too much of this neurotransmitter or too little of that neurotransmitter, but rather by any disruptions to the complex central noradrenergic system outlined above.

In the following pages, I'll describe some potential triggering events or possible malfunctions that may be responsible for starting the panic attack response.

PANIC AND HYPERVENTILATION

For years, researchers have been studying hyperventilation as a possible cause of panic attack. Hyperventilation describes involuntary rapid breathing in response to inordinately high concentrations of carbon dioxide in the blood. The stepped-up breathing rate brings more oxygen into the system and restores the balance of oxygen and CO_2. Sometimes, however, hyperventilation can result in too low levels of CO_2, resulting in a condition called *respiratory alkalosis.* Symptoms of alkalosis include light-headedness, dizziness, and numbness. The age-old cure for hyperventilation has been breathing into a paper bag. By rebreathing the same air, the patient takes in higher levels of CO_2 and the balance is restored to normal. (Ironically, for panic patients, breathing into a paper bag may be the *worst* "cure"—I'll explain this catch later in the chapter.)

Hyperventilation and panic disorder share a great many similarities:

- Both often occur after muscular exertion or while falling asleep or waking.
- Patients with both disorders experience similar physiological changes, including alterations in blood gases and pH factor.
- The symptoms of hyperventilation (rapid breathing, pounding heart, dizziness, feelings of suffocation, trembling, and so on) are nearly identical to those of panic attack.
- A significant number of hyperventilation patients also experience panic attacks, and vice versa.

Clearly, hyperventilation and panic disorder are closely related conditions. In studying this subject, researchers have addressed three obvious and logical possibilities:

1. *Hyperventilation causes panic.* Two studies involving agoraphobia patients have shown that hyperventilation may serve as a trigger for a panic attack. In both studies, the patients are intentionally hyperventilated. In one study, 61 percent of the patients experienced panic symptoms; in the other, 91 percent of the agoraphobic subjects reported symptoms of panic attack.

2. *Panic causes hyperventilation.* Some strong evidence weighs in against hyperventilation as a cause of panic. For instance, inhalation of carbon dioxide—the opposite of hyperventilation—is more effective in triggering panic attacks. Also, studies show that many of the stressors which cause hyperventilation don't necessarily result in panic, a finding you wouldn't expect to see if hyperventilation were a cause of panic.

3. *Both disorders have a common cause.* This theory is

based primarily on the striking similarities between the two disorders and on the fact that a distinct percentage of panic attack sufferers are also chronic hyperventilators.

One intriguing explanation for the relationship between panic and hyperventilation suggests that hyperventilation is a means of keeping blood levels of CO_2 low. If CO_2 is really a more potent provocation to panic than hyperventilation, this theory goes, then some panic patients become chronic hyperventilators to keep their CO_2 levels low. This theory has gained credence because of the far greater panic-inducing results achieved by CO_2 when compared to hyperventilation. For this reason, the hyperventilation cure of breathing into a paper bag may be the worst action for a panic patient to take, since the increased CO_2 may actually trigger a panic attack. In fact, CO_2 inhalation has been shown to be almost as effective as sodium lactate infusion in provoking panic attacks in panic-prone individuals.

SODIUM LACTATE, CO_2, AND PANIC

The similar panic-inducing properties of sodium lactate and CO_2 have led researchers to speculate that there is an underlying mechanism shared by the two substances. The body's metabolism of sodium lactate begins with the lactate being broken down and oxidized into bicarbonate ions. These bicarbonate ions cannot enter the brain, since they can't cross the blood-brain barrier; instead they circulate in the bloodstream, eventually hooking up with hydrogen ions to form carbonic acid. This carbonic acid will break down into . . . carbon dioxide. That's right, CO_2. My colleague Dr. Jack Gorman and his associates suggest that this CO_2 will then enter into the brain, where it may collect around the locus ceruleus and produce a panic attack, as inhaled CO_2 does. This theory implies that this concentration of CO_2 in the brain may cause the locus ceruleus to increase its activity and fire more neurotransmitters in response to a "suffocation alarm" in panic attack patients—the brain thinks it is suffocating to death, and orders the appropriate

134

responses. Therefore, the biological cause of panic attacks—or at least some types of panic attacks—may be hypersensitivity to the presence of CO_2 in the brain. In addition, the locus ceruleus may be overly sensitive to a number of different regulatory systems, resulting in an unnecessary panic response to other CNS "false alarms."

At this time, this theory is still just an intriguing possibility that definitely merits further attention. Nevertheless, I find the possibility that CO_2 and sodium lactate have similar mechanisms of action to be potentially very promising. Furthermore, this recent explanation of sodium lactate's possible role in panic attack has been strengthened by many years of research to establish the panic-inducing properties of lactate.

SODIUM LACTATE AND PANIC

Actually the evidence for sodium lactate's involvement in panic attacks began to appear twenty years earlier. In the 1940s, researchers studying why anxiety disorder patients experienced a worsening of their condition following vigorous exercise noted that patients with neurocirculatory asthenia (almost identical to what we call panic disorder) had higher levels of blood lactate following exercise, while normal subjects' levels were significantly lower. The question of whether lactate itself could precipitate a panic attack wasn't addressed until the 1960s, when researchers infused enough lactate into subjects to reach levels produced by strenuous exercise. From the very beginning patients with panic disorders have had attacks from lactate infusion, while the normal subjects, or controls, have not.

Traditionally, psychiatric research has been burdened by the inability to study certain psychiatric conditions in the laboratory. Instead, researchers have been forced to rely upon patient recollections or secondhand accounts for valuable information such as the onset, duration, symptoms, and consequences of the psychiatric episode. Panic disorder research was further hampered by the spontaneity of the attacks. With no

ACUTE PANIC INVENTORY (API)

The API is not included here as a "test" of a panic attack. There are no "right" or "wrong" answers in this inventory. Rather, the API should be used to evaluate a panic attack and to help the panic sufferer understand the emotional and physical components of an attack.

QUESTION: Not at all   Slightly   Moderately   Severely

1. Do you feel faint?
2. Are you afraid of dying?
3. Are you generally fearful?
4. Do you have heart palpitations?
5. Do you have any difficulty breathing, or are you breathing rapidly?
6. Do you have the urge to urinate?
7. Do you have the urge to defecate?
8. Do you feel light-headed or dizzy?
9. Do you feel confused?
10. Do you have a sense of unreality?
11. Do you feel detached from part or all of your body?
12. Is it difficult for you to concentrate?
13. Are you sweating?
14. Is it difficult for you to speak?
15. Would it be difficult for you to do a job?
16. Do you feel any shakiness, trembling, or twitching?
17. Do you feel nauseous?

From Dillon, JG, Gorman, JM, et al., "Measure of Lactate-induced Panic and Anxiety," *Psychiatry Research*, 20, 97–105, Elsevier Science Publishers, B. V. 1987.

way of controlling when an attack might occur, research relied only upon the subjective memories of the patients, thereby lessening the accuracy of the studies. The advent of sodium lactate infusion in the late 1960s gave psychiatry the tool it needed to study panic attacks in a controlled and objective environment.

The procedure for administering sodium lactate begins with a placebo infusion (usually saline solution). Then, at a time

---

SODIUM LACTATE AND BULIMIA

While sodium lactate infusion has not produced a significant rate of panic in other anxiety disorders, relatively higher rates of panic have been provoked by sodium lactate in bulimic patients. Following reports that bulimics often experience naturally occurring panic attacks, a study of bulimics who had *not* reported panic attacks nor met panic disorder criteria found that almost 50 percent of the bulimics experienced panic after lactate infusion. While the results of this study are preliminary, it does suggest that the binge eating of bulimics may be a form of a panic attack. This possible link between bulimia and panic disorders becomes even more intriguing since both conditions respond very well to the same tricyclic antidepressant medications.

---

unknown to the patient, sodium lactate will replace the placebo —this procedure verifies that panic attacks occur only after the lactate has been administered. The Acute Panic Inventory (API) scale (see box) assessed whether panic attacks induced by lactate were similar to spontaneous attacks. The overall results of the API indicated that patients gave the symptoms of their lactate-induced panic ratings, similar to those they gave to their naturally occurring attacks, strengthening the validity of sodium-lactate-induced panic attacks. Furthermore, sodium lactate's panic-inducing ability seems specific to panic disorder and agoraphobia with panic, since patients with other anxiety disorders (such as obsessive-compulsive disorders, generalized anxiety disorder, and social phobia) rarely experience panic during lactate infusion.

THE PANIC CHALLENGE

The use of sodium lactate to provoke a panic attack is sometimes referred to as a *challenge test.* While I view sodium lactate as currently the best measure for panic attacks, other agents have been used to precipitate a panic attack in panic disorder patients.

One of these other substances is caffeine. While caffeine has been shown to induce panic attacks in panic disorder patients, it can also produce panic in individuals with *no* history of panic attacks. Approximately ten cups of coffee will produce a panic attack in these normal subjects. While caffeine's role as a research or diagnostic tool in panic disorders remains uncertain, one conclusion can be drawn: Panic disorder patients should be advised to restrict or eliminate their caffeine consumption.

CO_2 is another such substance. Like so many discoveries in science, CO_2's utility as a challenge test was discovered inadvertently. A few years ago, researchers attempted to study the role of hyperventilation in panic by comparing its ability to precipitate panic to that of sodium lactate. As a control, 5 percent CO_2 was used to increase respiratory rate without causing the physiological changes associated with hyperventilation (these changes, primarily alkalosis, may be involved in the mechanism of a panic attack). To the surprise of the researchers, twice as many CO_2 controls panicked as hyperventilation subjects. At this time, the CO_2 inhalation results offer the promising, but very preliminary, possibility that CO_2 may develop into a helpful diagnostic and research tool in the future.

Other substances, including yohimbine, epinephrine, and isoproterenol, have also been studied. Of these, the most promising appears to be yohimbine, although more studies are needed to verify its panic-inducing abilities.

STRESS AND ANXIETY DISORDERS

Researchers have been fascinated by the connection between stressful life events and the onset of panic attacks. Many studies assessing their relationship have found an abnormally high incidence of stressful life events in the months preceding first panic attacks—for example, one study reported that 91 percent of first panic attacks were preceded by these stressors. According to one study done almost thirty years ago, 96 percent of agoraphobics reported background stress preceding their disorder. These life stressors were most likely to be death or serious illness of a close relative or friend, or serious illness of or danger to the patient. What makes this study interesting was the use of control groups: The agoraphobic patients were found to have significantly greater incidence of life stressors than patients suffering from other psychiatric "neuroses" or physical illnesses.

However, stress has been shown to be a precursor to a number of other conditions besides anxiety disorders. Some of these other conditions include cardiovascular disease, tuberculosis, multiple sclerosis, diabetes, arthritis, back pain, headaches, insomnia, depression, and complications during pregnancy and birth.

The usual explanation for these associations is that stress wears down our system. According to this theory, human beings may be prone to a number of conditions (like panic attacks) that might surface in a system weakened by stress.

But good common sense, plus research, tells us that not every individual develops panic attacks after even the most stressful events. This fact leads to a major question: Does stress merely weaken the system enough to allow any biological malfunctioning to surface, thereby leading to panic attacks, or does the stressful event itself cause the physiological changes that lead to panic attacks?

Researchers have known for years that the body, when under certain types of stress, especially physical stress, undergoes neuroendocrine changes, specifically in the hypothalamus, pituitary, and adrenal glands (called the HPA axis). The HPA axis secretes increased levels of the hormones ACTH and cortisol during physical stress, such as when a patient undergoes surgery. Some researchers had suggested that since the physical symptoms of a panic attack resemble the symptoms of physical stress, changes in hormonal levels might occur in panic attacks. Furthermore, if there were changes in hormonal levels, then these hormones might play a role in the genesis of panic attacks.

These theories, however, have not been generally supported by numerous studies designed to measure hormone levels in panic patients. A total of ten studies did not find significantly higher levels of hormonal activity in panic patients than in normal individuals. The slight elevation of hormonal levels may be due more to chronic anxiety than to panic attacks.

The failure to prove that elevated hormonal levels occur in panic attacks lends credibility to the theory that stress merely weakens the system to allow another, unrelated panic-prone tendency to surface.

PANIC ATTACKS AND SLEEP

Recently there have been reports on the high incidence of nocturnal panic attacks, with some patients reporting nighttime panic attacks that wake them from their sleep. Very preliminary studies indicate that when nighttime panics happen, it is almost always during the non-rapid-eye-movement (non-REM) periods of sleep. In the non-REM periods, dreaming does not usually occur, and sleep is not as deep as during the rapid-eye-movement (REM) period. The fact that panic attacks occur during the nondreaming state of non-REM sleep strengthens the biological basis for panic attacks, since it is difficult to believe that psychological or cognitive processes instigate an attack while the patient sleeps and is not dreaming. One report on sleep and panic attacks found that on nonpanicking nights, the patients had extended their REM sleep. This report suggested that perhaps patients had unknowingly extended their REM sleep as a means of protecting against panic attacks.

Interestingly, while other anxiety and depression patients report improvement following sleep deprivation, panic patients in one small study did not benefit. This study of twelve panic patients found that on the day after a sleep-deprived night, the majority of patients did not report any improvement, while 40 percent experienced a worsening of the anxiety and panic attacks.

The significance of this finding, as well as the overall relationship between nocturnal panic attacks and sleep, needs a great deal more examination before any truly meaningful conclusion or findings can be drawn.

THE PERIPHERAL NERVOUS SYSTEM AND PANIC DISORDERS

Another major theory for the possible biological cause of panic disorders is the *peripheral nervous system hypersensitivity* hypothesis. According to this theory, panic attacks may result from the physiological changes, such as high blood pressure and increased heart rate, that occur outside the central nervous system.

While I agree that these physiological changes are certainly a part—a major part, in fact—of a panic attack, I believe that they occur *because* of the panic attacks, but they do not precipitate the attacks. I base my reasoning on studies that show that panic patients do not have high blood pressure or increased heart rates at baseline (or during normal, nonpanic times), nor have they shown abnormally high or rapid physiological changes in response to everyday stimulations. For example, one study found that panic patients had normal responses to pain and cold. But of even greater significance has been the inability of medications that reduce the levels and symptoms of peripheral anxiety (such as the beta-blocker propranolol) to have any significant antipanic capabilities.

OTHER NEUROTRANSMITTERS AND ANXIETY DISORDERS

Other neurotransmitters, specifically the gamma aminobutyric acid (GABA) transmitters, have been studied for their possible role in the genesis of anxiety disorders. Interest into the GABA neurotransmitters has been spurred recently by the investigations into benzodiazepine medications. Until lately, benzodiazepine medications were thought to be ineffective antipanic agents. However, the recent success of alprazolam in treating panic disorder has led to a reevaluation of the other benzodiazepines and panic. While researchers study the antipanic efficacy of these other benzodiazepines, modern medicine has known for a long time that they are excellent anti-anxiety medications.

For years, we've known that benzodiazepines such as diazepam (brand name: Valium) and alprazolam (Xanax) were effective anti-anxiety drugs, but we didn't understand exactly how they worked. Now we are beginning to understand their action, and in the process, may be getting our clearest picture yet of the biological mechanics of anxiety.

The surface of neural cells contains various proteins, known as receptors, where specific neurotransmitters bind to the neuron. By anchoring to the neurons at these receptor sites, neurotransmitters can exert their chemical action on the neural impulses, regulating the flow of information to the brain and ultimately influencing human behavior.

Specific receptor sites will bind only with certain types of neurotransmitters. Receptor sites for GABA neurotransmitters are especially plentiful in the brain's limbic system, a fact which interests anxiety researchers because this system is composed of several brain areas known to influence a wide range of behavior, including anger, pleasure, and fear.

The nature of the link between the GABA system and benzodiazepine came into clearer focus when researchers discovered that certain nerve cells contain receptors with an affinity for benzodiazepine.

The benzodiazepine receptors are coupled to the receptors which attract the GABA neurotransmitters. We now believe that benzodiazepine accomplishes its anxiety-reducing effects by enhancing the inhibitory function of the GABA neurotransmitters, blocking the impulses which would otherwise stimulate the limbic system into triggering an anxiety response. This not only explains how the benzodiazepines work, but also suggests a discrete biological mechanism by which brain chemicals can generate and regulate anxiety.

Other neurotransmitter systems—the serotonin system, for example—may also be involved in the biogenesis of panic. But the important fact is that we are rapidly approaching the day when we can pinpoint the neural pathways of anxiety for anxiety and panic disorders, just as we now can trace the path of visual impulses along the optic nerve or aural impulses along the auditory nerve. We may soon be able to map the pathways of anxiety and identify the faulty chemical and electrical processes which garble neural messages and provoke inappropriate and pathological bursts of disabling anxiety and panic.

HORMONES AND ANXIETY

In further attempts to understand the biological basis of anxiety disorders, researchers have examined the role of hormones. Hormones are substances that travel through our blood to organs or tissues, where they enact modifications in function or structure. Examples of hormones include the corticosteroids, the thyroid hormone, growth hormone, and the catecholamines. A hormone can also be a neurotransmitter when it sends its chemical message over a short brain-synaptic distance. Neurotransmitters, such as norepinephrine, epinephrine, dopamine, and serotonin, are actually classified as catecholamine neurotransmitters (hormone-like chemical messengers that affect our nervous system).

Researchers have found that patients with anxiety disorders have different levels of circulating hormones than normal individuals. In most cases, anxiety disorder patients have elevated levels of hormones even in non-anxiety provoking situations—levels that normal individuals usually reach only under stress.

In their excellent review of the medical literature regarding hormonal and physiological abnormalities in anxiety disorders, my colleagues Oliver G. Cameron and Randolph M. Nesse hypothesize that:

> the "switch" or "trigger" which sets off an anxiety reaction is different, at least quantitatively and probably also qualitatively, in people with anxiety disorders vs. stress ("anxiety") in normals, but that once a reaction occurs, the physiological symptoms are fairly similar . . . (from Cameron, OG, and Nesse, RM. "Systemic Hormonal and Physiological Abnormalities in Anxiety Disorders." *Psychoneuroendocrinology,* Vol. 13, No. 4, p. 299)

The following table, based on the article by Cameron and Nesse, summarizes the role of hormones in normal individuals and anxiety disorder patients. This table compares normal individuals and normal individuals under stressful conditions with anxiety disorder patients. Note that the normal finding for the suppression of the corticosteroid dexamethasone (the Dexamethasone Suppression Test or DST) indicates that the panic patients are probably not suffering from a biological depression, since DST is often abnormal in depression. Also note that prolactin, the lactate hormone, while elevated in panic patients, does not increase following a cold stimulation test (In this test, cold temperatures are used to place the body under stress). Since prolactin levels in panic patients do not rise in response to cold, it appears that the higher levels of prolactin reflect an abnormality in the patient's responses to a panic situation, but not to a stressful situation.

GENETICS AND ANXIETY DISORDERS

Further investigation concerning the biological basis of anxiety disorders has focused upon genetics. Research from human family studies and experiments involving selective breeding in

HORMONAL LEVELS IN NORMAL INDIVIDUALS VS. ANXIETY DISORDER PATIENTS

Hormone	Normal Individuals	Normals under Stress	Panic and Agoraphobia Patients	Generalized Anxiety Patients	Phobic Patients
Catecholamines (norepinephrine, dopamine, epinephrine)	Not Elevated	Elevated	*Usually elevated in non-panic situations	Elevated	Elevated
Corticosteroids	Not Elevated	Elevated	*Normal or elevated *DST normal	Normal or elevated	Elevated
Prolactin	Not Elevated	Some Elevation	*Elevated in nonpanic situations *Normal cold stimulus *Elevated or normal response to lactate	Apparently normal	Normal
Thyroid	Not Elevated	Some Elevation	*Hyperthyroidism mimics panic *May be abnormal in some women	No information	Normal or elevated

animals are providing a growing body of evidence that suggests anxiety and fearfulness are genetically inherited traits.

In one study, a group of pointer dogs, chosen for traits of excessively fearful behavior, were bred with each other. Another group of pointers, chosen for more stable behavior, were also bred.

By the second breeding, 90 percent of the progeny of the fearful group also showed signs of extreme fearfulness and would cower, freeze, or flee when approached by strangers. But 80 percent of the offspring of the emotionally stable dogs showed no undue fear.

Similar results have been seen in selective breeding experiments with rats and mice, suggesting that fearful behavior can be passed down through the genes.

Evidence for the genetic inheritance of fearful traits has also been seen in a number of human studies. Some·of the most interesting findings have come from research involving sets of identical and nonidentical twins. Twin studies are used to measure the relative importance of environmental and genetic influences. If a condition is a learned response, you'd expect it to be present in both siblings in any set of twins, identical or nonidentical, since they were reared simultaneously by the same parents in the same environment. But a genetic disorder would be more likely to strike both siblings only in sets of identical twins, since they have a common genetic makeup. The frequency with which both twins share a given trait is known as the rate of concordance.

Studies of excessively fearful twins have revealed some solid evidence concerning the genetic aspects of anxiety:

- As children, identical twins showed a higher concordance rate than nonidentical twins in fear of strangers, shyness, tension, and emotionality. They also showed higher concordance for separation fears and overall nervousness.

- A study which rated adult twins by questionnaire showed that identical twins reported higher overall similarities for shyness, nervousness, and emotionality. More compellingly, identical twins reared separately, with entirely different environmental influences, showed higher concordance than non-identical twins reared in the same home. In fact, the rate of concordance seen in identical twins raised apart was very close to that of identical twins raised together—strong evidence that some people may be genetically predisposed to higher levels of anxiety.

Besides the genetic connection with panic attacks, ongoing research is beginning to pinpoint traces of genetic influence in the other anxiety disorders, including phobias.

There's fascinating evidence, for example, that people with blood-injury phobia, who faint at the sight of blood, may be suffering from a genetically based disorder.

Blood-injury phobia has the strongest family history of all the phobic disorders. Most blood phobics—68 percent according to one survey—have at least one close family member with the same phobia, and twin studies have shown a higher concordance for this condition among identical twins.

Investigators have noticed an unusual cardiac response in blood-injury phobics. Most phobia sufferers experience tachycardia, or rapid heartbeat, when exposed to the feared object or situation. Blood phobics, however, have a different, two-phase cardiac response. First there's tachycardia, but soon the heart slows into an abnormally slow rhythm, called bradycardia, which often goes far enough to cause the patient to faint.

Heart rates are controlled by the autonomic nervous system. Some researchers have proposed that the profound bradycardia seen in blood-injury phobics may be the result of a genetically inherited glitch in the autonomic response. In this view, patients who faint frequently and readily are more susceptible to the phobia.

THE GOOD NEWS

In this chapter, I've presented strong arguments in favor of the biological basis of panic disorders. We now know that people who suffer from them are not morally flawed; they are simply ill. Panic patients should be freed from the old accusations that their fears were due to their own character weaknesses. I believe that someday we will discover the reason, or reasons, why panic attacks occur. That day still lies in the future, but already we've made tremendous progress.

The next chapter takes a good long look at dozens of biological conditions which have been shown to produce mental and emotional symptoms which, without objective scientific testing, can easily be misdiagnosed as anxiety disorders. Read it carefully. As you realize how terribly wrong a diagnosis based on these psychiatric mimickers can be, you may wonder how long psychiatrists will continue to reject modern scientific diagnostic methods, and how long patients like Trip, Linda, and Andy will wait for the right treatment. But biopsychiatry helped them, and it can help you, too. For the most fundamental tenet of our approach to anxiety disorders is this: Many of these conditions have a biological basis, and anyone suffering from an anxiety disorder deserves the best possible, most careful diagnosis—and help—we can give.

CHAPTER SIX

THE
GREAT
MIMICKERS
OF
ANXIETY

MODERN PSYCHIATRY IS in trouble, and one of the most distressing signs is that too many patients are being treated for psychiatric problems they don't have. Instead, they suffer from biological disorders that cause symptoms usually associated with psychiatric disease.

There are from seventy-five to ninety-five physical conditions that can mimic psychiatric disorders, and over fifty conditions that can cause prominent anxiety symptoms! A number of these conditions, which must be ruled out when making a diagnosis of an anxiety disorder, are listed in the accompanying box. I call these conditions the Great Mimickers of Anxiety Disorders. Because they are able to imitate the outward signs of anxiety so convincingly, they are a major cause of psychiatric misdiagnosis.

These mimickers are insidious, deceptive, and almost impossible to detect without aggressive and sophisticated diagnostic testing. We know by now, of course, that most psychiatrists aren't likely to consider such tests. Instead, with the blessing of DSM-III-R, they assess their patients on the basis of these misleading symptoms and are fooled into making counterfeit diagnoses. The consequences, sadly, are borne by the patient in the form of inappropriate treatment and, in some cases, years of unnecessary misery.

It's estimated that 20 percent of the patients in an average psychiatrist's clientele, and up to one third of all hospitalized mental patients, are suffering from *physical* conditions which produce symptoms resembling those of purely psychiatric disorders. Almost half of all hospitalized psychiatric patients also have underlying, undetected physical problems which in some way aggravate their mental conditions.

At Fair Oaks Hospital, about 25 percent of all the patients we see have some sort of previously undiscovered physical ailment. There's a reason for that high percentage. For many, our clinic is a last resort. We get many patients who have been labeled "treatment failures" or "nonresponders." Before they get to us, they've been through several different psychiatrists, and as many unsuccessful treatment approaches. They come

DIFFERENTIAL DIAGNOSIS OF ANXIETY DISORDERS

The differential diagnosis of anxiety disorders involves the systematic elimination of the main conditions, both mental and physical, that can present symptoms similar to those of anxiety. The following is a list of the main mimickers that a psychiatrist should consider before making a diagnosis of anxiety disorder:

Endocrine Disorders
Hyperthyroidism (see page 156)
Thyrotoxicosis (see page 158)
Hypoglycemia (see page 158)
Diabetes mellitus (see page 159)
Cushing's syndrome (see page 160)
Pheochromocytoma (see page 160)
Carcinoid syndrome (see page 161)
Panhypopituitarism (see page 161)

Central Nervous System Disorders
Partial complex seizure (includes temporal lobe epilepsy and
  psychomotor epilepsy) (see page 162)
Postconcussion syndrome (see page 163)
Hyperventilation (see page 164)
Multiple sclerosis (see page 165)

Infectious Diseases
Infectious mononucleosis (see page 166)
Infectious hepatitis (see page 166)
Encephalitis (see page 167)
Brucellosis (see page 167)

Metabolic Diseases
Hypocalcemia (see page 167)
Hypokalemia (see page 167)
Niacin deficiency (see page 167)
Cobalamin deficiency (see page 168)
Wilson's disease (see page 169)
Systemic lupus erythematosis (see page 169)

DIFFERENTIAL DIAGNOSIS OF ANXIETY DISORDERS (*continued*)

Cancer
Brain tumor (see page 170)
Pancreatic carcinoma (see page 170)
Cardiovascular Disorders
Mitral valve prolapse (see page 171)
Cardiac arrhythmias (see page 172)
Myocardial infarction (see page 172)
Essential hypertension (see page 172)
Pulmonary embolism (see page 173)
Cerebral arteriosclerosis (see page 173)
Internal hemorrhage (see page 173)
Subacute bacterial endocarditis (see page 173)
Respiratory Disorders
Asthma (see page 174)
Bronchitis (see page 174)
Emphysema (see page 174)
Psychiatric Mimickers
Depression (see page 175)
Seasonal affective disorder (SAD) (see page 175)
Schizophrenia (see page 175)
Personality disorders (see page 176)
Drugs
Alcohol (see page 176)
Nicotine withdrawal (see page 178)
Marijuana (see page 178)
Cocaine (see page 179)
Amphetamines (see page 180)
PCP (see page 180)
Narcotics withdrawal (see page 180)
Medications
Lidocaine (see page 181)
Monoamine oxidase inhibitors (see page 181)
Disulfiram (see page 182)
Ethosuximide (see page 182)
Indomethacin (see page 182)

DIFFERENTIAL DIAGNOSIS OF ANXIETY DISORDERS (*continued*)

Vinblastine (see page 182)
Cycloserine (see page 182)
Nalorphine (see page 182)
Over-the-counter drugs
Diet pills (see page 182)
Laxatives (see page 183)
Caffeine (see page 183)
Aspartame (see page 184)
Environmental toxins
Mercury (see page 185)
Bismuth (see page 185)
Carbon dioxide (see page 185)
Volatile substances (see page 186)
Insecticides (see page 186)

here feeling like failures, blaming themselves for their own lack of progress. But often they've simply been misdiagnosed. We discover that they're suffering from undiagnosed biological conditions which account for their psychiatric symptoms, and for their long record as "nonresponders." Obviously, since their treatment plans ignored the cause of their symptoms, there's no way they *could* have responded.

HOW MIMICKERS CAUSE PSYCHIATRIC SYMPTOMS

When disease invades the body, certain chemical changes occur. Most body systems aren't affected in the earliest stages of the disease process, so physical symptoms may not emerge until the disease has progressed.

But the brain, the body's most sensitively balanced organ, can't tolerate the slightest abnormality in its biological makeup. It reacts immediately to the chemical changes caused by disease, producing alterations in mood, perception, and thinking that appear, to the superficial observer, to be purely psychiatric in nature. Since these "psychiatric" symptoms frequently occur long before any physical signs, there's often no reason to suspect physical disease.

Ruling out mimickers should be the first step in a thorough diagnostic process. That's the only way to ensure an incisive, successful course of treatment. Practitioners in all branches of medicine need to be aware of the danger these mimickers pose, but it's most crucial that we in the psychiatric field become expert in detecting their presence, since we are far more likely to encounter them than other doctors.

Clearly, it's our responsibility to know as much about these conditions as possible, and to suspect them routinely when we diagnose our patients. We've got to agree that no diagnosis is a sound one unless it has objectively ruled out the presence of these copycat disorders. Clearly, most psychiatrists are not philosophically or temperamentally inclined to believe that detecting medical problems is any of their business, but if the track record of psychiatric diagnosis and treatment is ever going to improve, that attitude has got to change.

In the rest of this chapter, I'll show you the Great Mimickers that are so often confused with the symptoms of anxiety disorders. And then we'll explain the kind of protocol we biopsychiatrists use to make a solid, medically oriented diagnosis. Sadly, after you've read the next few pages you'll probably know more about these mimickers than most psychologists, therapists, and mental health practitioners at work today.

The Great Mimickers of anxiety fall into several categories: endocrine disorders, disorders of the central nervous system, infectious diseases, metabolic problems, cancer, psychiatric mimickers, alcohol and drugs (including both medications and illicit drugs), environmental toxins, and cardiovascular disorders.

ENDOCRINE DISORDERS

The endocrine system is made of several hormone-producing glands, including the thyroid, the parathyroid, the adrenals, the thymus, the hypothalamus, and the pituitary, as well as the ovaries and testes.

The hormones of the endocrine glands work to keep the body in a state of balance, acting chemically on body organs to keep growth, appetite, blood pressure, heart rate, sexual drive, and other bodily processes running smoothly.

Certain glands have more responsibilities than others. The tiny hypothalamus acts as a kind of master gland, regulating all the body's processes, from the sleep/wake cycle to heart rate, hunger, and emotions. When it senses an imbalance, it orders the appropriate gland to produce the needed level of the correct hormone to reestablish equilibrium.

Most endocrine problems arise when a particular gland fails to produce the proper amount of hormone. When either too much or too little hormone is secreted, an imbalance results. The brain notices this imbalance immediately, and consequently the mind, emotions, and behavior can be affected long before the disorder has progressed to the point where bodily symptoms are seen.

The effects of the endocrine system on the mind can be profound. But they often go undetected, for two major reasons. First, there's nothing as obvious as a head injury or drug problem to account for the symptoms, so they're often ascribed to purely psychiatric causes. Second, the tests that can detect endocrine disorders tend to be complex and sophisticated. Most of these disorders can't be identified in the office. That means that psychiatrists need to become expert in spotting the signals of endocrine problems early on. If they never suspect them, they won't order the confirming tests.

Hyperthyroidism. Hyperthyroidism in its early stages can fool any physician into thinking it's an anxiety disorder or panic attack. It can also masquerade as depression or mania. It's one of the most common endocrine disorders and an important and widespread mimicker of many psychiatric conditions.

In hyperthyroidism, an overactive thyroid gland pumps high levels of thyroid hormone into the body, causing the patient's metabolic rate to rise. The effects include anxiety-like symptoms such as hyperactivity, shortened attention span, insomnia, and weight loss despite a heightened appetite and increased food intake. Heavy perspiration, fatigue, heart palpitations, and muscular weakness are also common. Men may experience some swelling of the breasts, and women may see their menstrual flow grow extremely light.

With these symptoms of hyperthyroidism, it's easy to see why it is so often confused with anxiety disorders. In one study, twenty-three of twenty-nine hyperthyroid patients had symptoms of anxiety that could have met DSM-III criteria for panic disorder. Incidentally, thyroid medication alone relieved these anxiety symptoms in 91 percent of the patients.

At Fair Oaks Hospital, we've seen a number of patients with "anxiety disorders" that turned out to be hyperthyroidism. Joan, for example, is an affluent housewife who's spent thousands and thousands of dollars for treatment at a famous university's phobia and panic clinic. When she called me, she was having several "panic attacks" and chronic anxiety most of each day.

When we talked to Joan, we learned that she was a virtual catalog of anxiety symptoms. She suffered from palpitations, chest pain, shortness of breath, hot flashes, and nausea. She wasn't housebound, but she avoided being alone. She was afraid of virtually everything—death, injury, public speaking, attorneys, divorce, dentists, fast cars, surgery, physicians, looking foolish, and losing control. She'd given up driving, but she could go just about anywhere as a passenger, whether it was in a limousine, a seaplane, or even a helicopter.

At the panic clinic, her doctors had tried imipramine, Parnate (tranylcypromine sulfate), and alprazolam—all accepted treatments for panic attacks—but none of them worked. Still, she said, they'd assured her that she would eventually respond "if we find the right medication."

I decided on a complete reevaluation. After all the tests were done and I told her what we found, she was chagrined.

"Your lactate test is negative. It's unlikely you're suffering from panic attacks," I said.

"What are you talking about?" She was almost angry. "Haven't you been listening?"

"I'm not done. Your TRH shows virtually no delta—"

"Meaning?"

"Meaning there's a good chance you're suffering from hyperthyroidism."

As it turned out, that's exactly what the problem was. Although Joan was doubtful at first that a mere hormonal imbalance could be causing her bizarre symptoms, she quickly became a believer. When she was treated correctly the panic and anxiety symptoms disappeared.

The similarities between the symptoms of hyperthyroidism and those of panic attacks has led researchers to study whether there may be a causal relationship between the conditions. While no direct relationship has been established, one study of panic attack patients revealed a prior history of thyroid disease in 10.8 percent of the patients—ten times the incidence in the general population. This study does suggest that in some cases of panic disorder, not only may a prior history of hyperthyroidism be the cause but the hyperthyroidism may still be present.

Thyrotoxicosis. A form of hyperthyroidism, thyrotoxicosis occurs owing to excessive amounts of the thyroid hormone in the blood stream. Symptoms of this condition include rapid heartbeat, tremor, anxiety, sweating, weight loss, and heat intolerance. Causes may include an overactive thyroid, a hormone-secreting benign tumor, a thyroid carcinoma, or Graves' disease.

Hypoglycemia. In this condition, the body's level of blood sugar falls to abnormally low levels, starving brain cells that depend on glucose to survive. The imbalance in brain chemistry can cause the kind of abnormal behavior that often gets hypoglycemic patients admitted to psychiatric wards. In mild cases, symptoms include trembling, confusion, and slurred speech, and the condition is often mistaken for drunkenness.

In more severe cases, hyperactivity and bizarre behavior may result. I remember the case of a woman who had appeared in a hospital emergency room. Her behavior was decidedly abnormal; she was loud and hyperactive, and had begun to remove her clothing in the waiting room when nurses restrained her. The woman was labeled as an obvious psych case, but blood testing soon showed she was suffering from extremely low blood sugar.

In chronic hypoglycemia, personality changes, attacks of paranoid psychosis, and eventual dementia are possible. In many cases, the agitated, disoriented behavior caused by this condition is taken as a sign of anxiety attack. Hypoglycemia often results when diabetics use too much insulin, but it can also be the result of insulin-secreting tumors of the pancreas. In some cases, early mild diabetes can cause "reactive" hypoglycemia, which strikes a few hours after a large meal laden with carbohydrates.

Diabetes Mellitus. In addition to the hypoglycemia caused by too much insulin and not enough carbohydrates, hyperglycemia (high levels of blood glucose) may also occur in poorly controlled diabetics (those who experience wide swings in blood glucose levels). Hyperglycemia will frequently occur when the diabetic consumes too much food to be metabolized by his or her insulin, resulting in higher than normal levels of blood glucose.

For many years physicians have known that psychological problems, such as too much stress, can affect glucose regulation in diabetic patients. Recently, researchers have studied whether the reverse would also be true—whether poorly controlled diabetes would cause psychological symptoms. In a limited but interesting study, two patients with insulin-dependent diabetes were studied over two consecutive nights. On one night the patients received a normal glucose infusion; on the other they received a higher-than-normal infusion. Neither patient was aware of how much glucose he had received. The study found that both patients responded to the hyperglycemic levels with symptoms "similar to that observed in psychiatric patients with severe anxiety."

This relationship between high glucose levels and anxiety levels may partially explain why so many diabetics report anxiety symptoms. One study of both insulin-dependent and non-insulin-dependent diabetes found the prevalence of generalized anxiety disorders to be six times higher in diabetics than in the general population.

Cushing's Syndrome. Also known as hyperadrenalism, this syndrome is due to an overabundance of the hormone ACTH in the body, caused either by hyperactivity of the adrenal cortex or by the action of ACTH-secreting tumors elsewhere in the body.

Cushing's syndrome is most common in women of child-bearing age. Its physical signs are distinctive, including a moon-faced appearance, weight gain, purple stripes on the abdomen, emotional changes, and the accumulation of fat pads known as buffalo hump. Kidney stones, easy bruising, bone weakness, and diabetes are also seen.

Ninety percent of Cushing's syndrome victims experience some disease-related effect on behavior. Depression is the most common "psychiatric" symptom, but the syndrome can also trigger anxiety. Cushing's syndrome can be treated by surgery, radiation, or drugs, depending upon the cause.

Pheochromocytoma. In pheochromocytoma, tiny tumors of the medulla secrete excessive levels of catecholamines, which throw off the body's hormonal balance and trigger a range of intense symptoms.

At some point in the progression of this disorder, patients will experience episodes of severe anxiety, pounding headaches, nausea, difficulty breathing, heart palpitations, pallor, and vertigo. You'll notice that these symptoms are deadringers for the physical signs of panic attack. Not surprisingly, pheochromocytoma is often misdiagnosed as a panic disorder.

High blood pressure is the most important symptom in recognizing this disorder. Unfortuntely, in some cases, it may occur only during attacks, when its significance is overwhelmed by the intensity of other symptoms.

Pheochromocytoma attacks can be triggered by sneezing, laughing, sexual intercourse, urinating, emotional stress, and other apparently unrelated phenomena.

Individuals with a family history of endocrine tumors seem to be more vulnerable to this condition. Also, since this is a disease primarily of the young, it should be routinely suspected in patients under twenty-five who are complaining of panic or severe anxiety.

Surgery cures this condition in 90 percent of cases.

Carcinoid Syndrome. This syndrome refers to a group of symptoms triggered by secretions of carcinoid tumors, which usually affect the endocrine cells in the small intestine, stomach, or appendix.

The symptoms of this syndrome include upper-body flushing, diarrhea, abdominal cramps, and color changes in the skin from pallid white to blue. Forty percent of patients who experience carcinoid syndrome also suffer some mental symptoms. One of the most common emotional reactions is heightened levels of anxiety.

The onset of carcinoid syndrome symptoms can be triggered by certain foods or alcohol, physical exertion, excitement, or the administration of epinephrine.

These tumors often spread to other organs, but patients can live for ten to fifteen years after diagnosis.

Panhypopituitarism. Tumors, injury, radiation, or infectious diseases can cause the anterior pituitary gland to lessen its production of hormones. The resulting imbalance leads to the condition known as panhypopituitarism.

Symptoms include lowered sex drive, infertility, hypoglycemia, hypothyroidism, hypotension, and susceptibility to infections. About 70 percent of patients experience psychiatric symptoms, including depression, anorexia nervosa, and anxiety.

Panhypopituitarism is treated by hormone therapy, which reestablishes the body's hormonal balance. In some cases, the pituitary gland must be removed.

DISORDERS OF THE CENTRAL NERVOUS SYSTEM

For obvious reasons, diseases of the central nervous system —the brain and spinal cord—are among the most common mimickers of psychiatric disorders. In fact, virtually every CNS disorder will have some effect on thinking, emotions, memory, or sensation. Some of the most common ones that can masquerade as anxiety disorders are described below.

Partial Complex Seizure. This term includes two types of seizure disorders, temporal lobe epilepsy and psychomotor epilepsy, which are most likely to produce psychiatric symptoms.

In epilepsy, the brain's normal electrical rhythms are interrupted by random bursts of electricity, scrambling brain function and resulting in seizure. Just prior to their attacks, most epileptics experience bizarre symptoms, which can include visual hallucinations, a sense of déjà vu, or mystical experiences.

The most common form of epilepsy involves episodes of incapacitating convulsions and loss of motor control, but not all epileptics experience that type of seizure. Some will simply cease all movement and stare off into space; others, experiencing a particularly mild seizure, may not even know it happened.

Between seizures, drastic personality changes can occur. One patient may become fanatically religious or intensely ethical, while others become antisocial, or suffer wild personality swings: righteous and ethical one day, mean and immoral the next.

At Fair Oaks Hospital, we treated a thirty-year-old woman besieged by anxiety and panic attacks. Her symptoms had begun four years earlier following a skiing accident in which she suffered a small cut on her head. For a week following the accident she felt weak and nauseous, but skull X-rays had shown no signs of fracture.

Her husband described her as a dynamic and confident person, very athletic, organized, and efficient. She was outgoing, athletic, well dressed, and sociable, and her small decorating business was doing quite well.

Following the skiing mishap, however, her husband noticed severe changes in her behavior. She seemed indecisive, uncertain, and irritable. Inexplicable feelings of anxiety began to dog her. Sometimes her heart would race, her arms would tremble, and she'd have to struggle for breath.

Her condition steadily grew worse. She began to suffer olfactory hallucinations, in which she smelled rotting garbage, sulfur, and burning rubber.

Meanwhile, sharp periods of anxiety would strike at least once a day. She began to avoid places where these attacks took place. Eventually she found it difficult to leave her home. After seeking help, she was hospitalized and diagnosed as a victim of panic attacks which had led to the development of agoraphobia.

Because of the abrupt changes that occurred soon after the skiing accident, we suspected that the accident itself was responsible. However, our tests of brain-wave activity were inconclusive. So before diagnosing Elaine as an epileptic, we first had to rule out the panic disorder.

We did that by administering a medication called desipramine, which makes panic attacks less severe, but can make epileptic seizures worse. Lo and behold, the panic symptoms abated, but her twenty-four-hour EEG results began to show more clearly the peculiar spiked pattern of temporal-lobe epilepsy. Elaine was treated with anti-epileptic drugs, which reduced the panic attacks, ended the hallucinations, and controlled the seizures.

Temporal-lobe epilepsy—TLE—is the real cause behind many misdiagnoses of anxiety, depression, hysteria, and "schizophrenia." One study examining ten patients not responding to treatment and originally diagnosed as "borderline state" or "latent schizophrenia" suffering from "attacks of anxiety" found that all ten were actually suffering from TLE. Mistaking TLE for panic attacks or severe anxiety is very unfortunate, since TLE, once diagnosed, can be controlled by anticonvulsant drugs or, in severe cases, surgery.

Postconcussion Syndrome. Jake was a forty-five-year-old loan officer for a large bank who came to us complaining of episodes of extreme anxiety that were wreaking havoc with his career. A phobic reaction to driving prevented him from driving his car. Anticipatory anxiety made him a basket case during important meetings and visits with clients. He also told us that he was deeply depressed, and had been so for a long time.

Jake had been under psychiatric care for years. Recently he had been hospitalized for his problems, and when we first saw him he was taking the antidepressive drug alprazolam (brand name: Xanax) four times a day. The psychiatrist who signed his discharge summary had apparently ordered a cursory physical exam by an internist, which turned up nothing which seemed significant. His diagnosis, a familiar one to Jake, was major depression, generalized anxiety, panic disorder, and phobia.

We put that diagnosis aside and began from square one, with a rigorous battery of lab tests and physical exams. It didn't take us long to find evidence of physical damage to the brain's temporal lobe. When we asked about it, Jake told us that he'd been in a car accident several years before and had taken a pretty good knock on the head. Since then, he said, he'd had trouble finding his way and recognizing new faces. Curiously, though, he didn't have any trouble recognizing customers he'd known *before* the accident.

More neuropsychological studies followed, and in the end we were able to determine that Jake's mental symptoms were caused by the almost forgotten accident, which had physically damaged the brain. We prescribed a course of rehabilitation, and Jake responded. The major symptoms of anxiety and panic disappeared, although he continued to feel mild twinges of fear as he drove his car. But he was driving again—in fact, he began to take long road trips just to prove to himself that he could. The anxiety he felt before business meetings had been reduced to what he considered manageable levels, and in general, his improvement, in his own words, was "amazing, fantastic, wonderful."

Jake's troubles are a clear example of postconcussion syndrome, a condition in which psychiatric and behavioral symptoms often appear as aftereffects of severe injuries to the head. Anxiety, depression, mood swings, and personality changes are all frequent results. Interestingly, this condition seems more common in head traumas caused by blunt, nonpenetrating force than in cases of more visible wounds that open the head.

Hyperventilation. This condition, which occurs when the breathing rate exceeds the oxygen requirement, is closely associated with anxiety disorders. In fact, some experts have suggested that it is hyperventilation that causes panic attacks. However, most experts believe that anxiety disorders cause the hyperventilation. Other causes of hyperventilation are asthma, exercise, head injuries, hyperthyroidism, hormones, and drugs.

Symptoms of hyperventilation include chest pain, faintness, dizziness, and numbness in fingers and toes. A thorough evaluation of hyperventilation's role in anxiety disorders may be found in chapter 5.

Multiple Sclerosis. This is a chronic, degenerative neurological disease that attacks the nerves' protective sheaths, resulting in the deterioration of bodily systems.

In the early stages, patients may experience tingling in the arms and legs, visual disturbances, and temporary weakness along with inexplicable euphoria or depression. As the disease takes stronger hold, a variety of degenerative symptoms emerge, possibly including loss of bladder and rectal control, impotency, slurred speech, and seizures. The MS patient may go through several periods of remission, after which the disease may return with more serious symptoms.

MS's effect on mood and behavior is often misread as the result of an emotional disorder, primarily because the symptoms aren't constant. They wax and wane, just as you'd expect symptoms of an emotional problem to do. Nuclear magnetic resonance (NMR) imaging, a technique using radio waves to record the structure and reactions of the brain, allows for early diagnosis of this condition.

When MS affects the frontal and temporal lobes of the brain, the result can be bizarre behavior which is often mistaken for psychiatric problems, including anxiety.

INFECTIOUS DISEASE

It makes sense that brain injuries and the like can cause psychiatric symptoms. But certainly it isn't possible to "catch" an anxiety disorder as you would a common cold. Right?

Wrong. Infectious diseases—viruses and bacterial illnesses —often have psychiatric manifestations. You may remember that I mentioned earlier that many cases of "schizophrenia" in the early part of this century were actually the late stages of syphilis. There are many other diseases that can mimic anxiety disorders as well, including the following.

Infectious Mononucleosis. Mononucleosis, often called the kissing disease, is caused by a type of herpes virus which attacks the body's disease-fighting white blood cells.

In four to seven weeks following infection, symptoms occur. In some patients, the disease may cause no more discomfort than a common cold, but others may suffer nagging headaches and fever, swollen glands, swollen eyelids, and persistent weakness.

Mono triggers depression and symptoms of anxiety, especially in women, which may persist for a year after the infection has been resolved.

This disease is diagnosed by blood tests, which often prove incorrectly negative the first time around. An accurate diagnosis may require a number of tests over a period of several weeks.

Infectious Hepatitis. This viral liver infection, one of the most common diseases in the world, is most prevalent in its Type A and Type B forms. Hepatitis A is caused by contaminated food or water. In hepatitis B, or serum hepatitis, the virus usually enters the bloodstream directly, through sexual intercourse or shared hypodermic needles.

Symptoms may not appear for from two to twenty-five weeks after infection. Initial symptoms include loss of appetite, nausea, vomiting, fever, aching joints, and itching. As the disease progresses, the patient's urine darkens and the skin and eyes show signs of jaundice or yellowing.

With proper care and strict bed rest, the body will fight off the hepatitis infection. In the meantime, a range of psychiatric symptoms, ranging from mild lethargy to full-blown psychosis, may appear. Some hepatitis patients have suffered delusions; even suicides have been reported. But the most common emotional complications are anxiety and/or depression.

Hepatitis is easily diagnosed through liver-function tests.

Encephalitis. Encephalitis is an inflammation of the brain that may result from a viral illness caused by a mosquito bite. Other possible causes are bacterial infection or allergic reaction to a viral illness or vaccination. Symptoms of some forms of encephalitis that may mimic an anxiety disorder include headache, nausea, muscle aches, vomiting, and visual disturbances.

Brucellosis. Brucellosis, also known as Malta or Mediterranean fever, is a chronic disease of farm animals caused by brucella bacteria. Contact with an infected animal or consumption of nonpasteurized infected milk can transfer this disease to humans. Untreated, the disease can last for years and develop into other, potentially fatal, conditions. The symptoms of brucellosis that resemble anxiety symptoms include fever, chills, sweating, and weakness.

METABOLIC DISEASES

The biochemical processes involving the movement of nutrients after digestion constitute the body's metabolism. Because the metabolic process is essential to maintaining life, any disruption can have wide-ranging consequences, including the following disorders:

Hypocalcemia. Hypocalcemia is a condition marked by too little calcium in the blood. The condition may result from hypoparathyroidism, kidney failure, pancreas inflammation, or lack of vitamin D. Anxiety-like symptoms of hypocalcemia include irregular heartbeat or muscle spasms.

Hypokalemia. Hypokalemia results from a lack of potassium in the blood and may be caused by malnutrition, by dehydration, or by treatment for diabetes, adrenal tumor, or hypertension. Patients taking diuretics (medications commonly used to lower blood pressure) should be advised to watch for symptoms of hypokalemia. These symptoms include weakness and nonrigid paralysis.

Niacin Deficiency. Pellagra, a disease caused by niacin deficiency in the diet, reached epidemic proportions in the first thirty years of this century. It is one of the greatest all-time mimickers. Because its symptoms so successfully mimic psychiatric disorders—dementia, psychosis, mania, and catatonia, to name a few—thousands of people suffering from this condition were inappropriately committed to mental institutions. It's estimated that nearly seventy thousand people were killed by pellagra in the first decades of this century. In the South, where many people lived on niacin-poor diets, almost half of all the patients in state mental hospitals were actually suffering from niacin deprivation.

The dietary importance of niacin was discovered in 1937, and as the vitamin was added to commercial food products, pellagra essentially disappeared. Today it is seen primarily in alcoholics, drug abusers, the elderly, and victims of liver disease. Also, some drugs used to treat Parkinson's disease can lower niacin levels in the body.

Anxiety and agitation are symptoms of the early stages of pellagra. If the disease has not progressed to the stage of dementia, niacin supplements usually provide a swift cure.

Cobalamin Deficiency. Cobalamin deficiency occurs when the body does not receive a sufficient amount of vitamin B_{12}, either because of a poor diet or because of the body's inability to absorb the vitamin. Vitamin B_{12} affects almost all of the body's tissues, but especially nerve cells and those cells containing rapidly dividing cells. The two most prominent side effects of cobalamin deficiency are anemia and neuropsychiatric disorders, including excessive anxiety.

Traditionally, neurologic symptoms were considered to be late signs of cobalamin deficiency that typically occurred only after anemia had developed.

However, a recent report examining patients with neuropsychiatric disorders due to cobalamin deficiency found that 28 percent had not developed anemia. The study also reported that for some of the patients, the correct diagnosis was delayed because cobalamin deficiency was considered unlikely without the presence of anemia. The study concluded that "neuropsychiatric disturbances due to cobalamin deficiency in the absence of anemia should not be considered rare. Abnormalities of the nervous system are typically such patients' first symptoms and may be associated with only minor hematologic abnormalities."

Wilson's Disease. This is a rare hereditary disease which impairs the body's ability to metabolize copper and leads to an excessive accumulation of that metal in body tissue.

Wilson's disease strikes young people, usually between the ages of six and twenty. With early detection and treatment, it's a reversible condition. Left untreated, it can be fatal.

The signs of this disease include distinctive golden-brown or gray-green rings around the corneas (present in about half of all cases). As the accumulation of copper increases, nerve cells are damaged, causing tremors, personality changes, and dementia. Some patients suffer liver damage.

Wilson's disease is associated with a variety of psychiatric symptoms, including anxiety and school phobia as in Trip's case, as well as depression, schizophrenia, hysteria, and hyperactivity. Often these symptoms occur independent of any physical manifestations, and as a result, misdiagnosis is common. In fact, Wilson's disease victims are more frequently referred to psychiatrists than to physicians.

Systemic Lupus Erythematosis. Lupus, or SLE, is a chronic disease involving the inflammation of the body's connective tissue. It is a serious, incurable, and unpredictable disease which usually strikes young women and develops slowly over a period of years. It may begin with a series of inexplicable fevers and progress to affect the lungs, spleen, kidneys, and heart. Common signs of lupus include disfigured joints, baldness, anemia, and rashes.

The psychiatric symptoms of lupus are often the first signs of the disease to present themselves. Lupus can mimic all types of mental symptoms, from anxiety to psychosis. Since these mental symptoms often arise independent of any physical symptoms, they're often misdiagnosed as purely psychiatric.

CANCER

In addition to the effects tumors can have on the endocrine system (see the endocrine disorders on pages 155–61, the following cancerous conditions can have many anxiety-like effects:

Brain Tumor. Brain tumors are associated with high rates of illness and death, although the truth is that many can be treated successfully by surgery or X-ray therapy. Symptoms of a brain tumor may include headache, nausea, vomiting, swelling of the optic disk in the eye, loss of sight, weakness, and confusion.

Pancreatic Carcinoma. This particularly lethal form of cancer attacks the pancreas, an organ which lies behind the stomach and secretes fluids necessary for healthy digestion. Of all the cancers which present psychiatric symptoms, pancreatic cancer is one of the most common and convincing mimics.

The first signs of this disease would appear, to the casual observer, to be entirely problems of mood: The patient is depressed, given to sudden bursts of weeping, anxieties, and insomnia. More obvious physical symptoms—pain, weight loss, and jaundice—don't appear until the disease has substantially progressed. In fact, one of the reasons that this cancer is so lethal is that it is shielded so long by the apparently psychiatric manifestations. When physical symptoms finally appear, at which point the diagnosis is much easier to make, it's often too late, and death may occur within the year.

CARDIOVASCULAR DISORDERS

The cardiovascular system is one of the most common mimickers for anxiety disorders. A report from the University of Missouri found that one out of three outpatients who see cardiologists for chest pain probably suffers from panic disorder. Conversely, recent studies have suggested that cardiovascular disease may account, at least partially, for the greater-than-expected incidence of mortality in panic disorder patients. While there is no definitive explanation for this association, one may assume that some patients being treated for anxiety disorders are suffering from one or more of the following cardiovascular disorders.

Mitral Valve Prolapse. This mimicker is one of the most widespread and easily misunderstood mimickers of anxiety states.

The mitral valve is a gateway on the left side of the heart, separating the atrium from the ventricle. In a normally functioning heart, oxygen-rich blood, flowing in from the lungs, collects in the atrium, which serves as a kind of antechamber. When a sufficient amount of blood has collected in the atrium, the pressure forces open the mitral valve, which allows blood to enter the ventricle. From there, heart contractions pump the blood through the body. As the pressure decreases, the mitral valve closes, sealing off the atrium from any backflow of blood.

In mitral valve prolapse, the mitral valve does not close completely, allowing a small amount of blood to flow back into the antechamber. The result is a minor heart murmur, which reveals itself to the stethoscope as a distinct click. In most cases, it's not a serious problem. Still, the sudden onset of its symptoms can be terrifying, especially in cases where the condition has not been diagnosed.

The most common symptoms of MVP are chest pain, palpitations, fatigue, difficult breathing, and anxiety. It's no wonder that so many MVP patients are diagnosed and treated as victims of panic disorders.

MVP may be difficult to diagnose, even during a physical exam, because the MVP click heard with a stethoscope may vary from patient to patient, and even within the same patient on follow-up examinations. Therefore, the most accurate method of detecting MVP is the echocardiography, specifically two-dimensional echocardiography.

MVP is so common that a study of five thousand individuals found a 5 percent rate for MVP in the general population. And females in their twenties had an MVP rate of 17 percent that steadily declined as the age increased.

Interestingly, MVP is not only an effective mimicker of panic disorder; there also seems to be a distinct hereditary link between the two conditions. Some studies show that mitral valve prolapse is found in one of every three panic attack victims. The exact relationship between the two conditions is not clearly understood, but the common occurrence of MVP—a hereditary defect—and panic disorders may suggest a hereditary component of pathological anxiety.

Cardiac Arrhythmias. Any change in the normal pattern of the heartbeat can be classified as an arrhythmia. Symptoms of an arrhythmia include palpitations, or rapid heartbeats, breathlessness, and chest pain. Since these symptoms are often also associated with anxiety disorders, there is a significant potential for confusion between the two conditions.

Cardiac arrhythmias may be caused by various conditions, including myocardial infarction (heart attack), a defect in the heart's electrical conduction, a side effect from some medications, or increased energy needs brought on by exercise or fever. Some arrhythmias can lead to heart attack—therefore great danger may result if this condition is ignored or undetected.

Myocardial Infarction. More commonly known as a heart attack, a myocardial infarction (MI) may be caused by a blood clot that interrupts the flow of blood, resulting in damaged heart tissue. In some cases the symptoms of MI are intense—a sudden and sharp pain that starts in the chest and may radiate to the neck, left arm, or upper abdomen. However, the symptoms are sometimes considerably milder, and may appear as indigestion, mild discomfort, or irregular heartbeat. These milder symptoms may be mistaken for those of an anxiety disorder. Prompt medical attention is the most important factor in improving both short-term survival and long-term prognosis.

Essential Hypertension. By far the most common type of hypertension (or high blood pressure), essential hypertension afflicts millions of Americans and has no single known cause. A number of conditions, such as adrenal, thyroid, and kidney disorders, may result in *secondary hypertension.* Both essential and secondary hypertension may be symptomless, or they may cause symptoms such as headaches, ringing in the ears, lightheadedness, and fatigue. These symptoms can be mistaken for those of anxiety disorders, a mistake made more likely by the widespread nature of these conditions.

Pulmonary Embolism. Pulmonary embolism occurs when an artery in the lung becomes blocked by tissue, air, fat, or blood clot. A pulmonary embolism may resemble a heart attack or a panic attack. Its symptoms include breathing difficulty, chest pain, shock, and bluish skin.

Cerebral Arteriosclerosis. Arteriosclerosis is a condition marked by the thickening, hardening, and loss of elasticity of the walls of the arteries. Arteriosclerosis may be caused by hypertension, kidney disease, diabetes, or excessively high levels of fats in the blood. Symptoms of cerebral arteriosclerosis that may resemble the symptoms of an anxiety disorder include headache, dizziness, and memory defects.

Internal Hemorrhage. An internal hemorrhage is a large loss of blood within the body from arteries, veins, or capillaries. Symptoms of a hemorrhage include a rapid pulse, low blood pressure, thirst, cold hands or feet, dizziness, fainting, and a sense of fear or restlessness. Any internal hemorrhage requires prompt medical attention.

Subacute bacterial endocarditis. Bacterial endocarditis is the inflammation of the lining of the heart or heart valves caused by bacteria. In its subacute form, the condition is not obvious—the patient may appear to be suffering only from anxiety-like symptoms such as weakness, loss of appetite, joint pain, and night sweats. Left undetected, subacute bacterial endocarditis may develop into potentially fatal heart valve damage.

RESPIRATORY DISORDERS

Since many panic disorder patients experience difficulty breathing—even hyperventilation—respiratory disorders that interfere with normal breathing are potential mimics of anxiety disorders. The following conditions are the most common respiratory disorders.

Asthma. Asthma is characterized by unpredictable periods of breathlessness and wheezing, usually caused by a sensitivity to a foreign substance (dust, pollen, pet hair, etc.) or environmental conditions (such as cold air, stressful situations, and strenuous exercise).

Symptoms of asthma that can mimic anxiety disorders include difficult breathing and tightness in the chest. Asthma is a serious condition and requires medical management.

Bronchitis. In this condition, the main breathing tubes (or bronchial tubes) become swollen and inflamed, causing the mucous glands in the tubes to expand and release mucous. The excess mucous combined with the already swollen bronchial tubes makes breathing difficult. Acute bronchitis (lasting less than six months) is most often caused by colds or the flu. Chronic bronchitis is usually caused by chronic environmental irritation from either cigarette smoke, air pollution, or occupational dusts. Many bronchitis victims also suffer from emphysema or other respiratory conditions called chronic obstructive pulmonary disease (COPD).

Emphysema. This disease occurs when the air sacs in the lungs where gas exchange takes place (the alveoli) become damaged or destroyed. Ultimately, emphysema leads to diminished oxygen in the blood and greater levels of carbon dioxide. As emphysema progresses, the lungs deteriorate, placing a greater burden on the heart and often leading to increased blood pressure. Symptoms that may mimic anxiety disorder include difficult breathing and fatigue.

THE PSYCHIATRIC MIMICKERS

The emphasis of this chapter is on *physical* conditions that can mimic anxiety, but we must be careful not to ignore the other *psychiatric* conditions that at first may appear to be anxiety disorders. A correct diagnosis is made more difficult by the frequent overlapping of anxiety disorders and other psychiatric conditions, such as depression. In Chapter 7, we'll examine the difficulties that occur when both anxiety and depression are present, but for now we will concentrate on the other psychiatric conditions that may be confused with anxiety disorders.

Depression. Although it is perhaps more likely that a person with an anxiety disorder will be treated for depression, the opposite situation also occurs. In general, although the DSM-III-R has numerous classifications for the different forms of depression (such as cyclothymia, dysthymia, and depressive disorder not otherwise specified), the most common depression symptoms, including insomnia, agitation, fatigue, and weight loss, can be mistaken for symptoms of anxiety.

The confusion between *bipolar disorder,* also called manic-depression, and anxiety may be greater. In this condition, periods of mania or euphoria are intermixed with periods of depression. Symptoms of a manic period that could mimic those of anxiety disorders are a decreased need for sleep, agitation, and increases in goal-directed activity. During the manic period, it is possible that the mania may be mistaken for excessive anxiety or obsession with a subject.

Seasonal Affective Disorder (SAD). Sometimes known as the winter blues, SAD occurs in certain individuals following a lack of exposure to sunlight. SAD symptoms, such as irritability, insomnia, and agitation, are often mistaken for symptoms of an anxiety disorder. This is likely to occur because many psychiatrists either fail to acknowledge SAD as a legitimate disorder or fail to detect the pattern of increased anxiety following lack of sunlight. Some psychiatrists have theorized that many people, perhaps even millions of Americans, suffer from undiagnosed SAD (for more information see pages 262–63).

Schizophrenia. Some people confuse schizophrenia with the very rare multiple-personality disorder, but schizophrenia actually encompasses a large group of mental disorders characterized by a patient's loss of a sense of reality and inability to think or act normally. Delusions and hallucinations may occur, but the symptoms that may be mistaken for those of anxiety disorders usually involve mood changes, extreme excitement, feelings of fear, social withdrawal or lack of desire to interact with others.

Personality Disorders. Personality disorders are deeply ingrained, inflexible, and harmful patterns of behavior, perception, and thinking that can impair normal functioning. The DSM-III-R defines sixteen different personality disorders, ranging from anti-social personality disorder to self-defeating personality disorder. Some of the personality disorders most likely to be confused with anxiety disorders are:

• Obsessive-compulsive personality disorder. The essential feature of this disorder is perfectionism and inflexibility, characterized by a preoccupation with rules, procedures, efficiency, and trivial details. Obviously, there is great potential for confusion between this condition and obsessive-compulsive disorder.

• Dependent personality disorder, in which the submissive person always relies upon another person, may be mistaken for agoraphobia.

• Avoidant personality disorder could be confused with agoraphobia or social phobias.

DRUGS

Every drug, illicit, prescribed, or over-the-counter, has side effects which can trigger psychiatric symptoms. Drugs, like physical diseases, throw off the body's chemical balance, and the brain, reacting to these changes, triggers changes in mood and behavior that are easily mistaken for signs of mental illness.

Since both therapeutic medications and illegal drugs are so widespread, since the symptoms they produce are so convincingly mental, and since so many psychiatrists fail to investigate thoroughly for drugs before diagnosing, I believe that drugs are the most dangerous and common of all the mimickers. As you'll see later, the first step in our diagnostic protocol at Fair Oaks is to rule out the presence of any drugs in the system.

Alcohol. Anxiety is a major symptom of alcohol abuse. In several well-known studies, researchers have agreed that sufferers of anxiety disorders seem to have a predisposition toward alcoholism. Some researchers have estimated that of all patients hospitalized for treatment of alcoholism, anywhere from 18 to 32 percent may be afflicted by panic disorder, disabling agoraphobia, or social phobias.

According to the research, alcoholics suffering from phobias usually develop their abnormal fears before their drinking problems have begun, suggesting that they drink in order to escape their crippling fears and the nagging anxiety that goes along with them.

In small doses, alcohol can quickly and quite effectively ease the terror of a panic attack. Unfortunately, the calming effects last only for a short time, after which the panic situation can rebound. If the panic sufferer then reaches for another drink, the cycle of dependence obviously begins. To make matters worse, it appears that as the condition progresses, more and more alcohol is needed to overcome the effects of the attack.

At the same time, the use of alcohol to relieve panic attacks seems to make subsequent attacks more likely.

Studies show that "severely" phobic patients develop alcohol dependency much more quickly than less intensely phobic individuals. In any case, at some point, alcohol becomes a factor in anxiety disorders, deepening the symptoms and prolonging its effects. In one study, most subjects reported that while their phobias had begun years before their drinking problems, their fears and anxieties were much worse after their alcoholism had taken hold.

Another study found that patients diagnosed as suffering from alcoholism and panic disorder were unable to distinguish between the symptoms of alcohol withdrawal and panic attacks. This finding led the researchers to speculate on the possibility that the two conditions share a common, or at least related, background.

A possible explanation for the high incidence of panic attacks among alcoholics may be the phenomenon of *kindling* (described below in the discussion of cocaine). Withdrawal from alcohol causes the brain to go through increased neural excitability—such as the jitteriness and DTs (delirium tremens) that alcoholics report. It is possible that repeated alcohol withdrawal may sensitize the brain to the point where kindling can occur, potentially resulting in panic attacks.

Nicotine Withdrawal. Eight of ten smokers who try to stop smoking experience withdrawal symptoms that mimic anxiety disorders. Other studies show that even smokers who are not trying to quit do regulate their nicotine levels. For example, smokers switching from cigarettes that have a high yield of nicotine to low-yield cigarettes smoke more frequently or more intensely in order to prevent the panic symptoms associated with lower nicotine levels.

ILLICIT DRUGS

Illegal drugs produce their mood-altering effects by interfering with chemical functioning in the brain. Over time, the drugs may replace the natural brain chemicals which normally regulate mood and perception. With prolonged use of drugs, the brain may cease to produce these chemicals at all, resulting in irreversible neurological damage.

Whether or not drugs cause permanent damage, they can produce a wide range of psychiatric symptoms, including, quite frequently, excessive anxiety and related disorders.

Marijuana. One side effect of marijuana intoxication is a phenomenon called *depersonalization,* in which users feel a sense of unreality, a lack of control over physical movement, even a feeling of being detached from the body, so that they can watch themselves from a distance.

This is also a common and especially disturbing symptom of panic attack. Researchers have traditionally thought that depersonalization in panic situations was a kind of defense mechanism, protecting the sufferer from the full impact of the panic-induced terror. That sense of detachment may provide some sense of safety during the attacks, but afterward it is one of the most troubling effects of the event, and it is part of the complex motivation that causes panic victims to begin a pattern of avoidance that eventually leads to phobic behavior.

During the marijuana-induced high, some people consider depersonalization as a nonthreatening and not unpleasant sensation. Knowing that the effect is directly related to smoking marijuana, they feel some sense of control over themselves. But if depersonalization subsequently occurs spontaneously, when those same people are "straight," it can be a terrifying event.

But for a significant number of agoraphobics, the first depersonalization experiences occurred as a consequence of marijuana use and were unrelated to any other anxiety symptoms. Still, the experience was jolting enough to trigger classic avoidance behavior, and as one survey shows, fear of the loss of control caused many of these people to choose avoidance behavior and then became agoraphobics.

Cocaine. Currently there is an epidemic of cocaine abuse in this country, an epidemic that has recently been augmented by the rapid spread of crack. While the effects of cocaine depend to some degree on whether the drug is sniffed, injected, or smoked (as freebase or crack), overall the same anxiety-mimicking side effects occur no matter the route of administration.

Cocaine's effect on the nervous system can be seen through its effects on the brain's electrical activity. EEG tracings of the brain after cocaine administration indicate activity in the same area of the brain responsible for the "flight or fight reaction," the very same reaction that is an integral part of panic disorder. No wonder that cocaine's side effects include increased heart rate, restlessness, irregular heartbeat, and high blood pressure —the same symptoms caused by a panic attack.

One survey conducted by the national helpline 800-CO-CAINE found that 50 percent of the callers reported cocaine-induced panic attacks! Other panic and anxiety-disorder clinics have noted the incidence of the onset of panic attacks beginning with cocaine use.

In fact, there is a strong possibility that the repeated use of cocaine may lead to spontaneous panic attacks, through a process called *kindling.* Apparently the phenomenon of kindling occurs after a part of the brain is repeatedly stimulated. This stimulation actually lowers the brain's activity threshold, so that eventually a level of stimulation that had previously been tolerated will now cause a reaction. If these kindled reactions are repeated enough times, the reaction may actually occur spontaneously, with no stimulation provoking the reaction.

How can cocaine abuse, through kindling, lead to spontaneous panic attacks? There have been reports of cocaine abusers who have repeatedly used cocaine without developing anxiety symptoms at first. Later, these cocaine abusers report that panic attacks may follow cocaine use. Eventually, the panic attacks strike without cocaine use. Even if cocaine use stops completely, the panic attacks can still persist. I believe that there is a very strong likelihood that cocaine abusers, given enough repetitions, may develop spontaneous panic disorder.

Amphetamines. Amphetamines were originally discovered in the 1920s by a scientist who was looking for anti-asthma medication. Amphetamines were soon found not only to reduce the bronchospasms of asthma but to produce side effects such as increased alertness and diminished desire for food. But soon, other less desirable side effects became apparent. These side effects include palpitations, rapid heartbeat, elevated blood pressure, overstimulation, and psychotic episodes—in short, many of the symptoms of anxiety disorders.

In addition, the abuse of amphetamines can produce drug dependence and withdrawal symptoms. The symptoms of amphetamine withdrawal, such as jitteriness and hyperactivity, can also mimic anxiety disorders.

PCP. PCP, or "angel dust," is a crystalline substance that can be sniffed, injected, or sprinkled on tobacco or marijuana and smoked. PCP can produce a violent state of panic, with a magnification of already present aggressive or hostile personality. Side effects of PCP may include sweating, drooling, flushing, constriction of the pupils, dizziness, uncoordination, slurred speech, and even psychosis.

In fact, PCP seems to play a role in psychotic behavior—one study found that up to one third of all involuntary admissions to psychiatric units were admitted PCP users.

Narcotics Withdrawal. Withdrawal from, or reduced dosages of, narcotics (such as heroin, methadone, and codeine) may cause several anxiety-like symptoms. The possibility of this mimicker going undetected is increased by the addict's tendency to conceal previous drug abuse.

MEDICATIONS

Without question, the widespread use of medications has been one of the most significant medical developments in the twentieth century and has saved millions of lives. The very power of these medications that accounts for their success also results in the potential for side effects. Unfortunately, some people taking medications fail to associate any of their anxiety-like symptoms with their medication. It is essential that patients report promptly to their physician any side effect from medications.

Lidocaine. First used as a general and local anesthetic, lidocaine has developed into the most widely used inpatient medication for the treatment of arrhythmias (irregular heartbeats). Although there is a tremendous overlap between cardiac and central nervous system disorders, there has been very little research into panic and anxiety symptoms in cardiac patients.

Recently a study of fifteen lidocaine patients who had psychiatric reactions to lidocaine found that 73 percent had "doom anxiety" reactions to the medication. The study noted other reports of doom anxiety in noncardiac patients after lidocaine had been used as an anesthetic. The authors of the study concluded that they hoped "the findings reported in this study will encourage physicians to more carefully consider lidocaine toxicity as a possible cause of these symptoms." I agree wholeheartedly.

Monoamine Oxidase Inhibitors. These antidepressant agents, which are structurally similar to amphetamines, can cause anxiety symptoms, nervousness, insomnia, and euphoria. While no one knows exactly how these MAOIs work, it appears that they interfere with the monoamine oxidase enzyme, an enzyme thought to be responsible for breaking down neurotransmitters once they reach individual brain cells. These neurotransmitters are believed to be critical ingredients in the brain's ability to regulate mood. The greater the inhibition achieved by MAOIs, the greater the incidence of anxiety side effects. If unchecked, these side effects can progress to symptoms that are virtually indistinguishable from panic, mania, or schizophrenia.

Disulfiram. This drug, best known under the trade name Antabuse, is often used in the treatment of alcoholism. It is meant to discourage drinking by causing severe nausea and vomiting when alcohol is ingested.

Disulfiram can cause anxiety, severe depression, and delirium. Treatment involves withdrawing the drug and replacing it with minor tranquilizers.

Ethosuximide. Primarily used in treatment of petit mal epilepsy, this drug causes a wide spectrum of psychiatric symptoms, including anxiety, depression, delusions, hallucinations, and even psychosis.

Indomethacin. This nonsteroidal anti-inflammatory agent has been shown to cause psychiatric symptoms after only one administration of the drug. Anxiety is a common side effect, along with hostility, disorientation, hallucinations, depression, and psychosis.

Vinblastine. Eighty percent of patients receiving this common anticancer drug experience symptoms of anxiety and depression within two or three days of treatment.

Cycloserine. Cycloserine is often used, in conjunction with other antibiotic drugs, to treat tuberculosis. However, it is sometimes used as the sole medication, and in these cases it can produce anxiety, nervousness, irritability, confusion, and paranoid delusions.

Nalorphine. This preanesthetic, administered before the main anesthetic is given, can cause immediate sensations of panic, suffocation, and fear of impending doom, all of which are classic symptoms of panic disorder.

OVER-THE-COUNTER DRUGS
Diet Pills. Drugstore shelves are loaded with pills and capsules which promise to depress your appetite and promote easy

weight loss. These nonprescription diet pills don't contain amphetamines, but their ingredients do include stimulants which can mimic the effects of amphetamines. Anxiety problems are a definite possibility with these drugs.

Laxatives. Some laxatives contain mercurous chloride. Overuse of mercury-containing laxatives can lead to mercury poisoning, which is associated with heightened anxiety and phobic behavior. (You'll find more about the anxiety-producing effects of mercury in the later discussion of environmental toxins.)

Caffeine. She was thirty-five, bright and attractive, and quite secure in her career as an executive secretary. She was regarded by coworkers as capable, collected, and utterly professional. But lately, her usually composed demeanor seemed to be falling apart. Out of nowhere, she'd begun to experience sudden, intense bouts of anxiety, complete with pounding heart, sweating palms, and rapid breathing. Her concentration would flag, and she found herself talking incessantly in a nonstop, rapid-fire style that had begun to concern her coworkers. She knew she was having panic attacks and was certain they would cost her her job.

The secretary sought psychiatric help, and fortunately it didn't take her psychiatrist long to put his finger on the problem. The young woman, he determined, wasn't panicked at all, she was simply suffering from a textbook case of caffeinism. By late afternoon, when her attacks always struck, she had usually gulped down six cups of coffee.

We all know that in moderate doses, caffeine can wake us up, improve performance in certain types of activities, and increase our alertness. Most of us are also familiar with the feelings that come from drinking one cup too many: edginess, nervousness, restlessness. If you really overdo it and take in more than 500 mg of caffeine a day, approximately five to eight cups of coffee, you may experience all the unpleasant symptoms of an anxiety disorder, as the young secretary now knows all too well.

But according to research, patients with phobic disorders

—associated with either generalized anxiety conditions or panic attacks—display a heightened sensitivity to the anxiety-producing qualities of caffeine. For these people, drinking just a few cups of coffee can trigger intense anxiety and even panic.

Aspartame. Annie loved diet colas, especially the ones sweetened with the sugar substitute known as aspartame or Nutrasweet. She'd drink several cans of it every day, and think nothing of it. But her case, which was recently reported in the psychiatric press, shows a possible link between this popular sugar substitute and panic disorder.

Annie was a cook and recently had taken a new job in a particularly hot kitchen, which caused her to boost her consumption of diet drinks dramatically. Sometimes she'd drink as many as twenty cans per day. Along with that, she'd drink one or two cups of aspartame-sweetened coffee each morning.

About a week after her heavy intake of aspartame-sweetened colas began, she began to feel symptoms of anxiety. She felt dizzy, her chest tightened and it was hard to breathe, and she felt the odd but terrifying certainty that she was dying.

Annie, of course, was suffering a panic attack. When she cut her cola intake to three cans or fewer per day, the symptoms ceased. When she went back to her twenty-can-per-day habit, the symptoms returned.

Annie's case was reported in an article in the psychiatric press, which explained that research has already implicated aspartame as a possible cause of seizures and mania. Now, it seems, there may be a link between the chemical and panic disorders. Interestingly, Annie also suffered from mitral valve prolapse, a condition which her doctor suggests may have increased her susceptibility to aspartame.

ENVIRONMENTAL TOXINS

The presence of even small levels of toxic elements in the bloodstream drastically affects the delicately balanced chemistry of the brain, and as we've seen before, that can trigger a range of apparently psychiatric symptoms.

Mercury. Mercury poisoning can result from inhaling mercury vapor, which occurs in certain industrial settings, from ingesting mercury-tainted food or water, or from using products such as skin creams, laxatives, and douches which contain mercury-based ingredients. The psychiatric symptoms of mercury toxicity include xenophobia (an abnormal fear or dread of strangers) and anxiety, as well as profound depression, mood swings, and severe irritability. If the source of mercury poisoning isn't discovered and eliminated, permanent dementia will eventually result.

Bismuth. In parts of Europe and Australia, bismuth is used in popular stomach medications. It's also a major ingredient in skin-lightening creams, which is significant, since this metal can be absorbed through the skin.

Bismuth toxicity works in two stages. In the first one to eight weeks of bismuth poisoning, the patient suffers anxiety symptoms, along with depression, feelings of apathy, and delusions.

As the condition progresses, more severe psychiatric symptoms emerge, including terrifying hallucinations, fluctuating states of consciousness, and language problems, in which speech sometimes degenerates to babble.

Bismuth poisoning is easily detected by measuring the level of its concentration in blood and urine. When the source of toxicity is cut off, improvement usually occurs within three to ten weeks.

Carbon Dioxide. The inhalation of carbon dioxide has been shown to provoke paniclike anxiety in patients already prone to panic attack. Carbon dioxide could also induce anxiety symptoms in subjects with no history of panic disorder, but several studies seem to indicate that panic sufferers are much more sensitive to the CO_2-induced attacks.

The precise mechanism by which carbon dioxide triggers anxiety is not completely understood. There is some thought that CO_2 overstimulates certain brain neurons, especially in the locus ceruleus, which seems to play a significant role in the biological aspects of the anxiety response (see pages 134–37 for more information).

Volatile Substances. Prolonged exposure to certain volatile hydrocarbons can trigger chemically caused bouts of anxiety and panic attack, along with personality changes, depression, and other psychiatric symptoms. High doses can lead to disorientation, confusion, and coma.

Painters, refinery workers, members of airport crews who refuel aircraft, and other individuals who inhale volatile fumes on a daily basis are especially at risk. So are people who sniff glue, gasoline, nitrous oxide, and other agents to get high.

Insecticides. In human beings, bug-killing chemicals containing organophosphates block the production of an essential brain enzyme. The physical result is a string of apparently psychiatric symptoms including anxiety, irritability, depression, restlessness, drowsiness, and decreased memory and attention span. The condition can usually be successfully treated with the intravenous administration of atropine.

MIMICKER DETECTIVES

I believe that developing a standardized, systematic, and scientific approach to detecting mimickers is crucial to the future of psychiatry. As the awareness of this prime cause of misdiagnosis grows, I think we'll see the emergence of a new group of experts specializing in studying the effects of these mimicking diseases.

CHAPTER SEVEN

BIOPSYCHIATRY'S DIAGNOSTIC APPROACH

"*L*OOK, DOC, I know I'm not the easiest person to work with. I don't have to tell you what my employees call me when they think I'm not listening."

I admit I had to force several choice adjectives out of my mind while I concentrated on her case. On the other side of my desk sat a forty-one-year-old divorced female, founder and president of a small but profitable marketing agency, whom I'll call Sheila. While I usually have a good rapport with my patients, I found this woman determined to be as disagreeable as possible. Nevertheless, Sheila had a very perplexing problem —one that had stymied five previous doctors. When she entered my office, she sat down abruptly, defiantly refusing to shake my hand. I had barely gotten my first question out when Sheila launched into her attack on the medical profession:

"Listen, I don't know why I'm here. You doctors are all alike. You don't know what's wrong, you don't know how to cure it, and you expect us poor patients to worship you. If I ran my company the way the medical profession works, then—"

"You're right," I interrupted. "It can be a travesty." Clearly, my comment surprised her. By stopping her before she could continue her somewhat valid, but unconstructive, criticisms, I had asserted my authority and defused her hostility. "Now," I said calmly, "why don't we start by discussing what's really bothering you?"

Sheila explained that she had been suffering headaches for the last three years. These headaches would appear almost every day around noon and last for ten to twelve hours. She described the headaches as a vise—always getting tighter— with dull, throbbing pain in a band around her head. Two internists, two psychiatrists, and one neurologist could find no "real basis for the headaches . . . they all said they were really just in my head." During the last three years, Sheila had been treated with anti-anxiety medications (diazepam and alprazolam), pain relievers, and ergotamine derivatives (antimigraine medications). The last doctor she had visited, a psychiatrist who ran a well-known panic clinic, prescribed the antidepressant imipramine. According to Sheila, none of the medications worked.

In fact, her headaches had worsened during the last two months and it was becoming increasingly difficult to keep working.

Further questioning revealed that eight years before, she had had what appeared to be a heart attack while driving to work.

"I can remember it exactly. It hit me on the morning of July 23, 1980, at precisely seven thirty-two A.M. The pain—it seemed to rip my chest, I couldn't breathe, and I could feel my heart racing. I pulled over to the side of the road and flagged down a state trooper. He took me to a local hospital, where I checked into what passes for their CCU. They ran their tests and then some idiot doctor just out of med school told me that I didn't have an attack. Instead he called it 'atypical chest pain.' What baloney."

When I asked her if she had had other similar attacks, she responded negatively, then hesitated and said she frequently had chest pains, but not as bad as the first attack. After having one other emergency room experience like the first one, she had endured these chest pains, rather than be "humiliated by medical incompetents too stupid to wipe their own noses." She worried about having a heart attack someday.

I decided to change the subject for a moment by asking her what she did when she felt the headaches beginning. Sheila replied that sometimes, if she had to, she stayed at work and "toughed it out." But lately she had been going home more often. "The sooner the better," she added, since the headaches usually didn't last as long if she went home. She told me that she liked to spend her weekends at home working because she didn't have time for a social life. When I asked her about her alcohol and drug use, she paused, then said quickly, "Well, I like to have some wine at home, like everyone else. But I never go out and drink, and I never ever drink during work hours." After some persistent questioning, she admitted that these "few drinks" amounted to almost a bottle of wine every day—although she continued to insist that she drank only at home and that it never interfered with her work.

A BIOPSYCHIATRIST'S DIAGNOSIS

Sheila's case presented a challenge, the type of challenge that motivated me to become a doctor. Just a few of the possible conditions that could have caused Sheila's condition include:

- A cardiac condition
- A lung condition
- Alcoholism
- Panic disorder
- Generalized anxiety disorder
- Agoraphobia
- Depression
- Migraines
- Brain tumor

Were any of the above responsible for Sheila's problems— or was it some other factor or factors, perhaps a mimicker, that was causing her symptoms? While speculation is tempting, as a doctor I must resist the urge to make snap decisions, the type of snap judgments that plague most psychiatric diagnoses. Since there were a number of physical and psychiatric conditions that might have been causing Sheila's headaches, the process of diagnosing her condition resembled the unraveling of a meticulously detailed mystery novel. My "detective" work followed the established biopsychiatric procedures of a thorough medical examination and diagnostic testing.

Before I could proffer a diagnosis I first had to gather as much information as possible. At the same time, the information Sheila provided did offer leads. Clearly, her substance abuse and chest pains bore closer examination. An anxiety disorder, perhaps panic with agoraphobia, was possible. Similarly, depression could not be ruled out. I decided to do a complete medical reevaluation of her case.

But before I reveal Sheila's correct diagnosis and how she

was treated successfully, I am going to divulge a secret: the "secret" of how a biopsychiatrist reaches a diagnosis and recommends treatment. The secret begins with . . .

STEP ONE: THE PATIENT'S HISTORY

One of the most effective diagnostic techniques, and one of the simplest, is to listen carefully as patients present their complaints. I usually begin the patient's first visit by asking him or her to describe the specific symptoms in great detail. Certain symptoms may indicate a particular diagnosis, or rule out another. For example, visual hallucinations or recent changes in vision often indicate the presence of a medical illness with psychiatric symptoms (such as a brain tumor). Although the patient may experience symptoms that resemble psychiatric conditions, the actual cause of these symptoms may be nonpsychiatric.

In anxiety disorders, the symptoms that a patient may describe may include rapid heartbeat, sweating, dizziness, trembling, nausea, shortness of breath, dry mouth, and diarrhea. Unfortunately, these symptoms are not very specific—literally hundreds of disorders can cause many of them. Despite this lack of specificity, this information is extremely important—although it does not provide us with the easy answer so many psychiatrists seek, it does contribute to the body of knowledge that a biopsychiatrist needs to make a diagnosis.

As part of the initial evaluation, I will ask the patient about his or her overall health, both currently and in the past—paying special attention to any medications, either prescription or over-the-counter, the patient may be taking or may have taken. Since many conditions may have genetic links, I will inquire of the health of family members, both living and dead. I note any recent memory loss or changes in weight, sleep patterns, appetite, taste sensations—actually, *any* physical or mental change can have significance. Since many of these changes may reflect alcohol and/or drug abuse, it is imperative that all physicians be aware of this problem. Unfortunately, even with 10 percent of the American population suffering from alcohol or drug addiction, many physicians—especially psychiatrists—pay only cur-sory attention to substance abuse. Since patients often deny any alcohol and drug use, the superficial approach of most physi-cians will usually fail to uncover the abuse.

ARE ALCOHOLIC WITHDRAWAL AND PANIC ATTACKS RELATED?

The relationship between substance abuse and anxiety disor-ders becomes even more complicated since a reported 20 to 30 percent of alcoholics also suffer from panic disorders.[1] One recent study found that alcoholics with panic disorders were unable to differentiate the symptoms of alcohol withdrawal from a panic attack, suggesting that the two conditions may have a related neurochemical cause in the central nervous sys-tem.[2] It may be possible that alcohol withdrawal makes the individual overact to a stimulus with a panic response.

In my evaluation—especially of patients who complain of anxiety or depression—I study the patient for any sign of sub-stance abuse. The symptoms that I look for are listed in the box on page 194. In addition to these signs, I will also note any behavioral and social problems, such as:

- Missed appointments
- Frequent employment changes
- Repeated tardiness at work
- Recent accidents
- Family problems
- Financial difficulties
- Violent or suspicious actions

Regrettably, even with my years of experience in the study of addictions and addictive behavior, I know that the power of observation has limitations. Substance abusers have remarkable abilities to deny and camouflage their substance abuse—abilities that will often thwart the most diligent interviewers. Accordingly, objective measures, such as urinalysis and blood alcohol screens, are needed to evaluate possible substance abuse.

However, most psychiatrists ignore these—and all other—objective laboratory tests. Incredibly, for these psychiatrists, the diagnostic process will end at the conclusion of the first fifty-minute-long interview. Perhaps no single aspect of traditional psychiatric practice both astounds and angers me more than this mad dash to reach a diagnosis and to begin treatment. For the biopsychiatrists, the diagnostic phase has only just begun.

PHYSICAL SYMPTOMS OF ALCOHOL AND/OR DRUG ABUSE:

- Puffiness of the face and/or hands
- Swollen or irritated nasal membranes
- Sudden vision difficulties
- Frequent infections
- Digestive problems
- Enlarged liver
- Tremors
- Lingering colds and flu
- Slurred speech
- Blackouts
- Changes in reflexes
- Loss of appetite
- Exercise intolerance

STEP TWO: THE MEDICAL EVALUATION

Actually this step begins the moment the patient enters my office, when I or my assistant measures the patient's height, weight, and blood pressure. And when I first meet the patient, I observe how the patient walks—his or her posture, coordination, and dexterity in simply entering my office, shaking hands, and sitting down. When I ask my opening questions, I assess sense of humor, concentration, and comprehension abilities. I pay special attention to the eyes—are they excessively vigilant (perhaps indicating paranoia), or are they unfocused, glazed over, and bloodshot (perhaps indicating substance abuse)? Does the patient's overall appearance indicate poor hygiene or nutritional deficiencies?

These observations, and countless others, race through my mind as I note areas to explore, either with follow-up questions or later during the physical examination. During the initial evaluation, my questions and actions must convey the implied message "I am your doctor, and it is my task to determine what is wrong."

This attitude, asserting the role of doctor, allows both biopsychiatrist and patient to move easily to the physical examination. While seeing a psychiatrist act as a physician may surprise some patients, most accept it far more easily than the traditional psychiatrist does. Most patients, especially anxiety disorder patients, expect to be examined by a doctor. Conversely, most psychiatrists refuse even to consider administering a physical exam. Some psychiatrists, especially those with a psychotherapy background, object to performing a physical exam because touching a patient might ruin their psychotherapy. Supposedly, a physical exam interferes with transference, a term used in psychotherapy to describe a patient's unconscious assignment of feelings for significant individuals in their earlier life to the psychiatrist. What nonsense! A psychiatrist should always be first and foremost a medical doctor, and medical doctors must be capable of examining patients.

Like any physician, the next step for a biopsychiatrist involves the hands-on, systematic examination of the various organs and systems of the body. Listening to the lungs, for example, may reveal the presence of infection, its location, and its severity. Heart sounds may indicate an unusual rhythm or the abnormal flow of blood through the vessels that may indicate mitral valve prolapse. A quick look at the ears, nose, and throat will immediately indicate the presence of certain infections. Some diseases such as diabetes produce changes in the structure of the eyes as a clue to their existence. Palpating (feeling) the neck provides information about the status of major lymph nodes there; an enlarged thyroid gland, for example, may indicate thyroid disease—a mimicker of anxiety. Similarly, palpating the abdomen can indicate whether such organs as the liver or the spleen are enlarged or have an unusual consistency, which may indicate alcoholism or other conditions. Even a glance at the ankles may reveal the presence of heart disease; if circulation is poor, fluids may accumulate in the ankles, causing swelling (edema).

After Sheila's initial interview and examination I suspected that she was suffering from a primary anxiety disorder. Her headaches—with their dull pain in a band around the head— did not suggest that any organic causes, such as a brain tumor, were involved. Sheila's headaches did resemble tension headaches caused by excessive muscle contraction. I suspected that she was suffering recurrent panic attacks, and that her frequent headaches resulted from the anticipatory anxiety that surrounds a panic attack. If my suspicions were true, then Sheila's avoidant behavior (leaving work to go home) and her excessive drinking were both attempts to overcome these panic attacks. However, before I settled upon this diagnosis and embarked upon a treatment plan, I needed both to verify my subjective suspicions with objective measures and, if possible, to identify any physical or biological basis for her panic attacks. These measures constitute the third step of the biopsychiatric approach.

STEP THREE: DIAGNOSTIC PROCEDURES AND LABORATORY TESTS

To verify Sheila's preliminary diagnosis, I recommended three diagnostic procedures: a twenty-four-hour ambulatory electrocardiogram (ECG) to measure cardiac performance, a two-dimensional echocardiogram to detect mitral valve prolapse or other cardiac abnormalities, and an electroencephalogram (EEG) to detect any tumors or forms of epilepsy that might be causing her symptoms. I also ordered basic and specialized medical tests (officially known as CBC and SMA-22 tests), a comprehensive urine test for drugs, a glucose tolerance test to check for diabetes, a blood-alcohol test, and a neuroendocrine test (a stimulation test using the thyroid-releasing hormone, or TRH). We drew the blood for the tests in my office. (Not surprisingly, a survey revealed that fewer than 75 percent of psychiatrists even had blood-drawing equipment available and fewer than 50 percent had blood drawn.)

Sheila was relieved, of course, when her EEG came back normal, indicating that neither cancer nor epilepsy was present. But I could sense her depression when I told her that both the ECG and the echocardiogram were also normal—she told me that she had secretly been hoping she had a mitral valve prolapse. When the EEG, ECG, and echocardiogram all came back normal, I recommended sodium lactate infusion, a test that has no effect on normal individuals but almost always causes a panic attack in patients suffering from panic disorders. The sodium lactate test did *not* provoke a panic attack in Sheila, confirming the previous failure of the antipanic drug imipramine and invalidating panic disorder as a diagnosis. I still suspected she was suffering from panic attacks, but now I focused on finding an organic cause for the attacks.

My suspicions were confirmed when all of the diagnostic tests came back normal except the TRH stimulation test. Follow-up endocrine evaluation confirmed that Sheila was actually suffering from hyperthyroidism, a condition that can mimic panic attacks. The diagnostic process did not stop there, however. I needed to rule out other factors that could *cause* hyperthyroidism, such as cancer, a malfunctioning pituitary gland, or an autoimmune disease. Follow-up tests eliminated these other conditions, and a specific diagnosis was made.

A thyroid hormone was prescribed to counteract the autonomous thyroid disease. Soon Sheila's chest pains and afternoon panic attacks disappeared. The headaches, however, did remain for a short time. The headaches and the excessive drinking, both part of her avoidant behavior, would linger unless corrected by additional therapy. Accordingly, Sheila enrolled in our outpatient alcohol treatment program here at Fair Oaks Hospital, where the efforts of a neurologist, internist, and psychiatrist provided her with the appropriate therapy to control her drinking and relieve her headaches.

Even Sheila's disagreeable nature had softened once her condition was recognized and treated. A few months after I last saw her, she sent a note thanking me for my help and apologizing for her earlier behavior. She added parenthetically, "If you'd felt the way I felt, you'd have acted like a monster too!" I knew exactly what she meant.

What happens, though, when other panic and anxiety disorders occur? How are they diagnosed and treated by biopsychiatrists?

DESCENDING BIOPSYCHIATRY'S DECISION TREE

The methodical approach seen in the first three steps of Sheila's treatment reflects the approach of the biopsychiatrist's decision analysis tree. Decision analysis aids like this one have become very popular recently. They help doctors comprehend the many variables that go into the diagnosis and treatment of a condition. Actually these decision analysis trees are not really new—they are merely graphic representations of the complex thought processes used by competent doctors for years. At first glance, this decision analysis tree for anxiety may seem bewildering. Don't worry—many psychiatrists are probably just as bewildered. Don't try to understand the whole tree immediately; rather, start at the top and work your way down slowly. To help you understand the decision analysis tree better, I've divided it into major levels (from A to G). The following paragraphs will help you navigate through these sections, giving you the chance to "play biopsychiatrist" as we analyze biopsychiatry's approach to diagnosing and treating anxiety disorders. Let's begin with a patient appearing at a biopsychiatrist's office with symptoms of anxiety.

Level A. The first and most important level of the decision

The Biopsychiatry Decision Analysis Tree for Anxiety Disorders:

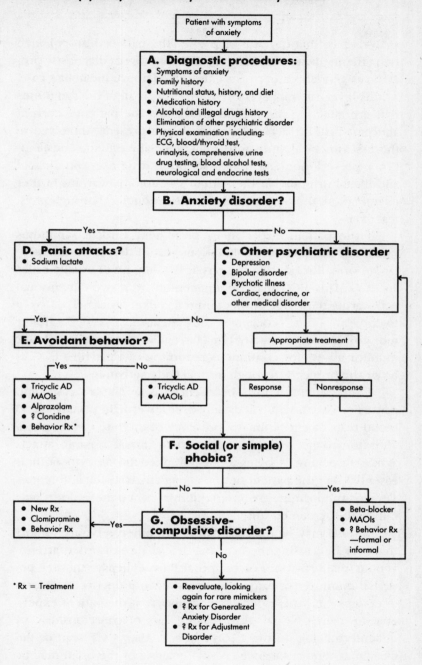

analysis tree incorporates step one (the patient history), step two (the medical examination), and step three (diagnostic procedures and laboratory tests), described above in Sheila's case. At this level, the biopsychiatrist must elicit all of the symptoms that are affecting the patient and assess the patient's current and past health. Factors—both past and present—involved in this assessment include nutrition (especially caffeine consumption), prescription and nonprescription drug use, and alcohol and illegal drug use. If the patient's symptoms warrant further examination, the biopsychiatrist will conduct a thorough physical exam.

If the patient experiences prominent cardiac symptoms (such as chest pain and palpitations) or if I detect cardiovascular abnormalities during the physical exam, I will usually order an ECG. This ECG may be augmented by a two-dimensional echocardiogram if I suspect mitral valve prolapse, or by a twenty-four-hour recording of the patient's ECG, called a Holter monitor, if I suspect arrhythmia (irregular heartbeat). A Holter monitor allows for continuous recording of a patient's ECG as he or she proceeds through normal daily activities.

If the patient reports headaches (as in Sheila's case) and nausea or sweating, I will usually order overnight urinalysis and blood tests to check for the presence of the rare cancer pheochromocytoma, whose symptoms can mimic a panic attack. While screening is being done for pheochromocytoma, it is essential that the patient not be taking any tricyclic antidepressants or monoamine oxidase inhibitors, since these drugs may nullify the screening test.

An EEG may be necessary to reveal other very rare tumors that may be causing the headaches, a seizure disorder, arteriovenous malformation, or temporal lobe epilepsy, another potential mimicker of panic attacks. An EEG to uncover this form of epilepsy may be especially appropriate if the patient experiences seizures, visual disturbances, loss of consciousness, or difficulty talking during a panic attack. Also, a CT scan or nuclear magnetic resonance (NMR) imaging of the brain may be necessary.

As part of an examination for panic and anxiety disorders, I will routinely order a series of laboratory tests designed both to assess the patient's overall health and to identify potential causes for the symptoms. These tests include a complete blood count (CBC) that assesses the total number of red and white blood cells in a millimeter of blood and can indicate the presence of infections and many blood diseases, and SMA-22, a blood test that measures the levels of twenty-two basic serum chemicals.

A battery of neuroendocrine tests designed to reveal abnormal function of the thyroid gland provides valuable information that may identify mimickers of psychiatric disorders, including anxiety and panic. Why is the thyroid gland so important? The metabolism of every cell in the body, including those of the brain, depends upon the thyroid hormones T_3 and T_4 to function correctly. This little gland determines the speed of all chemical reactions involved in consuming oxygen and burning energy in each cell. Normal growth and development are impossible when the gland is malfunctioning. In the previous chapter, I described hypothyroidism, a condition with depressionlike symptoms, results when the gland secretes too little thyroid hormone. Hyperthyroidism, a condition with anxiety and paniclike symptoms, occurs when too much thyroid hormone is secreted. The thyroid tests that I will order measure not only the levels of the thyroid hormones in the blood (the T_3 and T_4 screens), but also the body's ability to regulate the thyroid hormones (the TSH and TRH tests). Like Sheila, many patients suffering from hyperthyroidism are often misdiagnosed as anxiety disorder patients. One report, comparing the symptoms of anxiety disorders with hyperthyroidism, found that "many patients [with hyperthyroidism] in the study presented with symptoms very similar to patients with primary psychiatric disease. In fact, several had received psychiatric treatment (usually pharmacotherapy) and one had been hospitalized for psychiatric features of what eventually turned out to be thyrotoxicosis." (Thyrotoxicosis is caused by excessively high levels of the thyroid hormones in the bloodstream.) I suppose that my patient Sheila was lucky—at least she wasn't hospitalized.

Not only do the thyroid tests I recommend identify thyroid disease, but they may point to a biological basis for panic disorders: Several studies have found abnormal thyroid levels in panic disorder patients. In addition, one study found reduced or blunted TSH levels in panic patients that corresponded to levels found in depressed patients. This connection between panic and depression may account for the high percentage of depressed patients who show symptoms of anxiety.

Clearly, the complexity and importance of reaching a proper diagnosis cannot be overestimated. The failure by most professionals who treat panic patients to pursue the right diagnosis aggressively cannot be excused.

Level B. With the information provided by the patient's history, medical examination, diagnostic procedures, and laboratory tests the biopsychiatrist decides whether the patient is suffering from anxiety disorders. If the patient is diagnosed as suffering from anxiety disorder, then the question centers on identifying the specific anxiety disorder. Anxiety disorders may range from the situational or performance anxiety (such as fear of taking a test) that interferes with performance, to a generalized anxiety disorder (chronic and persistent fear not associ-

---

ANXIETY DISORDERS: WHAT'S THE THREAT?

In the different anxiety disorders, I try to identify what the patient perceives as threatening. An understanding of the threat, combined with the information gained from a patient interview and physical examination, helps to establish the correct diagnosis among the following anxiety disorders.

In *performance anxiety,* the threat is an anticipated event (such as taking a test) that causes higher-than-normal anxiety that interferes with the person's ability to perform a necessary event.

In *adjustment disorder,* the threat may be an everyday activ-

---

ANXIETY DISORDERS: WHAT'S THE THREAT? (*continued*)

ity that now provokes greater-than-expected levels of anxiety. For example, a recently divorced person may find eating dinner alone so unpleasant and anxiety-provoking that he or she cannot tolerate eating dinner at home. If this high level of anxiety occurs within three months after a stressful event and does not last longer than six months, then it is classified as adjustment disorder.

In *posttraumatic stress disorder* (PTSD), the threatening event is of such magnitude (such as murder, rape, war, a natural disaster, or a horrible accident) that it is outside the range of normal human experience.

In *simple phobia* (such as the fear of dogs), the actual threat is not normally dangerous or upsetting, but in this case it causes high levels of anxiety that may cause the person to avoid the threat.

In *social phobia*, patients feel threatened by the scrutiny of others, and hence they avoid events such as eating or speaking in public, where they feel vulnerable.

In *obsessive-compulsive disorder*, although patients will present other fears such as of uncleanliness and danger, the real threat is losing control. To avoid the anxiety caused by this loss of control, the patient follows ritual actions (compulsions) that prevent the loss of control.

In *agoraphobia with panic*, patients fear the possibility of powerlessness, and/or panicking while in vulnerable situations (elevators, cars, airplanes, stores, crowds, etc.). Theoretically, agoraphobia without panic can exist, but I believe it is extremely rare (if it exists at all).

In uncomplicated *panic disorder* (panic disorder without phobia), panic attacks occur without the patient's associating the attack with a specific threat or threats.

In *generalized anxiety disorder* (GAD), two or more threats that should not be anxiety-provoking provoke persistent and chronic levels of anxiety that cannot be attributed to any other disorder or organic cause.

DIAGNOSTIC CRITERIA FOR PANIC AND ANXIETY DISORDERS

Diagnosis	Symptoms	Stimuli	Response	Other
Panic disorder uncomplicated	Dizziness	None	Hypochondriac	3 Attacks/3 weeks
	Palpitations			4 Symptoms/attacks
	Dyspnea	Vistas (?)		Switchlike on
	Chest pain	Hot/humid (?)		Subpanics also
	Faintness	Novelty (?)		Females > males
	Choking			Asthenic body
	Flushing			Mitral prolapse
	Trembling	Lactate IV		
	Derealization			
	Paresthesias	β-Adrenergic		
	Apprehension	α_2-Adrenergic		
Limited phobia		Crowds	Social avoidant	Gradual onset
		Driving	If necessary	Anticipatory
		Elevators	Takes stairs	Fears > avoids
		Public transportation		
		Waiting lines		
Agoraphobia	Chronic fear	Separation	Avoids alone	High anxiety
		Distance home	Housebound	Panic stops (?)
Obsessive-compulsive behavior	Obsessions	Control loss	Noxious ideas	Ego alien
	Compulsions	"Germs"	Washings	Glove erythema
	Chronic fear	Unprepared	Listmaking	Restore control
	Chronic guilt	Did wrong	Checking	Preoccupation
			Rituals	
Generalized anxiety disorder	Trembling	Startle	Jumpiness	Chronic 1 month
	Restlessness		Strained face	Age > 18 yrs.
	Tics		Fatigue	
	Palpitations		Tachycardia	Sxs of 3 of 4:
	Flushing/chills		Cold hands/feet	1. Hypertonous
	Nausea/diarrhea		Vomiting	2. Hypersympathetic
	Total worry	Anxiety increases	Hypervigilance	3. Apprehension
	Nil threats		Disorganization	4. Hypervigilance
	Distractibility		Hypervigilance	
Social phobia	Blushing	Scrutiny	Hides out	Critical
	Shame	Authority		Projection
	Apprehension	Peers	Graded response	
	Tremor			
	Palpitations		Response	
	Sweating		Unconditioned, usually	No spontaneity
				Panic
	Dry mouth		Onset childhood	
	Avoids eye contact			

DIAGNOSTIC CRITERIA FOR PANIC AND ANXIETY DISORDERS

Diagnosis	Symptoms	Stimuli	Response	Other
Agoraphobia (only)	Chronic fear Low threat tolerance	Separation Trapped Distance	Avoids alone Housebound Home	Minor panic Rare
Simple phobia	Apprehension Hypersympathetic	Conditioned Noxiousness Reptiles graded Response Thunder Enclosure Heights		Common Treat if disabling

Posttraumatic
  stress disorder
	Psychic numbing
	Constricted affect
	Distractibility
	Chronic intense
	  fear
		Extreme noxious
		  exposure
		  (e.g, war,
		  murder)
		Reminders
			Potentiated
			Startle
			
			Increase fear	

Acute	Survivor guilt		Avoidance behavior	
Onset < 6 mos.	Irritability		Explosiveness	
Duration < 6 mos.	Obsessive recollection			
	Insomnia		Paranoia	
Chronic	Recurrent nightmares			
Duration > 6 mos.				
Delayed				
Onset > 6 mos.				

Reprinted with permission from *Diagnostic and Laboratory Testing in Psychiatry*, MS Gold and ALC Pottash, eds. New York: Plenum Press, 1986.

ated with a specific stimulus), to a simple phobia (such as fear of heights), to a social phobia (such as fear of eating or speaking in public), to agoraphobia, to obsessive-compulsive disorder, to posttraumatic stress disorder (PTSD). To identify the anxiety disorder, I consider first what is threatening to the patient, and second if panic attacks are associated with this threat. The box on pages 202–3 identifies the different threats associated with anxiety disorders, while the chart on pages 204–5 summarizes their diagnostic criteria.

Level C. Differentiating between anxiety disorders and other psychiatric conditions, such as depression, can be very difficult (see box on page 207). But if the biopsychiatrist suspects another psychiatric condition such as depression, bipolar depression (manic-depression), or psychoses (such as schizophrenia), appropriate therapy for that condition will be recommended. If the patient fails to respond to that therapy, the biopsychiatrist will reevaluate the patient for another psychiatric diagnosis— perhaps an individual originally suspected as suffering from depression may actually be suffering from manic-depression. A change in medication from antidepressants to lithium might prove beneficial. If the new therapy again proves inadequate, perhaps it will be necessary to do a complete medical reevaluation. All avenues must be explored before the patient should be described as treatment-refractory. Since the subject of this book is anxiety and panic disorders, we will focus on the other levels where the anxiety-disorder diagnosis can be made more specific.

Level D. If the patient is suspected of suffering from panic disorder or agoraphobia, I recommend a sodium lactate infusion to verify the diagnosis (as we saw above in Sheila's case). While I favor using sodium lactate as a diagnostic tool, its most common use has been in the research into panic attacks.

Despite its general acceptance as a research tool in accurately inducing panic, sodium lactate has not been widely used as a *diagnostic* aid. Resistance against using sodium lactate in diagnosis has centered on two areas. First, because it increases heart rate and blood pressure, sodium lactate is potentially dangerous for patients with a weakened cardiovascular system. Second, sodium lactate is not perfect: False negatives (cases in which panic disorder patients do not panic after lactate) and false positives (very rare cases in which people not suffering from panic attacks experience an attack following an infusion) may skew the results.

My response to these criticisms is simple. In the first case, I

DEPRESSION AND ANXIETY DISORDERS

Psychiatrists have long noted the connection between anxiety and depression. Recent studies have supported this connection: One study found that 50 percent of patients diagnosed as depressed first appeared for treatment with panic attack symptoms. Another study reported that the presence of major depression produced an 18.8-fold increased risk of panic disorder.

It is certainly understandable that many patients suffering from anxiety disorders are depressed. Living with excessive anxiety, disruptive phobias, and debilitating panic attacks could make anyone depressed.

Furthermore, anxiety disorder patients are often ashamed of their condition and find depression a more convenient explanation for their problems. A few years ago I had a college-age patient named Troy who initially complained of lethargy, boredom, and an overwhelming depression. As he put it, "There's nothing exciting going on in my life. I'm bored and I'm depressed. I want to change but I don't know how." My evaluation of Troy's case didn't support a depression diagnosis, however. His laboratory tests were normal, his school grades were good, and he participated in a number of outside activities—Troy gave every indication of being a quiet but successful student. It was only after more questioning that discrepancies in Troy's story appeared.

Initially, he told me he had a girlfriend and that they had "normal sexual relations." Later, when I asked him about his girlfriend and what he considered normal sexual relations to be, he became very flustered and blurted out, "Oh, five or six times a week." Given what I had already learned about Troy, I found this statement difficult to believe. And when I quietly questioned him again, he admitted that he had lied, that in fact he didn't even have a girlfriend. "Actually," he told me, "I'm a virgin. Fact is, I've never had a girlfriend—I get so nervous around women that I start sweating, I can't speak, and I get so

DEPRESSION AND ANXIETY DISORDERS (*continued*)

humiliated. I study a lot and I get involved in different activities so I don't have to feel like such a loser all the time. But it's not working. I see my friends going out on dates and having a good time, but I just can't get over my fear of talking to women."

No question that Troy was depressed, but it was a depression that derived from his fear of women. I recommended that Troy start a therapy program, and it was not long before his depression lifted.

Troy's case illustrates just one of the many problems that cloud the differential diagnosis of anxiety and depression. Other questions to consider are: Does the patient who has both anxiety and depression suffer from two separate illnesses? Is there a third condition, such as substance abuse, that is causing both the anxiety and depressive symptoms? Or, more theoretically, are anxiety and depression disorders really the same disease, just different sides of the same coin?

agree that sodium lactate does stress the cardiovascular system. However, before I recommend a sodium lactate infusion, I carefully screen out patients with any cardiovascular condition that might not withstand the lactate challenge. Patients whose cardiovascular system shows no abnormalities are then informed of the potential risk before agreeing to the lactate test. I assume that the research scientists have followed similar protocols before they administer lactate in their studies—and yet I am unaware of any claims that research scientists are endangering the lives of their subjects when they infuse lactate. Why then should it be assumed that a diagnostic administration of sodium lactate, under similar protocols, will endanger lives? Sodium lactate infusion, when done properly, is as safe in diagnosis as it is in research.

The second criticism, that lactate infusion is not perfect, mystifies me. In medicine, nothing is perfect. No diagnostic procedure or laboratory test, whether it is an X-ray, a CT scan, or a blood test, can claim 100 percent accuracy. And yet the orthopedist doesn't hesitate to X-ray a broken foot even though there is a chance that the X-ray will not detect the fracture, or that the radiologist will misread the X-ray. While lactate infusion is not perfect, it will accurately report panic attacks in approximately 80 percent of panic patients.

Even with an accuracy rate this high, a laboratory test should rarely be used by itself to provide a diagnosis. Instead it should be evaluated along with other clinical data and observations to reach the most accurate diagnosis possible. I believe that sodium lactate infusion should become an important diagnostic tool, especially since panic and anxiety disorder patients —and their psychiatrists—often have a difficult time distinguishing between intense anxiety and a panic attack. In addition, a sodium lactate infusion following the initiation of therapy can assess the effectiveness of therapy. Panic disorder patients, whose panic is well controlled through either medication or a combination of medication and behavior therapy, will usually not respond again to sodium lactate—even after their medication has been discontinued. This failure to respond proves to the patient that the therapy is working, an assurance that is often necessary, because recovering panic attack patients may mistakenly view their anticipatory anxiety as a failure of therapy.

If, after all the factors have been weighed (including a sodium lactate response), a diagnosis of panic disorder has been reached, then the next level concerns . . .

Level E. Avoidant behavior. Is the patient responding to a panic attack by using avoidant behavior? If the patient has responded to his or her phobias by avoiding situations that may entail "risk," then that is classified as avoidant behavior, and behavior therapy, as adjunct to medication, is indicated. If there is no avoidant behavior, then medication alone will suffice.

Level F. If panic attacks do not occur, then the next question concerns whether there is a social or simple phobia present. Treatment of first choice for phobias without panic is behavioral therapy. In many cases, patients can practice this treatment informally by themselves (see Chapter 9). Other more difficult problems may require formal therapy with a mental health professional. If behavior therapy alone does not provide the desired benefit, then medications, beginning with the beta-blockers, may be necessary.

Level G. If an anxiety disorder exists without panic attacks or social or simple phobias being present, then the next question is whether obsessive-compulsive behavior has developed.

Now, and only now, after having gone through these exhaustive diagnostic procedures, will the biopsychiatrist feel confident in recommending therapy. The following chapter details the most up-to-date therapeutic strategies, starting with panic disorders, then moving to the other anxiety disorders.

CHAPTER EIGHT

LET
THE
TREATMENT
BEGIN

TREATMENT OF PANIC DISORDERS
AND PANIC DISORDERS WITH PHOBIAS

Understandably, most of my panic disorder patients first arrive at my office in a very confused state, having seen other doctors without benefit. Not knowing what is wrong, they have been made to feel "crazy." Many family members, frustrated by panic attacks they don't understand, provide little emotional support. Alone, feeling weak and vulnerable, they have turned to a psychiatrist sometimes reluctantly, sometimes hopefully, as a "last-ditch" effort.

Imagine how happy I am to tell them, after a thorough examination, that they are suffering from panic disorder. When so much of modern medicine concerns caring for terminally ill patients, when the doctor can do little more than try to make the patient's remaining time as painless as possible, imagine how wonderful it is to tell people they have a treatable—even curable—condition. My enjoyment, of course, pales when compared to the patient's relief that they are not crazy, that there is something that can be done, that their life can be free from their fears. The patient's sense of relief usually does not happen immediately; often the patient is skeptical at first, perceiving me as just another doctor who makes promises he can't deliver.

For this reason, I must begin treatment by convincing my patients that I am a "one-stop shop" doctor—an M.D., diagnostician, and psychiatric specialist all rolled into one. For my treatment plan to be effective, the patient needs to believe that my approach will work. I should add here that my treatment plans for uncomplicated panic disorder (panic attacks without phobias) and panic disorder with phobias are almost identical. In fact, the only major difference concerns the avoidant behavior that is associated with phobias. (As I will describe, I prefer using behavior therapy for the treatment of avoidant behavior.)

To convince the patient and to make him or her a candidate for the "good news" approach, I start by explaining the possible biological causes of the panic attacks. I explain that the patient's

213

stimulus-response system has been malfunctioning, causing unexplained panic attacks. I will usually couch my explanation with references from the patient's own experiences. I admit to the patient that I do not know exactly what causes the panic, but I frequently mention that science doesn't know why people have high blood pressure or a whole host of other conditions, and yet no one blames the patient, or the patient's parents, for causing these other conditions.

For the patient who has panic disorder with phobias, I then proceed to establish how the patient, in response to panic attacks, can develop avoidant behavior and phobias. Again, whenever possible, I mention specific incidents from the patient's life. If the patient, especially an agoraphobic, cannot remember having specific panic attacks associated with the phobia, I explain that some patients may have what some experts call a "fear of fear." In this theory, specific panic attacks may not be necessary for the patient to have a phobia associated with an object or event; a phobia can be caused simply by a fear that a panic attack might occur. While it is difficult to prove this theory, it makes sense to me: One patient told me that while she was afraid of flying she had never even been near a plane.

In explaining the course of a patient's disorder, it is important to differentiate between a panic attack and the anticipatory anxiety that surrounds the attack. This can be difficult, because the word "panic" has a broader and very negative connotation in our society. People may say that they got lost while driving because they "panicked and forgot to turn left," or a basketball player may be accused of panicking and missing the last shot of a game. A patient should understand that when clinicians use the word "panic" to describe a panic attack, they are referring to a specific condition with real symptoms and sense of imminent death. This state of panic is so intense that it cannot last longer than approximately ninety minutes—the human body simply can't withstand the intensity.

Conversely, anticipatory anxiety is less intense than a panic attack. Anticipatory anxiety occurs when a person believes that an event or action will precipitate a panic attack. Differentiating between anticipatory anxiety and a panic attack may be diffi-cult, since anticipatory anxiety can be very upsetting (one pa-tient, attempting to overcome his fear of driving, said it was like "my first date, a job interview, and playing in the Super Bowl all wrapped into one every time I even think about getting behind the wheel"). Nevertheless, most patients can understand that the worry about a panic attack differs from the actual attack.

If it's feasible I will try to involve family members and/or friends in the recovery process. These individuals are often overlooked, but the majority of them have suffered from and been frustrated by their loved ones' phobias. Family members, once they understand panic attacks and phobias, can become valuable assistants in helping the phobic person through recov-ery.

Once patients understand the genesis of their panic attacks and the nature of the phobias that can develop, my next step is to correct their malfunctioning stimulus-response system through medication. Most patients accept the logic of begin-ning treatment with medication, but a few patients may have reservations. Some of these patients may be taking or may have taken medication without benefit; others may have already "failed" therapy with the same medication. I tell these patients there is more to successful therapy than just picking any medi-cation—the right drug, the proper dosage, and the proper du-ration of therapy are all equally important. I tell my patients that treatment for panic attacks proceeds on a trial-and-error basis. I will start with the medication that I think will work best. If necessary, I'll adjust the dosage. If, after sufficient time, a noticeable improvement has not been achieved, then other medications or treatment strategies may be tried. Medications commonly used in the treatment of anxiety disorders are listed in the box on page 216.

Other patients may object to pharmacotherapy, fearing that these psychiatric medications may be dangerous—an objection that may be more common in agoraphobics, who may fear that these medications will cause them to lose control over their actions and thus precipitate a panic attack. If I am patient but persistent I can usually assuage their doubts—I tell them of the hundreds of patients I have treated successfully with these medications and of the millions of people who have benefited from their use. These medications are not mood-altering; they do not make the patients lose control. In fact, they give patients control over their acts by preventing panic. I acknowledge that there is a risk of side effects, but at my usual low starting dose, this risk is minimal. Patients are told to call my office immediately if they do experience any side effects. Of course, most of them, even the ones that are most apprehensive about medications, never call.

MEDICATIONS USED IN THE TREATMENT OF ANXIETY DISORDERS

Generic Name	Brand Name(s) *1
ANTIDEPRESSANTS	
Amitriptyline	Elavil, Endep
Amoxapine	Asendin
Bupropion	Wellbutrin
Clomipramine	Anafranil
Desipramine	Norpramin, Pertofrane
Doxepin	Adapin, Sinequan
Fluoxetine	Prozac
Imipramine	Janimine, Tofranil
Maprotiline	Ludiomil
Nortriptyline	Pamelor
Protriptyline	Vivactil
Trazodone	Desyrel
Trimipramine	Surmontil
BENZODIAZEPINES	
Alprazolam	Xanax
Chlordiazepoxide	Librium
Clonazepam	Klonopin

1* The Brand Names listed in this section do not constitute a complete list, but merely reflect some of the more common brands.

(continued)

Clorazepate	Tranxene
Diazepam	Valium
Flurazepam	Dalmane
Halazepam	Paxipam
Lorazepam	Ativan
Oxazepam	Serax
Prazepam	Centrax
Quazepam	Dormalin
Temazepam	Restoril
Triazolam	Halcion

MAO INHIBITORS

Isocarboxazid	Marplan
Phenelzine	Nardil
Tranylcypromine	Parnate

OTHER MEDICATIONS

Baclofen	Lioresal
Carbamazepine	Tegretol
Clonidine	Catapres
Propranolol	Inderal
Verapamil	Calan, Isoptin

NEW MEDICINES†

Adinazolam
Alpidem
Fluvoxamine
L-deprenyl
Mianserin
Moclobemide
S-Adenosyl-Methionine (SAM)
Zimeldine

† While currently not available in the United States, many of these new medications may be approved for the treatment of anxiety disorders in the future.

I must emphasize that the treatment plan I am presently describing applies to panic disorders with agoraphobia or panic disorders with mixed phobias (cases in which there have been spontaneous panic attacks and resultant phobias, but not the travel restrictions associated with agoraphobia). For uncomplicated or simple phobias (cases in which a person has fears, but not panic attacks) I recommend a different treatment plan (see page 239 for more information). However, for panic attacks with phobias, I do recommend, as a treatment of first choice, medication, specifically the tricyclic antidepressants.

THE TREATMENT OF FIRST CHOICE: TRICYCLIC ANTIDEPRESSANTS

The ability of a tricyclic antidepressant (TCA) to block a panic attack was first noted over twenty-five years ago in pioneering research conducted by my colleague Dr. Donald Klein. Dr. Klein gave imipramine (a TCA) to patients hospitalized with phobias. Dr. Klein's work showed that imipramine effectively blocked the panic attacks, but had little effect on their anticipatory anxiety or avoidant behavior. The antipanic effect of imipramine has been well established by six double-blind placebo studies (in these studies neither the subject nor the research assistant know whether an active medication or an inactive substance was administered).

While the studies assessing the TCAs' efficacy have focused on imipramine, I have achieved similar treatment success with the other TCAs, such as desipramine, nortriptyline, and doxepin. Although I will usually begin treatment with imipramine, since its antipanic abilities have been the most thoroughly tested, I will not hesitate to switch to other TCAs if imipramine's side effects necessitate a change.

While no one knows exactly why TCAs like imipramine block panic attacks, some experts believe that the TCAs (as well as another type of antidepressant called monoamine oxidase inhibitors, or MAOIs) inhibit the activity of the locus ceruleus, a part of the brain believed to be involved in the fear/arousal response system (see Chapter 5).

Critics of TCAs in the treatment of panic attacks contend that any benefit of TCAs—if there is a benefit—is derived from their antidepressant mechanism and not from any antipanic efficacy. According to these critics, the studies showing TCAs' efficacy in treating panic attacks really reflect TCAs' antidepressant qualities; they claim that TCAs have little benefit in treating panic attacks when depression is not present.

As you may have guessed, I disagree with this criticism. First, I know how to diagnose depression and I know how to diagnose panic disorder, and I know how to tell the difference between the two. And while the two conditions may overlap (as one panic disorder patient expressed it, "Doc, if you had what I had, you'd be depressed too"), I have successfully treated uncomplicated panic disorder patients (i.e., those who did not have depression) with TCAs. Second, I, like other psychiatrists, have noted that panic disorder patients often respond to TCA dosages far lower than depressed patients require. If it's the depression that is really being treated, why are these lower dosages effective? One possibility is, of course, that these low dosages of TCAs are blocking the panic attacks but not treating depression.

Another possible explanation is that the panic disorder patients who respond to low dosages might metabolize TCAs slowly. (Metabolism is the process of breaking down and using a substance.) These slow metabolizers, because the medication stays in their system longer, might build up plasma levels of TCAs comparable to levels achieved in depressed patients. To assess this possibility, my Fair Oaks Hospital colleague Donald R. Sweeney, M.D., conducted a study of plasma blood levels following low-dose TCA therapy. After three weeks of therapy, the patients reported significant alleviation of the panic attacks. Analysis of their TCA plasma blood levels indicated that these levels corresponded closely to their low daily dosage—no buildup of TCA had occurred. This result implies that TCAs do, in fact, block panic attacks without affecting depression.

This implication has been verified by recent research indicating that the antipanic and antiphobic effects of antidepressants do not depend upon either the presence or the history of depression.

Because of the effectiveness of TCAs, I usually begin with a low daily dose of imipramine, such as 10 mg, and increase this dose gradually until the panic attacks stop or until the patient reports side effects. I usually recommend taking the dose at bedtime, since the drowsiness that can occur may help some patients sleep better. Some patients report a complete cessation of their attacks after only ten to fourteen days on dosages of 50 to 100 mg. If the panic attacks do not improve, it may be necessary to increase the dosage gradually up to 300 mg daily, and to maintain therapeutic doses for a period of at least six weeks.

If patients are not responding to the medication, I will first measure their plasma blood levels to verify that the patients have been taking the medication as I directed, and that their metabolism of the medication is not unusual, before trying another medication. Some nonresponding patients are actually not complying with their dosage. Some never even make it to the pharmacist. I've had patients swear that they have taken their medication as directed, only to have their blood tests fail to reveal any trace of it. Many of these noncompliant patients will start taking their medications once they realize that I intend to monitor their blood levels. Other patients stop taking the medication—without consulting me—after experiencing side effects. I stress to these patients, and to all of my patients, the importance of reporting all side effects to me. If I don't know about these side effects, there is little I can do to prevent or overcome them.

If side effects do appear, they will usually occur within three weeks of starting therapy—patients may report a feeling of being "tense," "jittery," or "spacey." This sensitivity to imipramine occurs in approximately 15 percent of the patients. Other patients may report experiencing a dry mouth, dizziness, or constipation. My response to these side effects depends upon a series of conditions:

- If the patient can tolerate these side effects, I will encourage him or her to wait if possible until at least three weeks have passed, since these side effects will often disappear in that time.
- If the patient's side effects cannot be tolerated but the panic attacks have improved, I will recommend a gradual reduction in dosage until the side effects disappear or until the drug stops working. If the side effects persist and they cannot be tolerated, it may be necessary to try another medication, preferably another TCA that is less likely to cause the side effects.
- If the patient cannot tolerate the side effects and the medication has not improved the panic attacks, I will usually recommend switching to another antipanic antidepressant, such as an MAOI.

I must stress that when administered properly, a TCA will work by itself in about one third of patients who have panic disorder with phobia. However, in the majority of cases, patients' avoidant behavior is so ingrained and their anticipatory anxiety so great that *behavior therapy* will be necessary. The type of behavior therapy I favor involves in vivo desensitization, or real-life exposure to phobias (see pages 245–54 for more information). In addition, there are cognitive strategies in which the patient is taught to recognize the "automatic" thoughts that occur when confronted with a phobia, and how these thoughts can be controlled and actually turned into positive forces.

While many patients, especially those with agoraphobia, need the guidance provided by a psychiatrist or a trained professional in conducting behavior therapy, other patients with less entrenched phobias may benefit from self-administered behavior therapy. In the next chapter, I'll explain the behavioral strategies for overcoming fears that individuals can practice on their own.

Once the proper dosage has been achieved, and with the patient practicing behavior therapy to overcome avoidant behavior and anticipatory anxiety, the next question is: *How long should the medication be taken?* While each patient's treatment plan must be assessed individually, I have found that the medication rarely needs to be used for more than one year. My experience indicates that maximum benefit occurs after therapy has been maintained for at least six months, but rarely will the patient continue to improve after twelve months. Usually, during this six-to-twelve-month period I will begin a slow tapering of the patient's imipramine dosage, sometimes as fast as 25 mg a day. Of course, if relapse occurs, I will reintroduce the medication and return to the lowest possible therapeutic dosage. Later, I will again attempt to discontinue the medication.

In almost all of my cases, my patients have been able to lead medication-free lives. However, we both know that if their panic attacks do occur, a successful and safe medication can provide freedom from these attacks.

WHY TREATMENT "FAILURES" OCCUR

Why doesn't every psychiatrist have the same success with TCA medications? One important reason is that many psychiatrists fail to implement aggressive behavior therapy in their treatment plans. Having heard of the antidepressants' success in treating panic disorders, they rely solely upon the medication. Without behavior therapy, many unfortunate patients will not have the necessary tools to overcome their avoidant behavior and anticipatory anxiety. Seeing themselves as failures, many patients will give in to their fears and drop out of therapy. In addition, very few psychiatrists ever recommend group behavior therapy, in which recovering patients help other patients to overcome their phobias. Often the sympathetic support and encouragement of a recovering patient will help the patient persevere. But if behavior therapy is rarely recommended, the recommendation for group behavior therapy is even rarer.

Other failures occur because the doctor doesn't follow prudent prescribing practice. Too much of the drug may be given too soon, causing too many side effects, or, more likely, too low a dose may be given for too short a time. The latter occurs more frequently for a variety of reasons.

First, patients may be expecting immediate results; when these fail to appear they may become discouraged and return to the doctor, demanding another medication. Many psychiatrists find that it's easier to give in to the patient than work for the best solution. Other doctors may fail to increase the dosage as necessary or they may wait only a few weeks before concluding that the medication is not working. Both failures result in the premature termination of therapy.

Second, many patients and psychiatrists mistake their anticipatory anxiety for a recurring panic attack and erroneously conclude that therapy has failed. I find that encouraging patients to maintain a diary or log of their actual panic attacks helps the patient to separate the anticipatory anxiety from the attacks.

If I suspect that the patient is actually experiencing anticipatory anxiety, but the patient continues to worry that he or she is still suffering panic attacks, I may recommend that another sodium lactate infusion be performed. Patients' failure to respond to the sodium lactate may prove to them that their attacks have been stopped and encourage them to proceed with their therapy plan. If the anticipatory anxiety continues to be a problem, a low dose of a benzodiazepine, or alprazolam, may be used as an adjunct to the antidepressant medications and behavior therapy. Usually the anticipatory anxiety will diminish as the patient realizes that the panic attacks have been successfully thwarted.

Occasionally, even with the high success rate possible with TCA and behavior therapy combined, some patients still experience recurring panic attacks. For these patients, I will recommend another very effective therapeutic tool: the monoamine oxidase inhibitors.

THE MONOAMINE OXIDASE INHIBITORS (MAOIs)

The first indication that the antidepressant MAOIs might be effective in the treatment of anxiety disorders occurred in the early 1960s when researchers noted that the first MAOI, iproniazid, seemed especially effective in treating "anxious" depressives. Then in the early 1970s researchers noted that depressed patients with symptoms of anxiety did very well following therapy with another MAOI, phenelzine (brand name: Nardil). The results of these studies led researchers to evaluate phenelzine in the treatment of anxiety disorders. Those studies have generally found phenelzine to have efficacy similar to imipramine's in preventing panic attacks. In fact, in patients with panic attacks and atypical depression (characterized by oversleeping, overeating, extreme muscle weakness, and sensitivity to depression), phenelzine achieved higher marks than imipramine. Why, then, haven't MAOIs such as phenelzine become as popular as the TCAs in treating panic disorders?

Years ago, MAOIs developed a reputation for extreme dangerousness, so psychiatrists stopped prescribing them. Today, we know that these risks have been overstated; yet I have encountered several psychiatrists who have never prescribed this medication. The avoidance of MAOI therapy stems from early uses of MAOIs that resulted in an extreme rise in blood pressure among some patients. This effect made MAOIs very controversial, and many psychiatrists avoided them.

Later, it was learned that these reactions of extreme high blood pressure occurred when the MAOIs were combined with other drugs or foods containing a substance called *tryamine.* Foods and medications containing tryamine are listed in the accompanying box. Unfortunately, many psychiatrists have failed to note that when these diet and drug restrictions are observed, MAOIs have proved to be a very effective antipanic medication.

Common sense, however, precludes me from recommending the MAOIs before the TCAs have been tried. Most panic disorder patients, especially those with agoraphobia, are extremely sensitive about their health. In fact, one report concluded that agoraphobics had virtually the same fears about their health as did patients suffering from hypochrondria (a condition marked by excessive preoccupation and worry over one's health). To these agoraphobic patients, the potential risks of MAOIs can appear to be very frightening, so frightening that it could cause them to drop out of treatment. For this reason, I prefer to keep MAOIs as an effective second line of defense for

FOODS AND MEDICATIONS TO AVOID WHILE TAKING MAOIs

1. *Foods and beverages to avoid*
   —Matured or aged cheeses such as blue, Swiss, cheddar, American, as well as processed cheeses and spreads, are particularly to be avoided. However, cottage, cream, or farmer cheese is permissible.
   —Red wines (Chianti in particular) and rose wines
   —Sherry, vermouth
   —Beer
   —Marmite, Bovril and similar yeast or meat extracts (beware of drinks, soups, or stews made with these products)
   —Yogurt not made by a reliable manufacturer
   —Broad bean, fava bean, or Chinese pea pods
   —Banana skins and overripe bananas
   —Any meat, fish, poultry or other protein food that is not fresh, freshly canned, or freshly frozen. (This includes game meats, offal, lox, salami, sausage, corned beef, and liver, including pate.)
   —Meat prepared with tenderizers
   —Pickled herring and pickled lox
   —Any food that previously produced unpleasant symptoms

2. *The following foods and beverages should be used with moderation, as they are occasionally associated with adverse reaction*
   —Caffeinated beverage, such as coffee, tea, cola
   —Chocolate
   —Alcoholic beverages of any kind*
   —Avocados
   —Soy Sauce
   * Distilled liquors (vodka, gin, rye, Scotch) will not produce a hypertensive reaction but will interact with Nardil to produce more rapid intoxication.

3. *Medications to avoid*
   —Cold tablets or drops

FOODS AND MEDICATIONS TO AVOID WHILE TAKING MAOIs
(*continued*)

—Nasal decongestants (tablets or drops)
—Hay fever medication
—Sinus tablets
—Weight reducing preparations—pep pills
—Anti-appetite medicine
—Asthma inhalants
—Demerol
—Other antidepressants
—Epinephrine in local anesthesia (includes dental)

4. Do not take any medicine, drugs, proprietary preparations (including cough and cold cures), or any other medication whatever without consulting your doctor.

5. Follow these instructions (and carry this with you) all the time while taking MAO inhibitors and continue to do so for two weeks after stopping medication.

Reprinted with permission from Fyer, AJ Sandburg, D. "Pharmacologic Treatment of Panic Disorder." *Review of Psychiatry*, Volume 7. Washington, D.C.: American Psychiatric Association Press, 1987.

---

the few patients who do not respond to the tricyclic antidepressants.

Besides phenelzine, the other currently available MAOIs are isocarboxazid (brand name: Marplan) and tranylcypromine (Parnate). Today, phenelzine is the most commonly prescribed MAOI in the treatment of panic disorders, followed by tranylcypromine. Tranylcypromine may be as effective as phenelzine (although studies confirming its efficacy are lacking), but it may be more difficult for the patient to tolerate.

When switching from a TCA to an MAOI, a drug-free "washout" period of seven to ten days had been standard procedure. However, recent studies have not found problems with introducing the MAOI while tapering the TCA dosage.

Usually, I will begin phenelzine therapy with a dose of 15

mg and increase this dose to a maximum of 90 mg if necessary. Before administering the MAOI, I will measure blood platelet monoamine oxidase activity; then during therapy I will measure this activity again—aiming for an 80 percent or greater inhibition of MAO activity. As with the TCAs, once the panic attacks have been controlled, the patient may require behavior therapy to overcome avoidant behavior and anticipatory anxiety. Similarly, a low dose of a benzodiazepine may be needed for patients who are especially sensitive to anticipatory anxiety.

In the unlikely event the patient does not benefit from either TCAs or phenelzine, I will then recommend therapy with alprazolam.

ALPRAZOLAM: PROMISE BEFORE PROOF?

As I stated earlier, alprazolam (brand name: Xanax) may develop into one of the most effective and well-established antipanic medications. Originally, some experts hoped that alprazolam, since it is very similar to a benzodiazepine (it's officially classified as a triazolobenzodiazepine), would not only block panic attacks but also quell the anticipatory anxiety. However, most reports have found that while alprazolam blocks panic attacks, it has little effect against the anticipatory anxiety. A few of these published reports compared alprazolam with either imipramine or phenelzine. While those reports found alprazolam to be at least the equal of the other drugs in preventing panic attacks, serious questions remain concerning alprazolam's withdrawal symptoms and relapse rate.

Some reports indicate that alprazolam may block panic attacks faster than imipramine, sometimes after only two or three doses. One study found that the benefits of alprazolam therapy appeared within one week, while imipramine required four weeks to achieve similar therapeutic benefit. However, it appears that after a few weeks of alprazolam therapy, panic attacks will return, requiring an increase in dosage from the initial 0.75 to 1.5 mg daily up to 6 mg daily (even 10 mg daily may be necessary). Besides the quick resurgance of panic attacks, another factor, potentially more serious, may undermine alprazolam therapy. This factor has been called "rebound anxiety."

Alprazolam is a short-acting medication, meaning that the effects of the drug will quickly wear off. Even patients taking alprazolam three or four times a day report feeling "edgy" and "nervous" just a few hours after their last dose. Some patients claim that they can tell time based on when they had their last dose. Other patients report a sense of "impending panic" if they are only one or two hours late in taking alprazolam. Some have established secret hiding places for their alprazolam to make sure that they will have it available when they need it, while others admit to feeling nervous if their supplies run low. Patients also report relief of their rebound anxiety within twenty to thirty minutes after taking alprazolam.

This rebound anxiety poses three significant problems:

First, the psychiatrist must strive for the proper dosage and dosage schedule to minimize this rebound anxiety.

Second, both the patient and the doctor must differentiate between this rebound anxiety and a recurring panic attack, a task made even more complicated if anticipatory anxiety is also present. A patient's failure to distinguish these anxiety levels may lead to the discouraged patient's dropping out of therapy, while the psychiatrist's failure to distinguish may lead to premature termination of therapy.

Third, and perhaps, most significant, this rebound anxiety may lead to alprazolam dependence, tolerance, and even addiction. I have spent a great deal of my professional career studying alcohol and drug addictions, and when I hear patients tell me that they can't wait till they take their next dose, well, my "addiction buzzer" goes off. While addiction to alprazolam or benzodiazepines may not be an issue for the majority of patients, other individuals with a history of alcoholism and drug addiction may not be so lucky. Alcoholics Anonymous and rehabilitation centers throughout the country are virtually overflowing with benzodiazepine abusers, many of them victims of the poor prescribing practices of psychiatrists and physicians.

Further problems with alprazolam often occur following its

discontinuation. As with the benzodiazepines, abrupt discontinuation of alprazolam may lead to severe withdrawal symptoms. Seizures have been reported following abrupt cessation, even after only eight weeks of therapy, or after dosages as low as 3 mg daily.

Even more troublesome have been the reports of withdrawal symptoms and the return of panic attacks even following a gradual tapering of dosage. One study found that fourteen of seventeen patients experienced at least two withdrawal symptoms (such as weakness, insomnia, and rapid heartbeat) during gradual discontinuation, and nine of the seventeen found these symptoms severe. However, this study found an even more alarming figure: Fifteen of seventeen subjects experienced a rapid recurrence or *increase* in panic attacks following gradual tapering of alprazolam, a rate that appears "considerably higher and more rapid in onset than panic patients tapered from tricyclic antidepressants or monoamine oxidase inhibitors." One possible explanation for this rapid recurrence may be that alprazolam blocks different pathways in the brain than the TCAs do, and these receptors along these pathways may become hypersensitive and overresponsive following alprazolam withdrawal. A larger and even more recently published study of alprazolam and panic disorder found a significant relapse rate within the four-week tapering period. The study concluded that a longer tapering period may be necessary.

Clearly, many questions regarding alprazolam therapy remain, questions that currently prevent me from using this drug as the treatment of first choice in panic disorder with or without phobia.

BENZODIAZEPINES

The efficacy of alprazolam in treating panic disorder caught many experts by surprise. For many years, conventional wisdom held that the benzodiazepines were effective against anxiety disorders, but not effective in the treatment of panic disorders. With the recent interest in alprazolam has come an increased effort at reevaluating the benzodiazepines, especially the high-potency benzodiazepines such as lorazepam (brand names: Temesta, Ativan), clonazepam (Klonopin), and oxazepam (Serax) in panic disorder. Like alprazolam, the benzodiazepines may promise rapid efficacy combined with fewer side effects than TCAs or MAOIs. The longer-acting and lower-potency benzodiazepines, such as diazepam (Valium) and halazepam (Paxipam), may allow easier discontinuation than does alprazolam.

But there simply isn't enough proof to support speculation and promises. More studies are needed before I will routinely prescribe benzodiazepines to block panic attacks as a first line of treatment. I am especially interested in future studies that examine whether benzodiazepines can actually thwart panic attacks, or if their primarily antipanic effect lies in reducing anticipatory anxiety. As I stated earlier, I currently use benzodiazepines in panic disorders only to reduce, when necessary, the anticipatory anxiety that may accompany an attack.

OTHER MEDICATIONS USED IN PANIC DISORDER

Beta-blockers, medications most often prescribed in the treatment of high blood pressure, have also been tried in the treatment of panic disorders. In general, most studies indicate that while these drugs may have some anti-anxiety effects, especially on performance anxiety, they have little impact on panic disorders. Their overall lack of efficacy in treating panic has been supported by the inability of propranolol, the most studied beta-blocker, to block sodium-lactate-induced panic attacks.

Other medications that have been tried include clonidine (brand name: Catapres), verapamil (Calan, Isoptin), baclofen (Lioresal), clomipramine (Anafranil), and carbamazepine (Tegretol). Of these agents, the medications most likely to become important antipanic therapies are clomipramine and clonidine. It appears that clonidine—a medication primarily used in the treatment of high blood pressure—may inhibit the locus ceruleus, a part of the brain whose activity may be a major component of a panic attack. In a recent study, clomipramine, used

THE GOOD NEWS ABOUT PANIC, ANXIETY, AND PHOBIAS

primarily to treat obsessive-compulsive disorder, has been shown to have a high success rate in treating panic attacks. Two other new antidepressant medications, bupropion (Wellbutrin) and trazodone (Desyrel) have not proven to be effective in treating panic. (Other promising medications that may be used in the future will be covered in Chapter 10.)

If all of medicine could match the success rate achieved in the treatment of panic disorders and panic disorders with phobias, then we would all live longer and healthier lives. The biopsychiatrist's approach of combining effective pharmacology with appropriate behavior therapy attacks panic disorders on *all* levels: The physiological, mental, and behavioral components are all addressed.

The following sections will cover biopsychiatry's approach to treating the other anxiety disorders: generalized anxiety disorder, social phobia (performance or situational anxiety), simple phobia (with no panic attacks), obsessive-compulsive disorder, posttraumatic stress disorder, and adjustment disorder.

TREATMENT OF
GENERALIZED ANXIETY DISORDER (GAD)

Previously known as "anxiety neurosis," this category at one time accounted for the overwhelming majority of psychiatric diagnoses. Since the 1960s, however, there has been a gradual migration away from GAD and toward a greater recognition of the panic disorders. Today, psychiatrists even debate the validity of GAD; critics claim that it should not exist as an independent category but is almost always associated with other conditions such as depression and alcoholism. And the distinction between GAD and panic disorders has become more ambiguous. At one time panic disorder and GAD were thought to be separate entities, primarily because they responded to different medications—the benzodiazepines worked in GAD, but not in panic disorders. Recently, the possibility that benzodiazepines may be effective in panic disorder may weaken this distinction. If benzodiazepines are effective in both conditions, is it because GAD patients really have undetected panic attacks? Or are panic attacks simply a more intense form of GAD? At this point, without much solid information available, these questions cannot be definitively answered. Especially since the effectiveness of all benzodiazepines in treating panic attacks has not been established—it may turn out that only a few benzodiazepines, perhaps only alprazolam, will have significant antipanic efficacy.

However, at this time, I believe that too many people are diagnosed as having GAD—especially since the majority of psychiatrists and nonpsychiatric physicians fail to detect underlying panic attacks, or conditions such as alcohol or drug abuse and depression. Instead the majority of patients will still be told that they are suffering from "anxiety and tension."

Nevertheless, I have found that some patients, while they may not meet the rather arbitrary criteria established by DSM-III-R, will qualify for a generalized anxiety diagnosis. However, I will make this diagnosis only after all other physical and psychiatric conditions have been ruled out and I am sure that the anxiety is not related to a specific event or object. And as you might expect, once this diagnosis has been made, my approach to treatment differs from that of the majority of psychiatrists.

The majority of psychiatrists and nonpsychiatric physicians will almost always begin treatment with benzodiazepines. After all, benzodiazepines have been shown to be generally very safe and effective in the treatment of anxiety. But benzodiazepines should not be prescribed so routinely. There is a problem of potential addiction associated with their use. Patients have grown very adept at procuring more prescriptions from their psychiatrists—very few, if any, of these psychiatrists will ever think to measure the patient's blood level of benzodiazepine, a measure that will indicate if the patient is self-administering too high a dose. Unfortunately, the patient's addiction may never be detected until it is too late.

Unlike these other psychiatrists, I first choose nonpharmacological treatment. Whenever possible, my treatment of first choice is the type of treatment that millions of people would benefit from, even if they are not suffering from any anxiety disorder. This treatment is exercise—vigorous, aerobic exercise.

EXERCISE: THE BEST TREATMENT FOR ANXIETY (AND YOUR HEART)

Some psychiatrists decline to recommend exercise to anxiety disorder patients, fearing that strenuous exercise might worsen the anxiety symptoms. In my opinion, any worsening of symptoms because of exercise means the patient has been misdiagnosed—the patient is actually suffering from panic disorder, since exercise raises blood levels of lactate and patients with panic disorder will respond by panicking. Of course, using sodium lactate infusion as a diagnostic tool would have identified these patients much earlier in the treatment process.

Conversely, I will strongly urge the majority of patients with anxiety disorder to begin a vigorous exercise program. Sometimes only a brisk thirty-minute walk every day is all that's needed to relieve their anxiety. Some tips for a simple but effective exercise program can be found in Chapter 9.

Unfortunately, some patients may not be able to comply with even the simplest exercise program, and others may find that while exercise does help, they are still bothered by anxiety disorder. For these patients I may recommend psychotherapy, biofeedback, cognitive and relaxation techniques, or short-term pharmacotherapy. Usually if pharmacotherapy is necessary, I will begin with a benzodiazepine.

BENZODIAZEPINES

In general, the benzodiazepines all share equal efficacy in the treatment of GAD. The main differences among the benzodiazepines lie in their pharmacology. The benzodiazepines can be classified according to their plasma half-life (see box below) —the shorter-acting drugs usually provide quick relief but do not sustain their effectiveness, while the longer-acting medications will usually not provide rapid relief but will maintain their effects over a longer period. The benzodiazepine that I prescribe depends upon my patient's needs. If the patient would have difficulty complying with multiple daily dosages, then a longer-acting benzodiazepine with once-a-day dosing would be called for. Similarly, if the patient has trouble sleeping, the longer-acting medications might provide relief throughout the entire night. However, these longer-acting benzodiazepines might cause too much sedation to combat daytime anxiety, and in that case the shorter-acting benzodiazepines would be pre-

---

DURATION OF EFFECTIVENESS OF BENZODIAZEPINES

Short
Alprazolam (Xanax)
Lorazepam (Ativan)
Oxazepam (Serax)

Intermediate
Chlordiazepoxide (Librium)
Diazepam (Valium)
Temazepam (Restoril)

Long
Clorazepate (Tranxene)
Flurazepam (Dalmane)
Halazepam (Paxipam)
Prazepam (Vestran)

---

scribed. Of course, if in the past the patient has responded favorably to a benzodiazepine, then that benzodiazepine would be used.

I will usually recommend the lowest possible dosage initially, and then increase the dosage if necessary. The most common daily anti-anxiety dosages for the benzodiazepines are:

Alprazolam	0.75 to 4 mg
Chlordiazepoxide	15 to 100 mg
Clorazepate	15 to 60 mg
Diazepam	4 to 40 mg
Flurazepam*	15 to 30 mg
Halazepam	20 to 160 mg
Lorazepam	2 to 6 mg
Oxazepam	30 to 180 mg
Prazepam	15 to 30 mg
Temazepam*	15 to 30 mg

* Flurazepam and temazepam are classified as hypnotic (or sleep-inducing) benzodiazepines.

From the very beginning, my patients understand that benzodiazepine treatment will be short-lived, and that the prescription will stop once the anxiety symptoms have been controlled. If during the course of treatment I suspect that the patient may be taking too many or too little, or abusing benzodiazepines, I will question the patient and the patient's family and test the patient's blood levels for unusual amounts of benzodiazepine.

The benzodiazepines are, by themselves, very safe medications. When combined with alcohol, however, they become very dangerous, and even lethal, drugs. This problem may be more likely to occur in patients with a history of alcohol or drug abuse. For these patients, I will often prescribe antihistamines, such as diphenhydramine. Antihistamines, ingredients in many over-the-counter cold and hay-fever remedies, when prescribed in larger doses can be effective anti-anxiety agents for patients with histories of alcohol and/or drug abuse. Similarly, for these patients a tricyclic antidepressant such as doxepin may be helpful.

The possibility of dangerous interaction with alcohol, combined with the benzodiazepines' potential for abuse, has led science to search for anti-anxiety agents without the problems posed by benzodiazepines. Recently, much attention has focused on a nonbenzodiazepine medication called buspirone (BuSpar).

Buspirone has been called a radical new advancement in the treatment of anxiety, since it promises to relieve anxiety without causing the drowsiness or worries about alcohol interaction associated with benzodiazepines. In addition, its abuse potential is limited, since high doses make individuals feel ill. If all of these claims are true, then buspirone would truly be an amazing medication.

However, buspirone does have drawbacks. It may take three or four weeks to reach therapeutic levels, and therefore has little value in acute anxiety treatment. Second, patients who previously took benzodiazepines (like many anxiety disorder patients) may not benefit from buspirone. Third, side effects such as nausea, headaches, and dizziness may limit its effectiveness. For these reasons, it appears that buspirone may help only a limited number of patients, such as the very few anxious patients who may require chronic, or long-term, treatment. Obviously, as with so many new medications, more experience and studies are needed before we fully understand buspirone's niche in the treatment of anxiety disorders.

Other potentially promising medications will be discussed in Chapter 10.

TREATMENT OF SOCIAL PHOBIA

For many people, especially psychiatrists, "social phobia" is a poorly defined term. Social phobia is not shyness. Rather it is the fear of embarrassment or humiliation that may occur when eating, drinking, speaking, or engaging in any other activity in front of others, a fear that results in avoidant behavior. One patient complained that he was absolutely certain that people could hear him swallowing when eating, and therefore he studiously avoided any business lunches or dinner meetings where "important people" might detect his "crudeness." Social phobics dread what they think will be humiliating situations and will go to great lengths to prevent their humiliation. When forced into these situations, social phobics report palpitations, sweating, trembling, and nausea, and they are convinced that others notice these reactions. Only fleeing the situation will relieve their reactions.

Social phobia bears a close resemblance to a similar but more limited condition called *performance anxiety* or "stage fright." Contrary to popular misconceptions, performance anxiety is not limited to "beginner's jitteriness" or "rookie's nerves." Rather, performance anxiety frequently strikes experienced performers, and may result in the ruin of brilliant careers.

Social phobia has national health consequences: Many social phobics turn to alcohol and/or illegal drugs for temporary relief from their fears, and social phobia is now seen as a cause of alcoholism and drug abuse.

Social phobics are often misdiagnosed as agoraphobics. However, there are two important distinctions. First, for social phobics, fear is confined to public activities that can be observed—when the same activity is done in private the social phobic experiences no anxiety. Conversely, agoraphobics may seek others to help them with their fears—for example, agoraphobics may ride in elevators or cross bridges when in the presence of others, but never alone.

Secondly, unlike agoraphobics, social phobics rarely respond to sodium lactate infusion. This lack of response to lactate indicates that spontaneous panic attacks are not involved in social phobia. While DSM-III-R claims that panic attacks can occur in simple and social phobias, my experience indicates that the presence of panic attacks rules out the uncomplicated phobia diagnosis in favor of the panic disorder with phobia diagnosis. In addition, social phobia may develop at an earlier age (typically between eighteen and nineteen years old) than agoraphobia (between twenty-three and twenty-four years old).

The accurate diagnosis of social phobia is important, since it effects treatment consequences. Many psychiatrists will misdiagnose social phobia as generalized anxiety disorder and opt for ineffectual treatment with benzodiazepines.

MY TREATMENT OF FIRST CHOICE: DO IT

For most social phobics, I recommend a very simple strategy: Just do it! The best way to overcome a fear of speaking in public is to speak in public. Simple, yes. But unaided, self-exposure is a very effective way of overcoming fears. In the next chapter, I will give self-help suggestions and behavioral modification tips that will facilitate the overcoming of these fears.

Some people, no matter how hard they try, simply cannot overcome their social phobia without the aid of medication. Usually I will prescribe a class of drugs called beta-blockers.

BETA-BLOCKERS AND SOCIAL PHOBIA

Beta-blockers are normally prescribed in the treatment of high blood pressure. Several years ago they were tried in the treatment of performance anxiety because of their ability to reduce the palpitations, sweating, blushing, and trembling associated with performance. Since that time, several studies have found that beta-blockers do work, and nervous performers report a more relaxed performance following beta-blocker therapy.

These studies indicated that beta-blockers may be useful in the broader category of social phobia. And while definitive studies showing beta-blockers' efficacy in social phobia are lacking, my clinical experience has shown that these medications do provide significant reduction of the anxiety associated with social phobia.

Among the beta-blockers (propranolol, atenolol, timolol, metoprolol, pindolol, nadolol), I frequently begin treatment with atenolol (brand name Tenormin) since this drug allows once-daily dosing and may have fewer side effects than the others. I often start with 50 mg daily and increase this dose only if necessary. I will usually tell my patients to take their own pulse frequently, and to call my office and stop taking the medication if the pulse drops to below fifty beats per minute.

If the patient does not benefit from beta-blockers, I may try a monoamine oxidase inhibitor, usually phenelzine (see pages 223–27 for more information on MAOIs). On a rare occasion, I may prescribe a tricyclic antidepressant.

It is essential throughout the treatment course that patients repeatedly test themselves through exposure to their phobias. Only through repeated exposure—at first with medication, later without—can patients overcome their fears.

TREATMENT OF SIMPLE PHOBIAS

My treatment recommendation for simple phobias (fear of dogs, snakes, driving, heights, etc.) is almost identical to my treatment approach for social phobias. With one exception: I will emphasize even more strongly the need for self-exposure in overcoming these fears. As one friend of mine said, "Doctor, the way I overcame my fear of flying was to learn how to fly." The next chapter will present behavior strategies that may help individuals overcome their fear.

As for the social phobias, I will recommend pharmacotherapy only for stubborn cases. Please see the above section on social phobias for information on the medications I use for simple phobias.

TREATMENT OF
OBSESSIVE-COMPULSIVE DISORDER (OCD)

For many years treatment for OCD struggled to be of any real benefits for patients with this condition. The psychodynamic therapies have not been effective. While the behavior therapies have helped to alleviate the compulsive rituals, they have not had the same success treating the obsessive thoughts. And until recently, pharmacotherapy did not provide much benefit: Medications had only the dubious distinction of relieving some of the anxiety associated with OCD, but no effect on the actual condition itself.

Recently, a tricyclic antidepressant not widely available in the United States called clomipramine (brand name: Anafranil) has brought renewed possibilities to the pharmacotherapy of OCD. Available in Europe and other countries for many years, clomipramine has not been marketed in this country, except on a "compassionate use" basis in the treatment of OCD. (We have used the medication successfully at Fair Oaks Hospital for many years on this basis.) However, it now appears that the drug may soon be more widely available in this country for patients with OCD. Studies have shown that clomipramine can significantly reduce obsessions and compulsions in 70 to 80 percent of patients. One study found a "striking superiority of clomipramine" over another antidepressant in adolescent patients, an especially significant result since half to one third of OCD cases begin during childhood or adolescence.

In addition, clomipramine appears to be more effective than other tricyclic antidepressants or monoamine oxidase inhibitors in treating OCD. While no one knows exactly why clomipramine is more effective, it may be because this drug has a greater affect on the neurotransmitter serotonin than do many other antidepressants. This serotonin hypothesis has led investigators to examine if other drugs with similar serotonin effects, such as fluoxetine (Prozac), have efficacy in treating OCD. These studies are still too preliminary to draw any conclusions, but the future pharmacotherapy for OCD appears promising.

Currently, the effective treatment plan would call for the combination of clomipramine and exposure-based behavior therapy (see Chapter 9 for more information on behavioral strategies), although studies proving the efficacy of this combined approach have not been done. Only time and more studies will tell if clomipramine (or another new medication) combined with behavior therapy will achieve significant results in OCD. However, for the first time in years, there has been a renewed excitement and hopefulness in the treatment of OCD.

TREATMENT OF POSTTRAUMATIC STRESS DISORDER (PTSD)

The traditional treatment options for PTSD are not as defined as other protocols described in this chapter. Our knowledge about the effectiveness of pharmacotherapy, psychotherapy, or behavioral therapy, either alone or in combination, is very limited.

Given these limitations, my treatment of choice combines psychotherapy with pharmacotherapy. Psychotherapy, or "talk therapy," with its ability to expose the guilt and shame that may torment the PTSD victim, is crucial to the recovery process. However, some individuals cannot proceed with psychotherapy because they simply cannot tolerate the feelings associated with the traumatic event. For these individuals and for those who do not benefit from psychotherapy alone, pharmacotherapy may be required.

Unfortunately, carefully controlled studies comparing the efficacy of different medications do not exist. Various medications have been used clinically, including tricyclic antidepressants (TCAs), monoamine oxidase inhibitors, beta-blockers, and benzodiazepines.

In general I initiate treatment with TCAs, usually amitriptyline. Amitriptyline is preferable because it may help treat the recurring nightmares that plague some PTSD victims. If TCAs provide only partial response, I will usually add a beta-blocker, such as propranolol. In addition, other medications, such as imipramine and alprazolam, may be tried. In any case, I must stress the importance of using pharmacotherapy as an adjunct to psychotherapy to help the patient explore the traumatic event and vent any repressed feelings.

TREATMENT OF ADJUSTMENT DISORDER (AD)

Like treatment for PTSD, treatment for adjustment disorder (AD) stresses psychotherapy, with pharmacotherapy used as an adjunct when necessary. The object of psychotherapy is to provide emotional support and empathy through trying times. If pharmacotherapy is necessary, the treatment of choice is benzodiazepine. Most often only short-term benzodiazepine therapy is required. When benzodiazepines are discontinued, the dosage should be tapered gradually.

In this chapter I have discussed the successful state-of-the-art treatments that can make modern medicine and biopsychiatry so successful. In general, these treatments require the guidance and administration of a qualified physician. In the next chapter I'll describe the procedures, tips, and techniques that individuals can try with or without the assistance of professionals.

CHAPTER NINE

HELPING
YOURSELF
TO A
BETTER
LIFE

N OT EVERY PERSON requires professional help for his or her phobias and anxieties. Some individuals may not have a severe problem, or may want to try overcoming their fears on their own before they call upon a professional. Many people, especially those not suffering from a phobia, see self-help as a very simple matter. They believe that phobics only need willpower, a "stiff upper lip," to pull themselves through their phobias. After all, can't we humans do anything if we just put our minds to it? This advice sounds terrific coming from a motivational expert, but real life is seldom that easy.

But it's not impossible to overcome your fears, either, especially with some general guidelines to help you through difficult times. In the first part of this chapter, I will provide information on how individuals can use behavior therapy on their own. This behavior therapy involves a gradual *exposure* or *desensitization* to a particular phobic situation. In the second part I will suggest relaxation techniques, exercise tips, and other strategies for reducing anxiety. These anxiety-reducing strategies are valuable even if you decide not to try the self-help approach.

Often, people with anxiety disorders feel powerless to live their lives the way they want. One patient said, "It's as if I'm watching a movie of someone else's life—there's nothing I can do to change the way the movie ends." In reality, there are many things a person can do to change his or her life, and not all of them require seeking professional help. Countless individuals have overcome their fears without seeking professional assistance, by exercising persistence and common sense. After all, there is nothing magical about professionally implemented behavior therapy—whether it is administered by an individual alone or under the guidance of a professional, behavior therapy is essentially the systematic implementation of some common-sense principles, principles that some individuals adopt without even knowing it.

Take, for example, Mason, a videotape producer in his mid-thirties. One day over lunch, after I had briefly described some of my current projects—including this book—Mason grinned and said: "Well, I guess you could say that I'm one that got away." After I asked him to explain what he meant, he replied:

"Not too many people know this, but I have a real fear of driving. For all of my adult life I've tried to keep this fear secret. Even if some bank clerk asked me for my driver's license I would lie about not having one and say I left it home. I even got a passport to go along with my credit cards for proof of identification."

When I asked him what he feared most about driving, he said, "I used to rationalize that a fear of driving made sense. After all, why trust some crazy nut with a two-ton car, driving eighty miles per hour, six inches on the other side of a white line? I mean, if you saw these same nuts in a supermarket aisle with a cart, you'd get out of their way fast. But really I was afraid of humiliation. What if I had to parallel-park in a tight space and I couldn't do it? What happens if I'm driving too slow and the person behind me gets angry? What if I panic and lose control of the car and kill someone? I couldn't stand being exposed as a failure. My heart would pound, I would get very nervous, and I would start to lock up whenever I even thought about driving. Most people think I must have had a bad experience driving when I was younger, but the truth is I was thirty-two years old before I ever got behind a wheel! And that was only when I forced myself to learn how to drive."

I then asked Mason what had led to his learning to drive.

"I got sick of always having to make excuses, of always having to figure out how to get somewhere without driving. And for a video producer, not driving is a real drawback. Sometimes you have to visit pretty remote locations where a car is a must. For years I would always budget for a production assistant just to drive me around. Now I am pretty tight with my money, and the thought of always paying someone to drive me around drove me crazy. Finally I said enough is enough. I knew that my fear was keeping me from a very necessary activity, and I knew I had to overcome this fear and learn to drive.

"I couldn't face the humiliation of asking one of my friends to teach me, so I signed up with one of those big driving schools. I figured if I couldn't stand the driving lessons, I would just quit. You know, just fade away quietly. What I didn't realize was that the way these driving schools make money is by getting you to *keep* taking lessons. At the beginning, I would try to postpone my first lesson, coming up with excuses why I couldn't make any appointments. Well, my instructor was a persistent SOB. He knew exactly what I was doing, and he wouldn't let me get away with any of my bogus excuses. Finally, I had to give in and make an appointment or let my instructor know that I was a real coward.

"So at seven o'clock on a Sunday morning I had my first lesson. Good weather, no traffic, and dual steering kept me from losing control. Oh, I was nervous, real nervous, but I only really came close to panicking twice in the hour. And each time I was able to recover, to calm down without losing it. The dual steering was the key—I knew that if I panicked, the instructor could take control of the car. He never had to, but just knowing he could made all the difference.

"I kept going back, my instructor kept pestering me, and I kept plunking down more money for lessons. Now, I'm not poor by any means, but let's say that money is very dear to me. The more money I gave that driving school, the more motivation I had to get my driver's license. And I did get that license —on the first try, to boot. Don't get me wrong—I'm no Mario Andretti by any stretch. I doubt that I'll ever find driving to be a picnic. But I *can* drive, and I got my picture on a license to prove it. Now I can actually talk openly about my fear of driving, acknowledge it, but not give in to it."

Mason's success is proof that many people can function with their fears, and even learn to overcome them without needing the assistance of a therapist.

In fact, psychiatrists, even biopsychiatrists, sometimes are bothered by excessive anxiety or fears. Younger psychiatrists especially may be nervous when presenting papers or delivering talks before other groups for the first time. Let me tell you about a trick I have used when "breaking in" junior members of my staff who had difficulty addressing large groups.

On a couple of occasions, when I was called upon to present a paper to a prestigious medical organization, I asked if a junior colleague could give the talk—*without* telling my colleague. Instead, I invited the less-experienced psychiatrist to "just accompany me and observe the talk." Then, the day of the scheduled talk, I would call the staff member and tell him that I was very sorry but I couldn't make the scheduled talk, and I would ask the younger psychiatrist to present the paper for me. "Don't worry," I would say, "here are the text and the slides. You have two hours to prepare."

The young psychiatrist would be flustered by this and occasionally would try to decline the opportunity. But I would insist that the only solution was for him to present the paper. I would recommend that he prepare the talk, then rehearse the speech—out loud—at least four times if possible.

My staff psychiatrists usually would spend the next two hours trying to master the paper's finer details and rehearsing before anyone who would listen. In fact, they would spend so much time concentrating on the paper and rehearsing that they wouldn't have time to worry about actually giving the talk. Now this may seem cruel at first, but invariably the talk has gone smoothly. And the psychiatrist, having succeeded once, would find future speaking engagements far easier.

My story and Mason's are just two examples of the countless methods individuals may use to overcome fear and anxiety without the assistance of a professional.

Remember, though, there is no shame involved in seeking or receiving professional help. Just as some people are natural athletes who can win championships on their own, others require outside coaching to reach their maximum potential. No one denies George Brett's ability to hit a baseball because he needs a hitting instructor. One person's phobia may be too entrenched, or there may be a slight abnormality in the person's panic response system that requires medication to offset. So there is absolutely no need to feel the slightest shame or remorse in seeking professional assistance for your condition.

ARE YOU A CANDIDATE FOR SELF-HELP BEHAVIOR THERAPY?

Any individual contemplating self-administered behavior therapy should take a few moments to answer the following questions.

- Do you have a history of heart trouble, high blood pressure, asthma, or peptic ulcers? (If you answer yes to this question, I would strongly urge that you consult a physician, preferably a biopsychiatrist, before you embark on any behavior-based therapy. If you do not, the strain of an exposure-based encounter with your phobia may prove to have a negative impact on your health.)
- Do you use drugs or rely on alcohol or other drugs (such as tranquilizers, marijuana, narcotics, etc.) to relieve your anxiety?
- Do you suffer from more than one phobia?
- Is it difficult for you to define your phobia in clear, distinct terms?
- Do you often think of suicide?
- Is it difficult or impossible for you to ask a friend or relative to help with your therapy?

An answer of yes to any of these questions may indicate that your problems require professional assistance. Even if you answered no to all of the questions, I would ask that you consider another very basic question: *Do you really want to live without your phobia?* Many people have grown accustomed to living with their fear and ultimately would rather accept it than deal with the trauma of confronting it. Acknowledging this fact now will save you from needless expense and pain. However, if you really would like a life free from your phobias, then read on.

BEFORE YOU BEGIN...

If after considering all of the above questions you have concluded that you would like to try self-administered behavior therapy, I suggest that you first understand these basic points of my behaviorally-based approach. These points are:

1. *You are not guilty.* Your suffering from a phobia does *not* mean either that you have brought this fear upon yourself or that there is a weakness in your personality or character. Accept the fact that you are suffering from a physical condition with real symptoms. Remember that you are not crazy, or losing your mind.

2. *Recognize your fear.* To overcome your fear, it is important that you learn to recognize its presence as well as the strategies and excuses you adopt to avoid confronting it. For example, the nausea you feel may be just an excuse to stay home and avoid the classroom discussion your professor has scheduled for today.

3. *Don't lose control of the situation.* The fact that your phobia is a physical condition with real symptoms does not exonerate you from remaining in control. By "remaining in control" I don't mean that you should try to suppress your anxiety. Rather I urge you to concentrate on understanding that you are not going to die (even though your heart may be pounding and you may feel as if you're suffocating) and on practicing the relaxation and breathing techniques described on pages 254–57.

4. *Persevere.* Understand too, that no matter how bad you feel, your anxiety will not last. Persevering through your phobia and repeatedly exposing yourself to the phobic situation are among the two most important actions you can take in overcoming your fears. As a friend of mine—now a pilot with a major airline—once said: "I overcame my fear of flying by forcing myself to learn to fly a plane." Simple advice, but effective —and not always as easy as it sounds.

Many individuals have found perseverance easier with the assistance of phobia self-help groups. These groups, comprised mainly of other phobia victims, frequently follow a twelve-step model similar to that developed by Alcoholics Anonymous.

THE TWELVE STEPS

Many self-help groups base their approach to overcoming fears on the twelve-step model first developed by Alcoholics Anonymous (AA) and later adapted by many other self-help groups, including Overeaters Anonymous, Gamblers Anonymous, and Cocaine Anonymous. Alcoholics have also used these twelve steps to battle the "dry drunks" that can occur when recovering alcoholics, who are still sober, begin acting irrationally, as if they had resumed drinking. Actually, these dry-drunk states resemble periods of excessive anxiety.

This is the twelve-step model created by AA:

Step One: "We admitted we were powerless over alcohol —that our lives had become unmanageable."

Step Two: "Came to believe that a Power greater than ourselves could restore us to sanity."

Step Three: "Made a decision to turn our will and our lives to the care of God as we understood Him."

Step Four: "Made a searching and fearless moral inventory of ourselves."

Step Five: "Admitted to God, to ourselves, and to another human being, the exact nature of our wrongs."

Step Six: "Were entirely ready to have God remove all these defects of character."

Step Seven: "Humbly asked Him to remove our shortcomings."

Step Eight: "Made a list of all persons we had harmed, and became willing to make amends to them all."

Step Nine: "Made direct amends to such people wherever possible, except when to do so would injure them or others."

Step Ten: "Continued to take personal inventory and when we were wrong promptly admitted it."

Step Eleven: "Sought through prayer and meditation to improve our conscious contact with God as we understood Him, praying only for knowledge of His will for us and the power to carry that out."

Step Twelve: "Having had a spiritual awakening as a result of these steps, we tried to carry this message to alcoholics, and to practice these principles in all our affairs."

The Twelve Steps, reprinted with permission of Alcoholics Anonymous World Services Incorporated.

STARTING BEHAVIOR THERAPY: SEVEN HELPFUL STEPS

1. Make a list of potentially frightening situations that you usually avoid, proceeding from the least threatening to the most. I call these situations your Personal Challenge List. For example, a person with a fear of elevators might begin this list with the least traumatic situation—staring at a picture of an elevator. For this person, the Personal Challenge List could end with being trapped alone in a dark elevator.

2. Record the physical symptoms that you normally feel when you are in these phobic situations. Do you feel nauseated? Does your heart beat faster? Do you begin to sweat profusely? Does your breathing become more rapid? Do you experience headaches? Do you feel you are suffocating? By recognizing these physical symptoms, you can use these symptoms as signals that it is time to implement the coping strategies described below.

3. Jot down some of the thoughts that occur during phobic situations. Often our negative thoughts and mental doubts are our worst enemy.

4. Record your *specific* goals that you would like to attain from the behavior therapy. Goals such as "I want to feel better" or "I want to do things I can't do now" are not very constructive. Instead, select goals that are both specific and attainable. For example, a person with a fear of driving (like Mason) may choose passing a driver's test as a goal.

5. Try to hook up with a friend or relative to help with your therapy. An assistant can provide valuable support and encouragement in your therapy plan. But make sure that this assistant is sympathetic to your fears and is willing and able to spend the necessary time. The absence of an assistant does make therapy more difficult, but it does not make it impossible.

6. Create a weekly plan. Look at your schedule for the next week and try to set aside at least one two-hour block of time for your behavior therapy. If a two-hour period is absolutely

impossible to establish, then settle for as long a continuous time period as you can manage. Remember, though, that a two-hour session is far more valuable than four half-hour sessions.

7. Prepare a log sheet for each exposure session. Specify an objective for each session *before* you begin. I suggest that your first objective be overcoming the least fearful situation you recorded in your Personal Challenge List (see paragraph 1 above). For example, your first session's task may be simply to look at a picture of a frightening object or situation. The objective of this session may be merely to describe the physical and mental symptoms this picture causes, and eventually to feel comfortable looking at the picture. This log should consist of:

DATE	TIME BEGAN	TIME ENDED	TASK	ANXIETY LEVEL	ANXIETY SYMPTOMS	OBJECTIVE	RESULTS

Rate your Anxiety level on a scale from 1 to 5, with 5 being the most anxiety and 1 the least.

DURING EACH SESSION . . .

1. Use *cognitive strategies* by identifying your negative doubts and substituting constructive thoughts. Self-defeating thoughts such as "I can't take this—this fear has been with me all my life, and there's nothing I can do about it" or "I know I'm going to die if I stay here" or "I know I'm going crazy" are not helpful and will only perpetuate your problems. Instead substitute positive thoughts: "I feel as if I am going crazy and am going to die, but I know that I'll be okay. Millions of other people feel the same way I do and I know they're alive and sane." Or "If other people can do this, so can I—there's nothing dangerous or deadly about this situation."

2. Practice your breathing and relaxation strategies (described below) at the first sign of anxiety.

3. Stay with it—don't give up. Tell yourself that you've allotted time to experience this fear, and since you know that

you're not going to die, concentrate on experiencing the symptoms of fear fully while you practice relaxation strategies.

Persistence is the key—as you continue to experience these previously frightening objects or situations, your body and mind should gradually become desensitized to them. I suggest that as you plan each session, keep your goal as a final objective and use your Personal Challenge List as an aid. Try to overcome your personal challenges as a means of reaching your objective. Immediately after the session you should record accurately all aspects of your encounter. When you reach the point where you can limit your anxiety, proceed to the next level along the path to your goal.

Even after you have reached your goal, it is very important to keep practicing, to keep experiencing the previously traumatic situations. Failure to do so may result in a return of your phobia and its avoidant behavior.

RELAXATION STRATEGIES

This section may be used by individuals undergoing exposure-based behavioral treatment as well as by those who wish to reduce the anxiety and stress in their lives.

BREATHING STRATEGIES

If during an anxiety attack you feel you can't breathe, can't catch your breath, or can't breathe deeply, try taking a single deep breath and concentrate on holding it for as long as you can. Doing this accomplishes two things. First, it puts you in control of the situation. By holding this deep breath you stop the runaway cycle of rapid, shallow breaths that may actually be contributing to your panic. Second, by concentrating on holding your breath, you stop focusing on your anxiety symptoms and may prevent these symptoms from escalating.

After your body forces you to exhale, try concentrating on inhaling and exhaling as slowly as possible, taking slow, deep breaths and gently exhaling. During this process, deliberately concentrate on the muscles of your diaphragm and visualize your lungs filling slowly with air and then deflating. If you find that you still can't breathe properly, try holding your breath again, and then repeat the slow breathing process.

PROGRESSIVE RELAXATION

Progressive relaxation is a process of tensing and relaxing various muscle groups in the body.

1. Begin by tensing and relaxing groups of muscles on your "dominant side" (the right side for right-handed people and left side for left-handed people). Tense the muscles of your hand by clenching your fist for a moment, then relax them and let your hand go loose. Try making your hand feel warm and heavy. Continue with the muscles of your forearm, then your upper arm, and then your shoulder. Eventually they will all become relaxed.

2. Next tense and relax the muscles of your foot and leg on your dominant side. Begin by curling your toes for a second or two, then relax them completely. Try making your foot feel warm and heavy. Continue tensing and relaxing muscles from your calf to your upper thigh. Eventually your entire dominant side should become relaxed.

3. Now repeat steps 1 and 2 on your nondominant side.

4. Then relax the muscles of your hips, buttocks, and pelvis, without tensing them first. Aim toward creating a wave of relaxation that spreads over your body from your pelvis to your stomach muscles and into your chest. This wave of relaxation should allow your stomach and diaphragm muscles to control your breathing.

5. Finally concentrate on relieving the muscles in your back, neck, jaw, face, and scalp. Focus on the muscles in your forehead and around your eyes.

For the best effect, you should repeat steps 1 through 5 *daily,* not only during periods of excessive anxiety.

MIND GAMES

After practicing the above relaxation techniques you may find that a few mental exercises will add to your relaxation:

1. Clear your mind of all thoughts. If negative or distracting thoughts occur, try to stop them with commands to yourself. These commands don't have to be elaborate—a simple "Let's go" will often suffice.

2. Imagine a very peaceful scene, such as a lake or white clouds in a blue sky. Concentrate on the details of the scene: the color of the water, the surrounding fauna or wildlife, etc.

3. If this doesn't work, try focusing on a boring, repetitive mental activity, such as repeating the multiplication tables, or repeating a list of names.

4. If even this fails to relieve your negative thoughts, try substituting positive thoughts, such as "I know I feel awful right now, but it won't last. Soon I'll feel better and I'll be able to learn from this experience."

The theory behind the relaxation abilities of such activities, which are technically known as *cognitive focusing,* is that the act of concentrating your attention on relatively pleasant, monotonous internal sensations is intrinsically incompatible with the thought and images that cause anxiety.

OTHER RELAXATION TECHNIQUES

Some of these may involve a greater investment of time and money:

Massage. The ancient techniques of massage are a very good means of reducing today's anxiety levels. Massage actually reverses the normal anxiety response. In a normal response to anxiety, the brain, perceiving the anxiety, orders the muscles to tense in preparation for the "flight or fight" response. Massage, by breaking down tension in these muscles, quite literally sends a "relaxation" message back to the brain. One friend of mine derives so much benefit from his New York City masseuse that he can barely tolerate going to the Hamptons for the weekend.

Transcendental Meditation (TM). In this process a person recites a repetitious phrase or sound, known as a mantra, as a method for inducing relaxation. It is similar to repeating multiplication tables or lists of names as suggested above.

Yoga. This is a Hindu exercise discipline, thousands of years old, involving control of the body and mind as training for the attainment of spiritual enlightenment and tranquility.

Biofeedback. This is a high-tech approach. Subjects are hooked up to a series of monitors that allow them to see the actual progression of their bodily processes—heartbeat, respiration, temperature, and so on. Eventually, subjects learn how to control these processes consciously to some degree, in order to modify their responses to stress, for example, by reducing the severity of illness or headache. Such a technique, however, may require a great deal of equipment, plus the participation of a trained supervisor, and it can be several months before subjects are able to create biofeedback effects on their own, independent of the machines. However, some individuals, especially those who like being in control of a situation, do very well with biofeedback. Interestingly, the progressive relaxation strategy described above, in which the individual concentrates on warming the hands and feet, is a simplified biofeedback technique. The process of warming the hands and feet increases blood flow to the outer extremities and decreases blood flow in inner tension centers (the forehead, neck, back, and jaw). This decreased blood flow helps to reduce muscle tension in these areas.

STOP DRUGS AND ALCOHOL

Substance Abuse. With an estimated 10 percent of the population—from twenty to twenty-five million Americans!—suffering from alcoholism or drug addiction, the role of substance abuse in any medical condition, especially the anxiety disorders, cannot be ignored. For many years, the relationship between substance abuse and anxiety disorders was seen as a one-way street: Anxiety disorder victims would turn to alcohol or drugs to alleviate their anxiety. While this view cannot be denied, we now know that substance abuse itself can cause anxiety. Any individual attempting to overcome their substance abuse must examine their alcohol and/or drug consumption.

Obviously, this examination can be very difficult. Denial among substance abusers is legendary—I've known addicts who have been arrested with a pile of coke in their laps, a loaded gun in their hands and no other remaining possessions to steadfastly deny that they had any problem with drugs. Many people naively claim that their drug use is "recreational." Perhaps no phrase upsets me more than the term "recreational drug use." Using the term "recreational" makes drug use sound like a game of ping-pong. There is *nothing* recreational about using dangerous, life-threatening drugs—as Len Bias and countless others have discovered.

While overcoming the denial that enshrouds substance abuse is the most important step, other aspects of treatment may prove equally difficult. For these difficult cases, professional intervention by alcohol and drug-abuse specialists is essential.

Anxiety disorder patients must remember that alcohol and drug abuse cannot continue if the individual truly wishes a life free from anxiety disorders.

CAFFEINE REDUCTION

Caffeine, a ubiquitous substance, should be considered a drug of the stimulant class capable of inducing panic attacks, although it is, of course, much less powerful than other stimulants such as amphetamines or cocaine. But caffeine has become so widespread and acceptable that some people really have no idea how much caffeine they consume each day.

Take, for example, one of my patients, a very successful sculptor, whom I'll call Gray. Approximately five years ago Gray came to me seeking help for daily panic attacks. His panic attacks had begun only six months before, but they were becoming so severe that they were interfering with his work. During our initial interview, Gray told me that his caffeine consumption was no more than normal, and that it had certainly not increased within the last six months. Well, his initial blood test

—and a confirmation test—told another story: His caffeine consumption had approached levels equivalent to twelve cups of coffee!

When I called Gray with these results, he admitted that he had really lost track of how many cups he drank each day. "I guess that sometimes I get so wrapped up in my work that I don't even realize how much coffee I drink," he said. But he insisted that he hadn't recently changed his coffee-drinking habits. In trying to unravel this mystery, I asked Gray again if there had been *any* changes in his personal or work situation within the last year. As it turned out, the only potentially significant change had occurred seven months before when Gray's longtime assistant had retired.

One quick telephone call to the retired assistant explained the mystery. Many years ago, having noted her employer's excessive coffee consumption and strong opposition to "fake" decaffeinated coffee, the assistant had surreptitiously switched to decaffeinated coffee. In fact, she had grown so accustomed to always ordering decaffeinated coffee that she had forgotten to tell the new assistant—who immediately began ordering and strongly brewing regular coffee. A switch back to decaffeinated coffee has resulted in a complete cure: Gray has gone over five years without a single panic attack.

But you need not drink fifteen cups of coffee—the amount of caffeine contained in even one cup is enough to affect the way your brain and body operate. Caffeine stimulates the flow of electrical signals to the muscles, which is why you may feel a "caffeine buzz" or notice a slight tremor in your hands or fingers after drinking coffee. With larger doses your heart rate and respiration speed up. You may even notice a ringing in your ears.

Caffeine is contained not only in coffee but in other products as well. In addition to caffeine, cocoa and tea provide additional doses of the mild stimulants theobromine and theophylline. A serving (five or six ounces) of instant coffee contains an average of 66 mg of caffeine, while percolated coffee has 110 mg. Coffee brewed by the drip method, probably the most common method today, has 146 mg per serving. Tea brewed for five minutes has 46 mg—nearly twice what tea left to steep for only one minute has. Coca-Cola and Dr Pepper each have over 60 mg per 12-ounce can; Tab contains 49 mg, Pepsi-Cola 43. Cocoa is the least stimulating caffeinated beverage, with only about 13 mg per serving; a chocolate bar has about twice as much.

There are 200 mg of caffeine in one tablet of such over-the-counter stimulants as Vivarin and Caffedrine. No Doz, Pre-mens Forte, and Aqua-Ban contain 100 mg each. Many pain relievers contain caffeine: Excedrin has the most with 64 mg per tablet; Vanquish, Anacin, Empirin, and Midol each have about 32 mg, and Dristan has 16 mg.

There are a number of steps you can take to restrict your caffeine intake. First, write down the amount of caffeine you ingest in the course of a day. Just seeing the total may help make you aware of the extent to which caffeine may be contributing to your anxiety.

Obviously, as in Gray's case, switching to decaffeinated coffee or tea can make a big difference. In response to public concern over caffeine intake, tea makers today are producing a variety of herbal and flavored teas, ranging from almond and apple to cranberry and cinnamon. Such products provide a soothing and palatable alternative to caffeine-containing drinks while satisfying the desire to drink a warm liquid. Most restaurants have decaf available for their customers who are watching their caffeine intake.

Some people, of course, find it virtually impossible to do without chocolate, but a number of caffeine-free snacks such as carob- or yogurt-covered peanuts—in moderation—may provide an adequate substitute.

If you can't go "cold turkey" and eliminate caffeine entirely, try cutting back. Look at your total caffeine intake and try reducing by a significant amount—a fourth, or a half—over a period of two weeks. Recently one coffee maker even introduced a "lite" coffee containing only half the usual amount of caffeine. Or try using a smaller coffee cup or limit the time of consumption to mornings only.

EXERCISE

Regular, vigorous exercise produces a world of benefits, including a reduction in anxiety. Studies have shown that exercise is an effective way to reduce anxiety, especially the anxiety that occurs in generalized anxiety disorder (GAD). I think so highly of exercise that I recommend it as the treatment of choice for some individuals suffering from excessive anxiety (especially those individuals in high-profile, high-stress jobs such as commodity brokers). Instead of a "power lunch," try jogging or racquetball at midday.

Space does not permit me to recommend specific programs of exercise best suited for different stages of life. However, many people feel that active walking and swimming are the best strategies, producing the best results with the minimum risk of strain or injury. Your own exercise regimen must suit your abilities and your life-style and should be undertaken only after consulting with a physician. Some other basic tips are:

• Plan on at least twenty minutes of exercise three times a week. Some experts feel this time should be extended to between thirty minutes and an hour five to seven times a week.

• Warm up before beginning; cool down after stopping.

• Exercise should be vigorous and continuous to the point where it produces muscle fatigue. It is really only after exercise, during the process of muscle rest and rebuilding, that improvements in tone and strength occur.

STOP SMOKING

Many people, including some strident antitobacco people, do not realize that cigarettes can cause anxiety. Nicotine—the stimulating ingredient in cigarette smoke—is absorbed through the mucous linings of the mouth and lungs, where it passes into the blood and circulates to the brain. There it triggers a variety of nervous-system responses, including alterations in the width of the airways in the lungs. Eventually nicotine reaches the hypothalamus, the control center of a number of vital functions, including appetite. Nicotine can also affect the cardiovascular system by causing tachycardia (excessively fast heartbeat), increased cardiac output, constriction of the blood vessels, and elevated blood pressure.

Quitting smoking provides benefits beyond reducing anxiety. Of course, quitting is notoriously difficult to do. Fortunately, there are a number of methods ranging from hypnosis to medications that may be effective in helping you to stop smoking. Nicotine gum, available by prescription, may satisfy the urge for nicotine and reduce the desire for cigarettes. Such gums, however, still introduce nicotine into the body and consequently may not help reduce anxiety. Recently, preliminary reports suggest the prescription medication clonidine may eventually develop into a safe and effective method of smoking cessation.

Even nonsmokers, through passive inhalation, may experience nicotine's effects. Passive inhalation may be especially troublesome in closed areas, where the air is recycled (such as airplanes).

GET MORE SUNLIGHT

Seasonal affective disorder (SAD) has somewhat inaccurately been referred to as the winter blues. In reality, SAD can occur at any time of the year when sunlight or a person's access to sunlight is limited. In addition, many experts now believe that in certain susceptible individuals limited exposure to sunlight may result in SAD, with the primary symptom of SAD being anxiety and not depression. Exactly how many people suffer from SAD is not known at this time, but estimates vary tremendously: Some experts have suggested that only 5 percent of depressed patients have SAD, while others suggest that as much as 5 percent of the general population may suffer from SAD.

While little is known about SAD, it appears that some people do experience anxiety or depression when their access to sunlight is limited, but feel normal during summer months or when their access to sunlight is acceptable. You may be a candidate for SES therapy if you find that your anxiety increases during winter months or overcast days (clouds reduce ultraviolet levels). Some experts now believe that morning light, with its higher concentration of ultraviolet rays, may best relieve the symptoms of SAD. Fortunately, exposure to ultraviolet light need not be for extended periods, greatly reducing the chance of developing skin cancer. Please note that sunglasses that block UV light may defeat exposure to morning light, since studies have shown that the light actually enters our system through our eyes! Some psychiatrists are now recommending that their SES patients try getting twenty to thirty minutes of sunlight every morning.

Some SAD patients, especially those whose climate limits exposure, have benefited tremendously from phototherapy using full-spectrum light boxes. These light boxes consist of a bank of full-spectrum light bulbs (similar to a plant growth lights). The patient sits in front of such a box for twenty to thirty minutes each day while reading or watching TV, periodically looking at the box. Some patients have even installed light boxes at their work sites and turn them on for brief intervals during the day.

In the next chapter, we will consider the work in areas of biopsychiatry that may, in the next few years, result in tremendous advances in our knowledge of anxiety disorders. Clearly, there is much more to be learned about the impact of biopsychiatry on anxiety disorders.

CHAPTER TEN

BIOPSYCHIATRY IN THE 1990s

B Y EXAMINING AND treating the physical nature of anxiety disorders, biopsychiatrists have been able to provide their patients with tremendous relief from their illnesses. In this chapter, I want to share with you some of the ongoing studies in biopsychiatry that make this field so exciting, and one I believe will have a tremendous impact on the lives of panic and anxiety victims. But to help you understand why I find the future of biopsychiatry so encouraging, I should explain why, years ago, I decided to become a psychiatrist.

Early in my medical studies I knew that psychiatry was not for me. Without question, I preferred neurology or neurosurgery to psychiatry, and I can remember a lunchtime conversation with my father during which I explained my preference. My father listened patiently as I ticked off my reasons: Although the neurologist and the neurosurgeon treated patients who were very sick, the technology at their disposal, especially microneurosurgery, was improving rapidly, and almost every day there were new breakthroughs in the treatment of seizures and other neurological disorders. Clearly, it was an exciting time for neurology and neurosurgery, and a time of great hope for the future.

Conversely, I explained, psychiatry was the pits. Too little medicine, too much baloney. At that time, psychiatrists weren't even expected to perform physicals (instead they simply called in an internist). And then there was the feud between the psychiatrists who relied (and overrelied) upon medications and those who saw themselves as "artists" rather than medical doctors. My own choice of discipline seemed obvious. I was certain my father would concur.

Instead, he surprised me. "Everyone knows a great neurologist," he said. "And nearly every community has a great neurosurgeon, but no one knows a great psychiatrist. You can be that psychiatrist." My father, a very pragmatic person, could see that psychiatry represented the greater challenge. Good paternal advice, and advice that I took.

Over time, I have realized that while the other medical disciplines certainly provide us with very valuable information about our health, only psychiatry combines the study of behavior and the study of the brain. How could I resist the challenge? Not to mention the challenge of encouraging psychiatry to move into the future (or "off the couch" and into the laboratories)?

Fortunately, other biopsychiatrists have also responded to this challenge. The human brain has gradually, almost grudgingly, revealed a few of its secrets, with more revelations looming as we intensify our study. It is these advances that I would like to discuss in this chapter.

NEW TESTS AND PROCEDURES

Until recently, psychiatry's study of the brain has been indirect, a consequence of our inability to peer within the brain to observe its functioning. As I described in earlier chapters, this lack of knowledge about the brain has resulted in some rather fanciful theories. But over the years these "creative" explanations for our actions have generally given way to more objective and scientific studies.

Within the last fifteen years, various brain-imaging techniques, such as computerized tomography (CT), magnetic resonance imaging (MRI), single photon emission computerized tomography (SPECT), and positron emission tomography (P.E.T.), have allowed scientists and psychiatrists to study brain anatomy in exquisite detail, and to observe and record changes in brain activity as the brain responds to specific challenges. For example, brain images—complex electronic pictures—of panic disorder patients have revealed unusually high levels of activity in certain areas of the brain. These brain-imaging techniques can actually record activity when a volunteer with a specific phobia imagines a phobic situation.

New research on obsessive-compulsive disorders (OCD) has used similar imaging techniques to isolate specific areas of the brain in which OCD patients appear to have abnormally high levels of activity. For example, researchers have found that OCD patients metabolize glucose at abnormally high rates.

Since glucose is the brain's source of energy, this increased activity potentially links this abnormal activity to OCD. Furthermore, the brain images of OCD patients who were responding well to drug treatment were different from the brain images of other OCD patients. In other studies, researchers using brain imaging techniques have uncovered clues that implicate OCD with specific areas of the brain associated with movement control, learned behavior, and methods of dealing with repetitive stimulations. The brain will reveal even more of its mysteries as the P.E.T. studies become more exact. Currently, the P.E.T. scans allow us to investigate whether specific abnormalities within the brain might cause a wide range of psychiatric disorders, ranging from Alzheimer's disease to panic disorders. As an article in the *Journal of the American Medical Association* expressed it:

> "If abnormalities are found, disease such as schizophrenia, manic-depressive illness, and Alzheimer's disease might one day join pellagra, neurosyphilis, and other diseases with defined biologic correlates of the mental dysfunction." (*JAMA,* 11/11/88, p. 2704)

In fact, P.E.T. scans can be used to examine in great detail *specific neurotransmitter receptors sites in a patient!* First, a substance with a known affinity for a specific receptor site is marked with a radioactive tracer. Later, when the tracer substance links with the receptor cite, a P.E.T. scan can record the density of these receptors in specific areas of the brain. In 1983, the first successful imaging of neurotransmitter receptors in a living human occurred when images of the dopamine receptor were recorded. Science has already begun to examine whether abnormal levels or concentrations of dopamine receptors cause schizophrenia. I expect P.E.T. scans to illuminate the serotoin system in OCD and the catecholamine system (i.e., norepinephrine and dopamine) in panic. P.E.T. scans, or a similar neurotransmitter scan, will be used to confirm psychiatric diagnosis. In other conditions, P.E.T. scans are already being used as diagnostic tools—for example, to help identify specific forms of epilepsy that will benefit from surgery.

But in my opinion, the most exciting future development with P.E.T. scans concerns their effect on treatment. If science can use the scans to identify any abnormalities in specific neurotransmitter receptor sites of panic disorder patients, and if it can be proven that these abnormalities cause panic attacks, then very specific medications that correct these abnormalities can be developed and refined. The possibility even exists that these medications will prevent panic disorder, phobias and anxiety disorders, just as the addition of a common nutrient, niacin, prevents pellagra.

But there are some drawbacks to using brain-imaging methods. They include the high cost of the scans and the technical problems inherent in studying so delicate an organ while it operates—even sensitive P.E.T. scans can be somewhat ineffective when it comes to depicting some of the brain's finer aspects. Basic questions remain, such as whether the increased activity detected by scans *causes* panic attacks or is a *result* of them. And if this increased activity is involved in causing panic disorders, then what causes the increased activity? And what specific areas of the brain actually cause anxiety?

These questions have been partly responsible for leading researchers to consider other methods of studying the brain's functioning, methods that may lead to the most dramatic and potentially exciting discoveries in the history of psychiatry.

Within the last ten years, psychiatry has begun to explore what I consider to be the most promising area for future psychiatric discoveries: our genetic composition and its impact on behavior.

THE GENETIC CONTROVERSY

Can our genetic structure influence our behavior? This question, which at first appears to be a simple, if significant, matter for scientific inquiry, has been the focus of great political and social controversy. For many years politicians and "scientists" claimed that genocide, mass extinction, and segregation are desirable because of the inherent genetic inferiority of certain races. "They can't help the way they act, it's in their genes" was—and is—used by racists to justify the most heinous crimes. And after so many years of these false and harmful claims, it is understandable that even legitimate work, by respected scientists regarding the possible link between genetic structure and behavior has been met with suspicion and criticism.

But in the mid-1970s a book by Edmund O. Wilson, *Sociobiology: The New Synthesis,* supported the legitimacy of the link between genetic makeup and behavior, arguing that human behavior, along with human physiology, had evolved genetically. According to this argument, our behavior, like our stereoscopic vision and bipedal mobility, resulted from the process of natural selection. Studies of fear and anxiety in animals have produced strong evidence supporting the theory that behavior could be genetically based.

THE GENETIC CASE GROWS STRONGER

Anxiety, in particular, is a good example of the inheritance of genetically influenced behavior, since anxiety and fear appear to be crucial to the survival of most, if not all, animals, including humans. If, for example, the antelope did not fear the lion, then the survival of its species would certainly be in doubt.

This process of natural selection may even explain why young women are particularly prone to agoraphobia. Recent theories have suggested that early humans feared attacks by other humans more than any other threat. And who would be more vulnerable to these human attacks than a young mother and her children?

Furthermore, there are a number of similarities between the fear and anxiety reactions of humans and those of animals—the "flight or fight" response described earlier is by no means limited to humans. You can see these nearly identical anxiety responses for yourself during a trip to the zoo: Monkeys wring their hands, bite their nails, lick their lips, pull their hair, tense their muscles, and pace back and forth when they're nervous. Very few people would disagree with the theory that the fear and anxiety responses of animals result from evolutionary forces. Is it then not probable that human anxiety is also a genetic product of evolution? And if our anxiety reactions are a genetic product, then might not other behaviors, such as aggression, timidity, and even depression, be genetically influenced? Research with animals has revealed that behavior, such as either boldly investigating a new environment or timidly remaining in a corner, can be inherited from the previous generation. But those studies involved rats or dogs, and some respected scientists dismissed the results as not applicable to the incredibly complex behavior of humans.

However, studies of human behavior have shown the tendency of many psychiatric problems to pass from generation to generation. Alcoholism, anxiety disorders, and depression are all more likely to occur if there is a family history of these conditions—even if a child is separated from his or her natural parents at birth and raised by others. The twin studies I cited earlier are even stronger proof of this possible link. In these studies, the incidence of anxiety disorders occurring in both twins was far greater if the twins were identical (that is, if they developed from the same egg) than if they were fraternal (if they developed from two different eggs).

Still, definitive, irrefutable proof has been lacking. Critics contended that other factors could account for these tendencies. After all, these critics claimed, the genetic structure of a single psychiatric condition had yet to be uncovered. And they were correct—until recently.

THE BREAKTHROUGH: GENETIC MAPPING
In the early 1980s, researchers studying a large Venezuelan family with a high incidence of Huntington's disease identified a genetic "marker" for Huntington's. Family members who had this marker also had Huntington's disease; those members without it did not have the disease. Huntington's disease, also known as Huntington's chorea or Woody Guthrie's disease, is

characterized by a gradual and ultimately fatal deterioration of movement and mental abilities. While medication can help control the irregular spastic muscle movements, little can be done to stem the mental deterioration. Huntington's disease usually appears between the ages of thirty and fifty, although the gene that eventually causes Huntington's is present at birth. For years geneticists have known that if one parent suffered from this disease there was a 50-50 chance that the offspring would develop Huntington's disease also.

The researchers were able to identify the genetic marker for Huntington's by using a process called *genetic mapping*. Individual genes reside on strands of chromosomes in a structure of DNA (deoxyribonucleic acid) sequences. In genetic mapping, researchers first chart a rough map of an individual's DNA sequences. Then, when certain sequences appear together, recently discovered *restriction enzymes* are used to recognize and isolate a specific DNA sequence, or "marker," for an inherited condition. Eventually, it is hoped, the individual gene responsible for Huntington's will be discovered.

By using these techniques, researchers have been able to identify the specific markers not only for Huntington's disease but also for Duchenne's and Beck's muscular dystrophy, for X-linked retinitis pigmentosa, and for fragile X-linked mental retardation. In the case of Duchenne muscular dystrophy, researchers identified both the gene responsible for the condition and the protein produced by the gene.

It is the identification of these protein by-products of genes that may have the greatest effect on future tests for disease and on treatment, since it is thought that these proteins may ultimately be responsible for bringing about the disease. With blood tests that reveal these markers, doctors will be able to positively identify panic disorder patients and institute treatment promptly, perhaps even on a preventative basis.

GENETIC MAPPING AND THE MIND

Research using genetic mapping techniques has been moving forward at extraordinary speed, and many psychiatric disorders have been studied. A very recent study of a form of manic-depression in the Amish population in Pennsylvania found a link between this condition and a genetic marker. And sitting near this specific marker is a gene that produces an enzyme called tyrosine hyroxylase, which is believed to be very important in causing mood changes.

I believe that a genetic marker for pain and anxiety disorders will be found in the near future. I base my belief on the family and twin studies I mentioned above, on the logical assumption that panic and anxiety disorders are a product of our evolution, and on the results of genetic research. Researchers studying the brains of mice have identified the genetic structure of the proteins that make up the brain's anti-anxiety receptor sites. These receptor sites allow the brain's anti-anxiety messenger, called GABA, to attach itself to individual cells, thereby inhibiting anxiety. Benzodiazepine medications, such as diazepam (brand name: Valium), enhance the link between GABA and its receptor sites, making the body's natural anti-anxiety process more efficient. You can think of these GABA messengers as the brain's "natural Valium." It may be that anxiety disorder patients suffer from a deficiency or abnormality in this "natural Valium," a condition that benzodiazepine medications can temporarily correct.

By understanding the structure of these anti-anxiety receptor sites and the gene that produces these receptors, science has potentially identified our anti-anxiety, or anti-fear, gene—a medical breakthrough made possible by gene mapping. It seems logical that it is only a matter of time before researchers will identify the opposite gene, the one that produces fear.

GENETIC MAPPING: THE QUESTIONS

Although the promises of genetic mapping are exciting, they raise complicated moral, ethical, and legal questions. Will prospective parents choose to have only "perfect" babies, free from even the possibility of developing conditions such as manic-depression, Huntington's disease, or cancer? Will employers require their present and future employees to be genetically screened? Will doctors be required to tell patients that they face a future of muscular or mental deterioration? Would someone married to or engaged to a person who faced such deterioration have a right to know?

Questions like these abound whenever there is a new technological or medical breakthrough. They are questions that I am not qualified or prepared to answer. But as a physician, I see the exciting potential of genetic mapping. With the advent of genetic mapping, science has developed, and is continuing to develop, superior means of predicting a wide range of physical and psychiatric conditions, which may have a tremendous impact on their diagnosis, treatment, and prevention. As a physician I see not only the questions raised by genetic mapping but also the contribution it may make to freeing the world from many of the disabling diseases and psychiatric conditions that afflict us today.

THE GOOD NEWS CONTINUES

Genetic mapping is not the only promising development with respect to anxiety disorders. As I see it, the primary problem today with anxiety and panic disorders lies not in treating them but in identifying the untreated individuals who suffer from them. Ideally, in the future we will be able to predict which individuals are likely to suffer from these disorders and to take preventative measures that will block the panic attacks before they occur or provide remedies when the attacks do occur. For example, we may be able to identify an individual whose genetic structure indicates a likelihood of developing seasonal energy syndrome. Such an individual would be advised of this condition and encouraged either to live in the Sunbelt or to use phototherapy in the northern climates.

MAO ACTIVITY AND BEHAVIOR

One potentially significant predictor of potential psychiatric problems may be low levels of the enzyme monoamine oxidase

(MAO). You may remember that in the treatment section we discussed MAO inhibitors as a very effective means of treating panic attacks. I realize that this may sound contradictory: After all, why should naturally occurring low levels of MAO be a marker for psychiatric problems even though MAO inhibitors, which work by lowering levels of MAO, effectively treat many of these same psychiatric disorders? In the box on page 267, I speculate on some potential reasons for this apparent contradiction, but for now let's explore the link between lower levels of this enzyme and the incidence of psychiatric disorders.

For many years, low levels of MAO activity have been associated with a wide range of psychiatric disorders such as schizophrenia, manic-depression, alcoholism, and addictive drug use. (The association between alcoholism and MAO levels may be especially significant for anxiety disorder patients since there is a high correlation between anxiety disorders and alcoholism.) One problem with using low levels of MAO activity as a possible predictor of psychiatric disorders is that these levels are measured after the individual has been diagnosed with the psychiatric condition, and the possibility exists that the low levels may actually be caused by the disorders, or result from some treatment the patient may already have received.

To assess the possibility that low MAO activity may predict psychiatric problems, researchers measured the MAO levels of 375 college students and university employees (ages eighteen to thirty-eight). The researchers then selected groups with the lowest 10 percent and the highest 10 percent of MAO activity levels. Interviewers who were unaware of the laboratory findings then questioned the volunteers.

The initial results of this study found that the low-MAO-activity individuals had twice as many non-job-related contacts with psychiatrists or psychologists than did the high-MAO-activity group. The low-MAO-activity males had more arrests and convictions for serious offenses and greater incidence of addictive drug use than did the high MAO-activity group—suggesting that these low-MAO-activity males were stimulus seekers or risk takers. And the relatives of the low MAO-activity individuals had *eight times* the suicide and suicide-attempt rate of the relatives of the high-MAO-activity group!

Two years after this initial report, these same groups were evaluated in a follow-up study. In comparison with the high-MAO-activity group, the low-MAO-activity individuals reported

- Greater job instability
- Less progress in school, with more low-MAO-activity males dropping out of school and entering the work force
- Much greater incidence of cigarette smoking (unfortunately, because telephone interviews were used in the follow-up study, inquiries regarding illegal drug use were not made)
- More major and minor medical health problems
- More mental health problems in their relatives, including a greater incidence of depression, alcoholism, and suicide attempts

The authors of this study concluded: "Overall, the low-MAO subjects continue to show signs of poorer functioning in almost all areas of their life that we examined. . . . The low-MAO group continued their pattern of high activity, low stability found in previous studies" [from Coursey, RD, Buchsbaum, MS, and Murphy, DL. *Neuropsychobiology,* 8:51–56 (1982)].

ARE LOW MAO ACTIVITY LEVELS GENETIC?

One area of this study that I found particularly interesting was the high incidence of mental health problems in the relatives of low-MAO-activity individuals. This correlation is another indication that behavior, or at least psychiatric disorders, might be genetically transferred. To assess whether the low MAO activity level might also be determined genetically, researchers measured the MAO activity of patients suffering from manic-depression and of their relatives. This study found that both the manic-depressive patients and their relatives had significantly lower than normal levels of MAO activity.

This study also found that 27 percent of the relatives had some sort of affective (or mood) disorder. Not all of these relatives with psychiatric disorders had low MAO levels, while some of the relatives with no psychiatric disorder had low levels. This finding tends to support the assumption that low levels of MAO activity do not *result* from psychiatric disorders.

WHY THE MAO CONTRADICTION?

Earlier in this section, I commented upon an apparent contradiction: Why might low levels of MAO activity predict some psychiatric disorders, although therapy with MAO inhibitors, which act to reduce MAO levels, proves effective in the treatment of some of these same conditions? Logically, I admit, this doesn't seem to make sense.

But the basis for this apparent contradiction may lie in our understandable—but perhaps misleading—attempts to simplify the brain so that we can better grasp its role. As we have seen, the body, with all of its regulatory and counterregulatory systems, is very complex—so complex that in many cases it resists a simplified approach. It would be very neat and logical if too much or too little of one substance could produce this or that effect. It would make my job, and the jobs of other researchers, far easier. Unfortunately, our physiology is not always so cooperative. When MAO inhibitor medication is administered and MAO activity levels drop, the MAO inhibitor may actually be affecting more than the MAO activity levels. In fact an entire chain reaction of events may occur, with one or more of the subsequent effects accounting for the medication's therapeutic benefits. I feel that this apparent contradiction may disappear when our knowledge of the exact processes involved in these psychiatric disorders improves.

WILL MAO LEVELS BE USED TO PREDICT PSYCHIATRIC DISORDERS?

Although MAO activity levels may become an effective means of predicting which individuals may develop anxiety disorders or other psychiatric disorders, there are several problems that must first be resolved. MAO activity levels are only a *general* indication of potential psychiatric problems; direct correlations between specific conditions and MAO levels have not yet been established. And there is no definitive explanation for why some individuals with low MAO activity levels do not develop psychiatric problems.

For these reasons, I feel that while MAO levels have some potential, the best possibility for an accurate prognosticator lies with genetic mapping. In addition, the challenge tests we discussed earlier, such as sodium lactate infusion, yohimbine administration, and CO_2 inhalation, may eventually be used not only to diagnose panic disorders and to assess when treatment is complete but to predict who might suffer from these conditions.

But research into the various means of diagnosing and predicting the anxiety disorders may also lead to improvements in treatment options, especially in the area of psychopharmacology.

NEW MEDICINES OF THE MIND

Since current pharmacological treatments for anxiety and panic disorders are so effective, and since any major pharmacologic breakthroughs derived from genetic mapping may be years away, recent attention has focused on creating treatments that have fewer and safer side effects. In the following section, I will briefly discuss some of the more interesting medications that may become valuable treatment options in the years to come.

Mianserin. Widely used in other countries, mianserin has not been marketed in the United States. Mianserin is an antidepressant with efficacy similar to that of the tricyclic antidepressants (TCA) but a different mode of action. Like the TCAs, mianserin appears to be effective in treating panic attacks, although double-blind studies have yet to validate its effectiveness. The medication also appears to have strong sedative and anti-anxiety properties. As is the case with most medications, no one knows exactly how mianserin works. However, indications are that the drug may work by blocking the alpha$_2$ receptors, receptors that are believed to be involved in storing the neurotransmitter norepinephrine. Blocking these alpha$_2$ receptors may result in more norepinephrine being released, and since both norepinephrine and alpha$_2$ receptors regulate the locus ceruleus (the area of the brain thought to be involved in panic attacks), any alteration in norepinephrine availability may have anti-anxiety and antipanic effects.

In addition, mianserin appears to lack some of the side effects associated with the TCAs, such as increased heart rate and other cardiac abnormalities. But there have been a few disturbing reports from Europe that suggest mianserin may induce generalized seizures and potentially fatal blood disorders. Therefore, the future availability of this medication in this country remains in doubt.

Adinazolam. Very similar to the very popular triazolobenzodiazepine alprazolam (brand name: Xanax), adinazolam has been used in Europe as an antidepressant. Preliminary reports suggest that this medication has anti-anxiety benefits similar to those of alprazolam, suggesting that adinazolam may have antipanic effects as well; however, it may also share some of alprazolam's negative side effects, such as withdrawal symptoms and potential for physical dependence (see pages 227–29 for a discussion of alprazolam therapy). Given alprazolam's wide popularity, chances are good that adinazolam will be available in this country if future studies support the drug's efficacy and indicate relatively few side effects.

Alpidem. The potential side effects associated with the anti-anxiety benzodiazepines has stimulated the search for safer anti-anxiety agents. Although chemically different from the benzodiazepines, alpidem is apparently active near the same GABA receptors that are affected by benzodiazepines. Preliminary studies with human volunteers have indicated that alpidem may have anti-anxiety effects with less sedation, muscle relaxation and memory impairment than the benzodiazepines. One preliminary study of alpidem found significant improvement in 67 percent of the patients, with mild side effects (the most common being headaches). Interestingly, the study did not report any signs of rebound anxiety or withdrawal symptoms that significantly hamper benzodiazepine therapy. Although promising, many more studies must be done before the true safety and effectiveness of this agent will be known.

Fluoxetine. Recently approved for use in the United States and marketed under the brand name Prozac, fluoxetine is the very first medication from a new class—called serotonin reuptake inhibitors—to be released in this country. Fluoxetine appears to have antidepressant effects similar to those of the TCAs, without the TCAs' potentially serious cardiac side effects. However, fluoxetine has a different set of side effects, such as nervousness, insomnia, headaches, and nausea, that may limit its effectiveness in panic or anxiety disorder patients. In one study of sixteen panic disorder patients, 50 percent found that they could not tolerate fluoxetine's side effects of nervousness and agitation. While its use in panic disorders may be limited, early reports of its effectiveness in treating obsessive-compulsive disorder have been promising. Also, fluoxetine may be helpful in treating eating disorders, especially bulimia and obesity. Studies are under way to evaluate this medication's possible weight-loss benefits in nondepressed patients.

Fluvoxamine Like fluoxetine, fluvoxamine is classified as a serotonin reuptake inhibitor. Two recent studies have shown fluvoxamine to be effective in treating panic disorder. The success of the serotonin reuptake inhibitors—especially when compared to noradrenergic medications such as maprotiline (Ludiomil)—have led some researchers to suggest that the neurotransmitter serotonin may be directly involved in causing panic attacks. However, other researchers have disagreed, claiming that the maprotiline dosages may have been too low to prove effective. Interestingly, one study of fluvoxamine reported that the panic attacks initially worsened, before improving after 1–2 weeks of therapy. Like other serotonin reuptake inhibitors, this medication may someday prove effective in the treatment of obsessive-compulsive disorder.

Zimeldine. Another promising serotonin reuptake inhibitor, zimeldine—in one double-blind study—was shown to be more effective than even imipramine in the treatment of agoraphobia with panic attacks. Unfortunately, because of the potential for serious side effects the drug may never be approved. However, derivatives of zimeldine may prove to be useful in panic and OCD.

Trazodone. Introduced into the United States in 1982, trazodone (brand name: Desyrel) has rapidly become one of the most popular antidepressant medications. Chemically and pharmacologically different from other antidepressants, trazodone may have fewer of the side effects associated with other antidepressants (such as constipation and cardiovascular changes). While its primary side effects are drowsiness and dizziness, trazodone may also, rarely, cause priapism (sustained and painful erections) in males.

Since 1982 trazodone has been used successfully in the treatment of anxiety disorders and bulimia. In addition, very preliminary reports suggest that the medication may be very useful in obsessive-compulsive disorder. In published reports, five OCD patients report significant improvement in their symptoms while taking trazodone. However, preliminary studies have reported mixed results in the treatment of panic disorder with trazodone.

L-deprenyl. Although it is related to most other MAO inhibitors currently available, l-deprenyl (also known as selegiline) may lack the potentially serious hypertensive side effects associated with the MAO inhibitors. Whether the medication has the same antidepressant and antipanic efficacy as the MAO inhibitors remains to be proven. Interestingly, a recent study suggests that l-deprenyl may improve the mood, memory, and behavior of some Alzheimer's patients.

Moclobemide. Unlike all other currently available MAO inhibitors, moclobemide is a reversible MAO inhibitor. (The other MAO inhibitors are irreversible; as a result, strict dietary restrictions are necessary, and the prolonged presence of the medication in the body following termination of therapy makes a switch to another antidepressant medication difficult.) Preliminary results indicate that moclobemide is an effective antidepressant that lacks the potentially serious hypertensive effects of other MAO inhibitors. As with all experimental medications, additional studies are required before the drug's overall safety and effectiveness can be established.

S-Adenosyl-Methionine (SAM). Different from any other currently available antidepressant, SAM is a naturally occurring substance found in the central nervous system. When given intravenously in European and British studies, SAM demonstrated rapid antidepressant effects, without significant side effects. Controlled evaluations of SAM should reveal whether this medication has significant antidepressant, antipanic, or anti-anxiety benefits. Whether or not this drug will ever become available in this country cannot be determined at this time.

ENVIRONMENTAL PSYCHIATRY

In the last chapter, I discussed how seasonal affective disorder (SAD) may cause anxiety and depression. Briefly, it now appears that in some individuals the absence of sunlight, or specifically the ultraviolet light contained in sunlight and full-spectrum lights, causes psychiatric disorders. If this theory holds true, and indications are that it will, then the acceptance of SAD as a viable cause of some psychiatric conditions may usher in a new era of *environmental psychiatry.*

If sunlight, or the absence of sunlight, can have such a profound effect on our behavior, then might not other environmental factors have equally serious affects? These environmental factors could range from pollution, food additives, and high noise levels to crowded living conditions, and even humidity or temperature levels. When so many of us readily acknowledge that pollution or harmful additives can cause cancer and other physical diseases, why have we hesitated to consider that these same factors might have psychiatric effects? And if the absence of sunlight can cause anxiety and depression, might not cold temperatures also cause these conditions? These questions, plus many more, remain to be answered.

Without question, the future looks very bright for those who suffer from panic and anxiety disorders. The possible developments that I have described in this chapter may ultimately lead to a world free from the panic, anxiety, and phobias that torment so many people today.

But perhaps the most important point to remember is not that the future looks promising, but that the treatments that biopsychiatry has available *today* are so effective. In fact, they work so well that approximately 90 percent of patients with panic and anxiety disorders can find effective relief.

Nothing I write in this book can ever top that good news.

RESOURCES and STATE-BY-STATE LISTING OF EXPERTS

For more information on evaluation and treatment, you may contact:

Fair Oaks Hospital
19 Prospect Street
Summit, NJ 07901
1 (800) HELPLINE

ALABAMA

Michael J. Kehoe, M.D.
University of Southern Alabama
2451 Fillingim Street
Mobile, AL 36617
(205) 479-3072

John R. Smythies, M.D.
Departments of Psychiatry &
   Neurosciences
University of Alabama Medical Center
University Station
Birmingham, AL 35294
(205) 934-2011

ARIZONA

Allan Beigel, M.D.
430 N. Tucson Blvd.
Tucson, AZ 85716
(602) 325-4837

Janice Bebe Dorn, M.D., Ph.D.
Biological Psychiatry
4227 North 32nd Street
Suite 108
Phoenix, AZ 85018
(602) 224-9277

Dennis C. Westin, M.D., P.C.
5240 E. Knight Drive
Tucson, AZ 85712
(602) 795-0309

ARKANSAS

Frederick Guggenheim, M.D.
University of Arkansas for Medical
   Sciences
4301 W. Markham, Slot 589
Little Rock, AR 72205
(501) 686-5483

CALIFORNIA

Monte Buchsbaum, M.D.
University of California/Irvine
California College of Medicine
Room D402
Irvine, CA 92717
(714) 856-4244

John Deri, M.D.
2154 Broderick Street
San Francisco, CA 94115
(415) 921-3311

John Feighner, M.D.
University of California/San Diego
San Luis Rey Hospital
1011 Devonshire Drive, Suite E
Encinitas, CA 92024
(619) 753-2301

Robert Fusco, M.D.
French Hospital Medical Center
4131 Geary Boulevard

San Francisco, CA 94118
(415) 944-1733 or 666-8877

Robert H. Gerner, M.D.
12301 Wilshire Boulevard
Suite 210
Los Angeles, CA 90025
(213) 207-8448

Michael J. Gitlin, M.D.
UCLA Neuropsychiatric Institute
Center for Mood Disorders
12301 Wilshire Blvd/Suite 210
Los Angeles, CA 90025
(213) 207-8448

Daniel X. Freedman, M.D.
Department of Psychiatry
UCLA Neuropsychiatric Institute
760 Westwood Plaza
Los Angeles, CA 90024
(213) 206-0213

Geoffrey J. Newstadt, M.D.
Cedars-Sinai Medical Center
8700 Beverly Blvd.
Los Angeles, CA 90048
(213) 855-3465

Ferris N. Pitts, Jr., M.D.
170 N. Daisy Avenue
Pasadena, CA 91107
(818) 568-1310

Victor I. Reus, M.D.
University of California, San Francisco
Medical Director
Langley-Porter Institute
401 Parnassus Avenue
San Francisco, CA 94143
(415) 476-7478

David A. Sack, M.D.
Assistant Clinical Professor of UCLA
5911 Heil, Suite E
Huntington Beach, CA 92649
(714) 840-8615

Harvey A. Sternbach, M.D.
UCLA Neuropsychiatric Institute
2730 Wilshire Blvd., Suite 325
Santa Monica, CA 90403
(213) 828-7879

Forest S. Tennant, Jr., M.D., Ph.D.
University of Southern California
Community Health Projects, Inc.

336½ South Glendora Avenue
West Covina, CA 91790
(818) 919-1879

COLORADO

Kenneth L. Weiner, M.D.
University of Colorado Medical Center
6300 South Syracuse Way
Suite #655
Englewood, CO 80111
(303) 220-1655

CONNECTICUT

Dennis Charney, M.D.
Yale University School of Medicine
333 Cedar Street
New Haven, CT 06510
(203) 789-7329

Earl L. Giller, Jr., M.D., Ph.D.
Professor of Psychiatry
University of Connecticut Health
  Center
Department of Psychiatry
Farmington, CT 06032
(203) 679-2705

Wayne K. Goodman, M.D.
Yale University School of Medicine
333 Cedar Street
New Haven, CT 06510
(203) 789-7336

Malan Hale, M.D.
University of Connecticut Health
  Center
263 Farmington Avenue
Farmington, CT 06032
(203) 679-4281

Selby C. Jacobs, M.D.
Yale University School of Medicine
Yale New Haven Hospital/2039CB
333 Cedar Street
New Haven, CT 06510
(203) 785-2619

J. Craig Nelson, M.D.
Yale University School of Medicine
Yale New Haven Hospital
20 York Street
New Haven, CT 06504
(203) 785-2157

Laurence Rossi, M.D.
Institute of Living
400 Washington Street
Hartford, CT 06106
(203) 241-8000

L. Michael Sheehy, M.D.
Columbia College of Physicians and
  Surgeons
Silver Hill Foundation
P.O. Box 1177
New Canaan, CT 06840
(203) 966-3561

WASHINGTON, DC, AREA

Robert L. DuPont, M.D.
Georgetown University
6191 Executive Boulevard
Rockville, MD 20852
(301) 231-9010

John E. Meeks, M.D., Medical Director
Psychiatric Institute of Montgomery
  County
14901 Broschart Road
Rockville, MD 20850
(301) 251-4500

David Pickar, M.D.
National Institute of Health
Clinical Center, NIH,
9000 Rockville Pike
Bldg. 10, 4N214
Bethesda, MD 20892
(301) 496-4303

Robert M. Post, M.D.
National Institute of Mental Health
Bldg. 10, 3N212
9000 Rockville Pike
Bethesda, MD 20892
(301) 496-4805

William Z. Potter, M.D., Ph.D.
National Institute of Mental Health
Bldg. 10, 2D46
9000 Rockville Pike
Bethesda, MD 20892
(301) 496-5082

Judith Rapoport, M.D.
National Institute of Mental Health
Bldg. 10, Room 6N240
9000 Rockville Pike
Bethesda, MD 20892

S. Charles Schulz, M.D.
Georgetown University
National Institute of Mental Health
5600 Fishers Lane
Rockville, MD 20857
(301) 443-4707

Thomas W. Uhde, M.D.
Chief, Unit on Anxiety & Affective
  Disorders
Room 3, South 239
National Institute of Mental Health
Biological Psychiatry Branch
9000 Rockville Pike
Bethesda, MD 20205
(301) 496-6825

FLORIDA

James Adams, M.D.
2329 Sunset Point Road, Suite 203
Clearwater, FL 33575
(813) 796-0038

John Adams, M.D.
University of Florida Medical School
Dept. of Psychiatry, Box J-256, JHMHC
Gainesville, FL 32610
(904) 392-3681

Cesar Benarroche, M.D.
Fair Oaks at Boca/Delray
5440 Linton Blvd.
Delray Beach, FL 33484
(407) 495-1000

Todd Wilk Estroff, M.D.
Harbor Oaks Hospital
Fort Walton Beach, FL 32548
(904) 863-4160

Irl Extein, M.D.
Medical Director
Fair Oaks at Boca/Delray
5440 Linton Boulevard
Delray Beach, FL 33484
(407) 495-1000

Abraham Flemenbaum, M.D.
2500 E. Hallandale Beach Blvd.
Suite 508
Hallandale, FL 33009
(305) 454-5544

David A. Gross, M.D., Medical Director,
Neurobehavior Treatment Center

Fair Oaks at Boca/Delray
5440 Linton Boulevard
Delray Beach, FL 33484
(407) 495-1000

Richard C. W. Hall, M.D.
University of Florida College of
    Medicine
Clinical Professor of Psychiatry
Florida Hospital
601 East Rollins Street
Orlando, FL 32803
(407) 897-1801

Arnold L. Lieber, M.D.
University of Miami
St. Francis Hospital
Neuroscience Unit, 11th Floor
250 West 63rd Street
Miami Beach, FL 33141
(305) 868-2747

Otsenre Matos, M.D.
150 Sunset Blvd., Suite 12
New Port Richey
Tampa, FL 33552
(813) 849-2005

William Rea, M.D.
Lake Hospital of the Palm Beaches
1710 Fourth Avenue North
Lake Worth, FL 33460
(407) 588-7341

David Sheehan, M.D.
University of Southern Florida
Psychiatry Center
3500 E. Fletcher, Suite 321
Tampa, FL 33613
(813) 974-3344

Steve Targum, M.D.
University of South Florida
Sarasota Palms Hospital
1650 South Osprey Avenue
Sarasota, FL 33579
(813) 336-6070 Ext. 3851

Brian Weiss, M.D.
University of Miami
4300 Alton Road
Miami, FL 33140
(305) 674-2194

GEORGIA

Ronald C. Bloodworth, M.D.
Charter-by-the-Sea
2927 Demere Road
St. Thomas Island, GA 31522
(912) 638-1999

John Curtis, M.D.
650 Oglethorpe Avenue
Suite #6
Athens, GA 30606
(404) 354-4045

Mark Gould, M.D., Medical Director
Brawner Psychiatric Institute
3180 Atlanta Street, S.E.
Smyrna, GA 30080
(404) 436-0081

Luther Smith, M.D.
Arnold Kelz, M.D.
1953 Seventh Avenue
Columbus, GA 31904
(404) 324-5447

Arnold Tillinger, M.D.
515 East 63rd Street
Savannah, GA 31405
(912) 352-2921

HAWAII

John McDermott, M.D.
Chairman, Department of Psychiatry
John A. Burns School of Medicine
1960 East West Road
Honolulu, HI 96822
(808) 948-8287

ILLINOIS

John M. Davis, M.D.
University of Illinois
Illinois State Psychiatric Institute
1601 West Taylor
Chicago, IL 60612
(312) 413-1065

Jan Fawcett, M.D.
Rush Presbyterian/St. Lukes Medical
    Center
1720 West Polk Street
Chicago, IL 60612
(312) 942-5372

THE GOOD NEWS ABOUT PANIC, ANXIETY, AND PHOBIAS

Dale Giolas, M.D.
University of Illinois
Hartgrove Hospital
520 N. Ridgeway
Chicago, IL 60624
(312) 722-3113

Stuart Yudofsky, M.D.
Professor & Chairman
Department of Psychiatry
University of Chicago
Box 411
5841 South Maryland Avenue
Chicago, IL 60637
(312) 702-6192

INDIANA

Suhayl J. Nasr, M.D.
Kingwood Hospital
3714 S. Franklin Street
Michigan City, IN 46360
(219) 873-1614

John Nurnberger, Jr., M.D.
Indiana University Medical Center
791 Union Drive
Indianapolis, IN 46223
(317) 274-8382

Iver Small, M.D.
Indiana University School of Medicine
Larue D. Carter Memorial Hospital
1315 W. Tenth Street
Indianapolis, IN 46202
(317) 634-8401

Joyce Small, M.D.
Indiana University School of Medicine
Larue D. Carter Memorial Hospital
1315 W. Tenth Street
Indianapolis, IN 46202
(317) 634-8401

IOWA

Nancy C. Andreasen, M.D., Ph.D.
Department of Psychiatry
University of Iowa
500 Newton Road
Iowa City, IA 52242
(319) 356-1553

William Coryell, M.D.
University of Iowa College of Medicine

500 Newton Road
Iowa City, IA 52242
(319) 356-1351

George Winokur, M.D.
University of Iowa College of Medicine
500 Newton Road
Iowa City, IA 52242
(319) 356-1533

KANSAS

Thad H. Billingsley, M.D.
The Benessere Center
4501 College Blvd.
Suite 350
Leawood, KS 66211-2328
(913) 432-9900

Sam Castellani, M.D.
School of Medicine at Wichita
University of Kansas
1010 North Kansas
Wichita, KS 67214
(316) 261-2647

Donald Goodwin, M.D.
University of Kansas
Department of Psychiatry
39th and Rainbow
Kansas City, KS 66103
(913) 588-6402

Sheldon H. Preskorn, M.D.
University of Kansas Medical School
Chief of Psychiatry
VA Hospital #116
5500 East Kellogg
Wichita, KS 67218
(316) 685-2221 X 3386

David Sternberg, M.D.
University of Kansas
The Kansas Institute
555 E. Santa Fe
Olathe, KS 66061
(913) 782-7000

KENTUCKY

Karley Y. Little, M.D.
University of Kentucky Medical Center
Annex 2
Lexington, KY 40536
(606) 233-5552

Daniel Nahum, M.D.
University of Kentucky
Department of Psychiatry
John Chambers Bldg.
820 South Limestone
Lexington, KY 40536
(606) 233-5444

John J. Schwab, M.D.
University of Louisville School of
    Medicine
Department of Psychiatry, RM 503
Louisville, KY 40292
(502) 588-5387

LOUISIANA

Rudolph Ehrensing, M.D.
Ochsner Clinic
1514 Jefferson Hwy
New Orleans, LA 70121
(504) 838-3000

Wayne Julian, M.D.
Tulane University
5610 Read Boulevard
New Orleans East, LA 70127
(504) 244-5661

Greg Khoury, M.D.
Medical Director, Depression Clinic
Jo Ellen Smith Psychiatric Hospital
4601 Patterson Road
New Orleans, LA 70131
(504) 367-0707

Michael R. Madow, M.D.
CPC Coliseum Medical Center
3601 Coliseum Street
New Orleans, LA 70115
(504) 897-9700 or 891-2500

Stanley Roskind, M.D.
Tulane University
Medical Director
Jo Ellen Smith Psychiatric Hospital
4601 Patterson Road
New Orleans, LA 70131
(504) 367-0707

Gene L. Usdin, M.D.
Louisiana State University
Ochsner Clinic
1514 Jefferson Hwy
New Orleans, LA 70121
(504) 838-3965

MAINE

Alan Elkins, M.D.
Chief of Psychiatry
Maine Medical Center
22 Bramhall Street
Portland, ME 04102
(207) 871-2355

MARYLAND

Frank J. Ayd, Jr., M.D.
1130 East Cold Spring Lane
Baltimore, MD 21239
(301) 433-9220

Paul R. McHugh, M.D.
Johns Hopkins University School of
    Medicine
Johns Hopkins Hospital
6000 North Wolfe Street
Baltimore, MD 21205
(301) 955-3130

Solomon Snyder, M.D.
Johns Hopkins University School of
    Medicine
Wood's Basic Science Bldg., Rm 813
725 North Wolfe Street
Baltimore, MD 21205
(301) 955-3024

Bruce T. Taylor, M.D.
Taylor Manor Hospital
College Avenue, P.O. Box 396
Ellicott City, MD 21043
(301) 465-3322

MASSACHUSETTS

Paul Barreira, M.D.
Department of Psychiatry
University of Massachusetts Medical
    Center
55 Lake Avenue, North
Worcester, MA 01605
(508) 856-4087 or 752-4681
    Ext. 263

Jerrold G. Bernstein, M.D.
280 Ward Street
Newton Centre, MA 02159

Jonathan O. Cole, M.D.
Harvard Medical School
McLean Hospital
115 Mill Street

Belmont, MA 02178
(617) 855-2901

Michael Jenike, M.D.
Massachusetts General
244 Grove Street
Reading, MA 01867
(617) 726-2998

Jeffrey M. Jonas, M.D.
Cape Cod Hospital
27 Park Street
Hyannis, MA
(508) 790-2101

Jack H. Mendelson, M.D.
McLean Hospital
115 Mill Street
Belmont, MA 02178
(617) 855-2716

Harrison G. Pope, Jr., M.D.
Harvard Medical School
McLean Hospital
115 Mill Street
Belmont, MA 02178
(617) 855-2911

Alan F. Schatzberg, M.D.
Massachusetts Medical Health Center
74 Fernwood Road
Boston, MA 02115
(617) 734-1300 Ext. 119

Lloyd I. Sederer, M.D.
McLean Hospital
115 Mill Street
Belmont, MA 02178
(617) 855-2108

MICHIGAN

Raymond E. Buck, M.D.
Psychiatry Center of Michigan
Moross Road
Detroit, MI 48236
1-800-537-7924

George C. Curtis, M.D.
University of Michigan Medical Center
Med. Inn Bldg., Room C-444
1500 E. Medical Center Dr.
Ann Arbor, MI 48109-0840
(313) 764-5348

John Francis Greden, M.D.
University of Michigan School of
Medicine
1405 E. Ann, Box 11
Ann Arbor, MI 48109
(313) 763-9629

MINNESOTA

Paula J. Clayton, M.D.
University of Minnesota
Department of Psychiatry
Box 77 Mayo Memorial Bldg.
420 Delaware Street, S.E.
Minneapolis, MN 55455
(612) 626-3532

Dallas Erdmann, M.D. &
Gary Christenson, M.D.
Directors, Mood Disorders Clinic
Box 393
420 Delaware Street
Minneapolis, MN 55455
(612) 626-3698

James Halikas, M.D.
University of Minnesota
Department of Psychiatry
Box 393 Mayo Memorial Bldg.
420 Delaware Street, S.E.
Minneapolis, MN 55455
(612) 626-6361

Yasyn Lee, M.D.
Park Nicollet Medical Center
Mental Health Department
5000 W. 39th Street
Minneapolis, MN 55416
(612) 927-3371

MISSISSIPPI

Howard Freeman, Jr., M.D.
Charter Hospital of Jackson
East Lakeland Drive
Jackson, MS 39216
(601) 939-9030

MISSOURI

C. Robert Cloninger, M.D.
Head, Department of Psychiatry
4940 Audubon Avenue
St. Louis, MO 63110
(314) 362-7005

NEW HAMPSHIRE

John Docherty, M.D.
Nashua Brookside Hospital
11 Northwest Blvd.
Nashua, NH 03063
(603) 886-5000

NEW JERSEY

Charles Ciolino, M.D.
Summit Medical Group
120 Summit Avenue
Summit, NJ 07901
(201) 273-4300

James A. Cocores, M.D.
ORC
1 West Ridgewood Avenue
Paramus, NJ 07652
(201) 670-7788

Charles A. Dackis, M.D.
Medical Director
Hampton Hospital
Rancocas Road
P.O. Box 7000
Rancocas, NJ 08073
(609) 267-7000

Peter Herridge, M.D.
Fair Oaks Hospital
19 Prospect Street
Summit, NJ 07901
(201) 522-7000

Stuart Kushner, M.D.
One Prospect Street
Summit, NJ 07901
(201) 522-7095

Robert Moreines, M.D.
Fair Oaks Hospital
19 Prospect Street
Summit, NJ 07901
(201) 522-7000

Peter S. Mueller, M.D.
601 Ewing Street
Princeton, NJ 08540
(609) 924-4061

Michael Orlosky, M.D.
Rutgers University Medical School
133 Franklin Corner Road
Lawrenceville, NJ 08648
(609) 896-1211

Donald R. Sweeney, M.D., Ph.D.
Yale University School of Medicine
Fair Oaks Hospital
19 Prospect Street
Summit, NJ 07901
(201) 522-7000

NEW YORK

Richard Altesman, M.D.
Harvard School of Medicine
Stony Lodge Hospital
P.O. Box 1250
Briarcliff Manor, NY 10510
(914) 941-7400

Robert Cancro, M.D.
NYU School of Medicine
550 First Avenue
New York, NY 10016
(212) 340-6214

Max Fink, M.D.
State University of New York School of
  Medicine
P.O. Box 457
St. James, NY 11780
(516) 444-2918

James W. Flax, M.D.
242-D North Main Street
New City, NY 10956
(914) 638-3358

Alexander Glassman, M.D.
Columbia University School of
  Medicine
NY State Psychiatric Institute
722 W. 168th Street
New York, NY 10032
(212) 960-2200

Jack Gorman, M.D.
Columbia University School of
  Medicine
NY State Psychiatric Institute
722 W. 168th Street
New York, NY 10032
(212) 960-2200

Larry Kirstein, M.D.
Columbia University College of
  Physicians and Surgeons
Regent Hospital
425 E. 61st Street

New York, NY 10021
(212) 935-3400

Donald F. Klein, M.D.
Columbia University School of
    Medicine
722 West 168th Street
New York, NY 10032
(212) 960-2307

Dr. V. Klopott
144 Dunbarton Drive
Delmar, NY 12054
(518) 382-0925

Michael Liebowitz, M.D.
Columbia University
161 Fort Washington Avenue
New York, NY 10032
(212) 305-5341

H. Rowland Pearsall, M.D.
Stony Lodge Hospital
P.O. Box 1250
Briarcliff Manor, NY 10510
(914) 941-7400

Arthur Rifkin, M.D.
Hillside Hospital
263 Street & 76th Avenue
Glen Oaks, NY 11004
(718) 990-3551

Andrew E. Slaby, M.D., Ph.D., M.P.H.
Psychiatrist-in-Chief
Regent Hospital
425 East 61st Street
New York, NY 10021
(212) 935-3400

NORTH CAROLINA

Bernard J. Carroll, M.D., Ph.D.
Duke University
P.O. Box 3950
Durham, NC 27710
(919) 684-5616

Alan L. Krueger, M.D.
Medical Director
Appalachian Hall
P.O. Box 5534
Asheville, NC 28813
(704) 253-3681

Anthony J. Weisenberger, M.D.
Clinical Director

Appalachian Hall
P.O. Box 5534
Asheville, NC 28813
(704) 253-3681

Charles B. Nemeroff, M.D., Ph.D.
Duke University
P.O. Box 3950
Durham, NC 27710
(919) 684-6562

OHIO

Gregory B. Collins, M.D.
The Cleveland Clinic Foundation
9500 Euclid Avenue, Desk P68
Cleveland, OH 44106
(216) 444-2970

Murray D. Altose, M.D.
Chief of Staff
Cleveland Veterans Administration
    Medical Center
10701 East Boulevard
Cleveland, OH 44106
(216) 526-3030 Ext. 225

A. James Giannini, M.D.
Ohio State University
Northeast Ohio Medical College
3040 Belmont Avenue
Youngstown, OH 44504
(216) 759-8685

Marcia Kaplan, M.D.
University of Cincinnati Medical School
7303 Medical Arts Bldg.
231 Bethesda Avenue
Cincinnati, OH 45267
(513) 475-8700

Matig Mavissakalian, M.D.
Ohio State University
Department of Psychiatry
Room #169, Upham Hall
473 West 12th Avenue
Columbus, OH 43210
(614) 293-5130

Herbert Y. Meltzer, M.D.
Case Western Reserve University
2074 Abington Road
Cleveland, OH 44106
(216) 844-8750

OKLAHOMA

Gordon H. Deckert, M.D.
University of Oklahoma College of
   Medicine
P.O. Box 26901
Oklahoma City, OK 73190
(405) 271-5272

OREGON

Alfred Lewy, M.D.
Oregon Health Sciences University
L-469, Department of Psychiatry
Portland, OR 97201
(503) 279-7746

PENNSYLVANIA

Edna Foa, M.D.
3200 Henry Avenue
Philadelphia, PA 19129
(215) 842-4010

David Kupfer, M.D.
University of Pittsburgh School of
   Medicine
3811 O'Hara Street
Pittsburgh, PA 15213
(412) 624-2353

Joseph Mendels, M.D.
Medical Director
Philadelphia Medical Institute
1015 Chestnut Street-Suite 1303
Philadelphia, PA 19107
(215) 923-2583

Joaquim Puig-Antich, M.D.
University of Pittsburgh School of
   Medicine
3811 O'Hara Street, Rm. E720
Pittsburgh, PA 15213
(412) 624-1436

Kenneth R. Sandler, M.D.
University of Pennsylvania School of
   Medicine
Fairmount Institute
561 Fairthorne Street
Philadelphia, PA 19128
(215) 487-4000

Troy Thompson, M.D.
Department of Psychiatry & Human
   Behavior

Room 321-B, Curtis Building
1015 Walnut Street
Philadelphia, PA 19107
(215) 928-6912

Daniel P. van Kammen, M.D., Ph.D.
University of Pittsburgh School of
   Medicine
VA Medical Center/Psychiatry Services
Highland Drive
Pittsburgh, PA 15206
(412) 363-4900 Ext. 4223

Peter Whybrow, M.D.
University of Pennsylvania
305 Blockly Hall
Philadelphia, PA 19104
(215) 662-2818

RHODE ISLAND

Richard Goldberg, M.D.
Brown University
Rhode Island Hospital APC-9
593 Eddy Street
Providence, RI 02902
(401) 277-5488

Stephen Rasmussen, M.D.
Brown University
Butler Hospital
345 Blackstone Boulevard
Providence, RI 02906
(401) 456-3852

SOUTH CAROLINA

Raymond F. Anton, Jr., M.D.
Medical University of South Carolina
VA Medical Center
109 Bee Street
Charleston, SC 29403
(803) 577-5011

James Ballenger, M.D.
Medical University of South Carolina
171 Ashley Avenue
Charleston, SC 29403
(803) 792-2010

R. Bruce Lydiard, M.D., Ph.D.
Medical University of South Carolina
Department of Psychiatry
171 Ashley Avenue
Charleston, SC 29403
(803) 792-4032

TENNESSEE

Hagop Souren Akiskal, M.D.
University of Tennessee School of
  Medicine
66 North Pauline Street
Suite 633
Memphis, TN 38163
(901) 528-6449

TEXAS

R. Michael Allen, M.D.
800 W. Arbrook Blvd., Suite 325
Arlington, TX 76015
(817) 468-9130

James Buckingham, M.D.
4800-A Northeast Stalling Drive
Nacogdoches, TX 75961
(409) 564-9785

Lee Emory, M.D.
1103 Rosenberg
Galveston, TX 77550
(409) 763-0016

Frederick Goggans, M.D.
University of Texas, Dallas
Health Science Center
1814-B Eighth Avenue
Ft. Worth, TX 76110
(817) 924-1036

Edward Gripon, M.D.
University of Texas Medical Branch
3560 Delaware, Suite 502
Beaumont, TX 77706
(409) 899-4472

James Maas, M.D.
University of Texas Health Science
  Center
7703 Floyd Curl Drive
San Antonio, TX 78284
(512) 567-5396

John Rush, M.D.
University of Texas Health Science
  Center
5323 Harry Hines Blvd.
Dallas, TX 75235
(214) 688-3992

Alan C. Swann, M.D.
University of Texas Medical School
6431 Fannin Street

Suite 5218
Houston, TX 77030
(713) 792-5541

UTAH

Bernard Grosser, M.D.
University of Utah Medical Center
50 North Medical Drive
Salt Lake City, UT 84132
(801) 581-4888

VIRGINIA

Charles M. Davis, M.D.
Charter Westbrook Hospital
1500 Westbrook Avenue
Richmond, VA 23227
(804) 261-7124

C. Gibson Dunn, M.D.
Springwood Psychiatric Institute
Route 4, Box 50
Leesburg, VA 22075
(703) 777-0810

Robert O. Friedel, M.D.
Medical College of Virginia
Charter Medical Corporation
1001 Chinaberry Boulevard
Suite #319
Richmond, VA 23225
(804) 272-1050

Neil Price, M.D.
Assistant Professor, Psychiatry
Department of Psychiatry & Behavioral
  Science
Eastern Virginia Medical School
Pembroke 5/Suite 331
Virginia Beach, VA 23462
(804) 490-1641

WASHINGTON

Gary Tucker, M.D.
University of Washington
R.P. #10
Seattle, WA 98195
(206) 543-3750

David Dunner, M.D.
University of Washington
Harborview Medical Center
325 Ninth Avenue, ZA#15
Seattle, WA 98104
(206) 223-3404

WEST VIRGINIA

James M. Stevenson, M.D.
West Virginia University School of
Medicine
Morgantown, WV 26506
(304) 293-2411

WISCONSIN

Barry Blackwell, M.D.
Sinai Samaritan Medical Center
2000 W. Gilbourn Avenue
Good Samaritan Campus
Psychiatry Department/Corporate 4
Milwaukee, WI 53233
(414) 937-5300

Burr Eichelman, M.D.
University of Wisconsin Medical School
VA Hospital
2500 Overlook Terrace
Madison, WI 53705
(608) 262-7015

Herb Roehrich, M.D.
St. Catherine's Benet Lake Center
12603 224th Avenue
Benet Lake, WI 53102
(414) 396-4360

CANADA

Paul Garfinkel, M.D.
Clarke Institute of Psychiatry
250 College Street
Toronto, Ontario
M5T 1R8 Canada
(416) 979-2221

Russell T. Joffee, M.D.
Toronto General Hospital
200 Elizabeth Street
Toronto, Ontario
M5G 2C4 Canada
(416) 340-3043

Guy Chouinard, M.D.
4015 Trafalgar Road
Montreal, Quebec
H3Y 1R1 Canada

Morton Beiser, M.D.
University of British Columbia
Health Sciences Center
2255 Westbrook Mall
Vancouver, BC V6T 2A1
Canada
(604) 228-7327

Jean-Guy Fontaine, M.D.
McGill University
36 Claude Champagne
Outremont, Quebec H2V 2X1
Canada
(514) 739-6692

GREAT BRITAIN

Malcolm Lader, M.B., Ch.B., PH.D., M.D.
Institute of Psychiatry
DeCrespigny Park
Denmark Hill
London SE5 8HF
Great Britain

PUERTO RICO

Robert Stolberg, M.D.
(809) 723-3294
(Bilingual)
Mon., Tues., Thurs.

In addition you can contact:

CHAANGE
2915 Providence Road
Charlotte, NC 28211
(704) 365-0140

Freedom From Fear
308 Seaview Avenue
Staten Island, NY 10305
(718) 351-1717

National Depressive and
Manic Depressive Association
222 South Riverside Plaza
Suite 2812
Chicago, IL 60606
(312) 993-0066

The Phobia Society of America
P.O. Box 42514
Washington, DC 20015-0514

TERRAP Programs
648 Menlo Avenue, #5
Menlo Park, CA 94025
1-800-2-PHOBIA

Obsessive-Compulsive Disorder Foundation
P.O. Box 573
New Haven, CT 06535

SOURCES and BIBLIOGRAPHY

Alcoholics Anonymous World Services, Inc. *Twelve Steps and Twelve Traditions.* Alcoholics Anonymous World Services, Inc. (1976).

Allman, WF. "How The Brain Really Works Its Wonders." *U.S. News and World Report,* (June 27, 1988) 48–54.

American Psychiatric Association. *Diagnostic and Statistical Manual of Mental Disorders.* 3rd edition, revised. Washington: American Psychiatric Press, 1987.

Anath, J. "Clomipramine: An Antiobsessive Drug." *Can J Psychiatry* (April 1986); vol. 31:253–58.

Ascher, LM. "Employing Paradoxical Intention in the Treatment of Agoraphobia." *Behav Res & Therapy* (1981), vol. 19, 533–42.

Babcock, HH. "Integrative Psychotherapy: Collaborative Aspects of Behavioral and Psychodynamic Therapies." *Psychiatric Annals* (May 1988), 18:5:271–72.

Ballenger, JC, Burrows, GD, DuPont, RL, et al. "Alprazolam in Panic Disorder and Agoraphaobia: Results From a Multicenter Trial." *Arch Gen Psychiatry* (May 1988); 45:413–22.

Ballenger, JC. "Recent Developments in the Causes and Treatments of Panic Disorder." Psychiatric Grand Rounds, Fair Oaks Hospital, Summit, NJ. April 27, 1988.

Ballenger, JC. "Pharmacotherapy of the Panic Disorders." *J Clin Psychiatry* 47 [6, Suppl] (June 1986), 27–32.

Balon, R, Pohl, R, Yeragani, VK, et al. "Lactate- and Isoproterenol-Induced Panic Attacks in Panic Disorder Patients and Controls." *Psychiatry Research* (1988); 23, 153–160.

Barlow, DH, Blanchard, EB, Vermilyea, JA, et al. "Generalized Anxiety and Generalized Anxiety Disorder: Description and Reconceptualization." *Am J Psychiatry* (January 1986); 143:40–44.

Barlow, DH, DiNardo, PA, Vermilyea, BB, et al. "Co-Morbidity and Depression Among the Anxiety Disorders." *J of Nervous and Mental Disease* (February 1986) vol. 174; no. 2; 63–71.

Barlow, DH, Shear, MK. Foreward to Section I in *Review of Psychiatry: Volume 7.* RE Hales and AJ Frances, eds. Washington: American Psychiatric Press, 1988.

Barlow, DH. "Behavioral Conception and Treatment of Panic." Pharmacology Bulletin (1986); vol. 22, no. 3:802–6.

Barlow, DH. "Current Models of Panic Disorder and a View from Emotion Theory." Chapter 1 in *Review of Psychiatry: Volume 7.* RE Hales and AJ Frances, eds. Washington: American Psychiatric Press, 1988.

Barnett, JE, Barrett, JA, Oxman, TE, Gerber, PD. "The Prevalence of Psychiatry Disorders in a Primary Care Practice." *Arch Gen Psychiatry* (December 1988), 45: 1100–6.

Baron, M. Rainer, JD. "Molecular Genetics and Human Disease: Implications for Modern Psychiatric Research and Practice." *British J of Psychiatry* (1988), 152, 741–53.

Beitman, BD, Mukerji, V, Flaker, G, Basha, IM. "Panic Disorder, Cardiology Patients, and Atypical Chest Pain." *Psychiatric Clinics of North America* (June, 1988), vol. II, no. 2, 387–97.

Benowitz, NL. "Pharmacologic Aspects of Cigarette Smoking and Nicotine Addiction." *NE Journal of Medicine,* November 17, 1988, vol. 319, no. 20, 1318–30.

Berlant, JL, Extein, I, Kirstein, LS, eds. *Guide to the New Medicines of the Mind.* Summit, NJ: PIA Press, 1988.

Bernstein, GA, Garfinkel, BD. "School Phobia: The Overlap of Affective and Anxiety Disorders." *J Amer Acad Child Psychiatry* (1986), 25, 2:235–41.

Birtchnell, J. Evan, C, Kennard, J. "Life History Factors Associated with Neurotic Symptomatology in a Rural Community Sample of 40 to 49-Year-Old Women." *J of Affective Disorders* (1988), 14, 271–85.

Blazer, D, George, LK, Landerman, R, et al. "Psychiatric Disorders: A Rural/Urban Comparison." *Arch Gen Psychiatry* (July, 1985) vol. 42, 651–56.

Boffey, PM. "Publicized Tranquilizer Getting Mixed Reviews." *New York Times.* May 26, 1988; B6.

Bootzin, RR, Acocella, JR. *Abnormal Psychology: Current Perspectives,* 5th Ed., New York: Random House, 1988.

Boulenger, JP, Uhde, TW. "Caffeine Consumption and Anxiety: Preliminary Results of a Survey Comparing Patients with Anxiety Disorders and Normal Controls." *Psychopharmacology Bulletin* (October 1982); vol. 18, no. 4, 53–57.

Bowen, RC, Cipywnyk, D, D'Arcy, C, Keegan, D. "Alcoholism, Anxiety Disorders, and Agoraphobia." *Alcoholism: Clinical and Experimental Research* (January/February 1986) vol. 8, no. 1, 48–50.

Breier, A, Charney, DS, Heninger, GR. "Major Depression in Patients with Agoraphobia and Panic Disorder." *Arch Gen Psychiatry* (Dec 1984), 41: 1129–35.

Breslau, N. Davis, GC, Prabucki, K. "Searching for Evidence on the Validity of Generalized Anxiety Disorder: Psychopathology in Children of Anxious Mothers." *Psychiatric Research,* 20, 285–97.

Brody, JE. "Panic Attacks: The Terror is Treatable." Personal Health Column in *New York Times,* October 19, 1983.

Brownstein, M, Solyom, L. "The Dilemma of Howard Hughes: Paradoxical Behavior in Compulsive Disorders." *Can J Psychiatry* (April 1986), vol. 31, 238–40.

Buigues, J. Vallejo, J. "Therapeutic Response to Phenelzine in Patients with Panic Disorder and Agoraphobia with Panic Attacks." *J Clin Psychiatry* (February 1987) 48: 55–59.

Cameron, OG, Lee, MA, Curtis, GC, McCann, DS. "Endocrine and Physiological Changes During 'Spontaneous' Panic Atacks." *Psychoneuroendocrinology* (1987), vol. 12, no. 5, 321–37.

Cameron, OG. "The Differential Diagnosis of Anxiety Disorders: Psychiatric and Medical Disorders." Symposium on Anxiety Disorders. *Psychiatric Clinics of North America,* vol. 8, no. 1. (March 1985), 3–23.

Cameron, OG, Nesse, RM. "Systemic Hormonal and Physiological Abnormalities in Anxiety Disorders." *Psychoneuroendo* 1988, 13(4); 287–07.

Carr, DB, Sheehan, DV, Surman, OS, et al. "Neuroendocrine Correlates of Lactate-Induced Anxiety and Their Response to Chronic Alprazolam Therapy." *Am J Psychiatry* (April 1986); 143: 483–94.

Charney, DS. "Dysregulation of Noradrenergic Neuronal Systems in Panic Disorders." IV World Congress of Biological Psychiatry. Philadelphia, 1985.

Charney, DS, Goodman, WK, Price, CH, et al. "Serotonin Function in Obsessive-Compulsive Disorder: A Comparison of the Effects of Tryptophan and M-chlorophenylpiperazine in Patients and Healthy Subjects." *Arch Gen Psychiatry* (1988) 45: 177–85.

Charney, DS, Heninger, GR, Jatlow, PI. "Increased Anxiogenic Effects of Caffeine in Panic Disorders." *Arch Gen Psychiatry.* 42 (1985); 233–43.

Charney, DS, Heninger, GR, Redmond, DE. "Yohimbine-Induced Anxiety and Increased Noradrenergic Function in Humans: Effects of Diazepam and Clonidine." *Life Sciences,* vol. 33, no. 1 (1983), 19–29.

Charney, DS, Redmond, DE. "Neurobiological Mechanisms in Human Anxiety: Evidence Supporting Central Noradrenergic Hyperactivity." *Neuropharmacology,* vol. 22, no. 12B (1983), 1533–36.

Charney, DS, Woods, SW, Goodman, WK, et al. "The Drug Treatment of Panic Disorder: The Comparative Efficacy of Imipramine, Alprazolam, and Trazodone." *J Clin Psychiatry* (1986); 47: 580–86.

Charney, DS, Woods, SW, Goodman, WK, Heninger, GR. "Neurobiological Mechanisms of Panic Anxiety." *Am J Psychiatry* (1987); 144: 1030–36.

Cheever, S. *Home Before Dark: A Biographical Memoir of John Cheever.* Boston: Houghton Mifflin Company, 1984.

Ciraulo, DA, Barnhill, JG, Boxenbaum, HG, et al. "Pharmacokinetics and Clinical Effects of Alprazolam Following Single and Multiple Oral Doses in Patients with Panic Disorder." *J Clin Pharmacol* 1986: 26: 292–98.

Cloninger, CR. "Recent Advances in the Genetics of Anxiety and Somatoform Disorders." Chapter 94 in *Psychopharmacology: The Third Generation of Progress.* Edited by Herbert Meltzer. New York: Raven Press 1987.

Clouse, RE. "Anxiety and Gastrointestinal Illness." *Psychiatric Clinics of North America* (June 1988) vol. II, no. 2, 399–417.

Cocores, JA, Davies, RK, Dackis, CA, Gold, MS. "Propranolol and Stuttering." *Am J Psychiatry,* 1986, 143(8): 1071–72.

Cole, JO. "The Drug Treatment of Anxiety and Depression." *Med Clin North America* (1988); 72(4); 815–30.

Coryell, W, Endicott, J, Andreasen, NC, et al. "Depression and Panic Attacks: The Significance of Overlap as Reflected in Follow-up and Family Study Data." *Am J Psychiatry* 145: 3 (March 1988), 293–300.

Coryell, W, Noyes, R Jr, House, JD. "Mortality Among Outpatients with Anxiety Disorders." *Am J Psychiatry* (April 1986); 143: 4; 508–10.

Coryell, W. "Panic Disorder and Mortality." *Psychiatric Clinics of North America* (June, 1988) vol. II, no. 2, 433–39.

Council on Scientific Affairs Report of the Positron Emission Tomography Paniel, "Positron Emission Tomography—A New Approach to Brain Chemistry." *JAMA,* November 11, 1988, 260: 2704–10.

Coursey, RD, Buchsbaum, MS. "The Relationship of Platelet MAO Activity to Psychological Variables Underlying Psychiatric Diagnoses." Platelet MAO

Activity and Psychiatric Diagnoses, pages 97–109 in *Biological Markers in Psychiatry and Neurology*. Usdin, Hanin, eds. New York: Pergamon Press, 1982.

Coursey, RD, Buchsbaum, MS, Murphy, DL. "Two-Year Follow-Up of Subjects and Their Families Defined as at Risk for Psychopathology on the Basis of Platelet MAO Activities." *Neuropsychobiology* (1982) vol. 8, 51–56.

Cowley, DS, Hyde, TS, Dager, SR, Dunner, DL. "Lactate Infusions: The Role of Baseline Anxiety." *Psychiatry Research* (1987), 21, 169–79.

Cowley, DS, Roy-Byrne, PP. "Hyperventilation and Panic Disorder." *The American J of Medicine* (November 1987), vol. 83, 929–37.

Craske, MG. "Cognitive-Behavioral Treatment of Panic." *Review of Psychiatry: Volume 7*. RE Hales and AJ Frances, eds. Washington: American Psychiatric Press, 1988.

Crayton, JW. "Adverse Reactions to Foods: Relevance to Psychiatric Disorders," *J Allergy Clin Immunol* (July 1986); vol. 78, no. 1, part 2; 243–50.

Crowe, RR, Noyes, R Jr. "Panic Disorder and Agoraphobia." *Disease-a-Month* (July 1986); 32(7).

Dackis, CA, Gold, MS, Pottash, ALC, Sweeney, DR. "Evaluating Depression in Alcoholics." *Psychiatry Research,* 1986, 17: 105–9.

Dager, SR, Comess, KA, Saal, AK. Dunner, DL. "Mitral Valve Prolapse in a Psychiatric Setting: Diagnostic Assessment, Research and Clinical Implications." *Integr Psychiatry* (1986); 4: 211–23.

Dager, SR, Holland, JP, Cowley, DS, Dunner, DL. "Panic Disorder Precipitated by Exposure to Organic Solvents in the Work Place." *Am J Psychiatry* (August 1987); 144: 1056–58.

Dager, SR, Khan, A, Comess, KA, et al. "Mitral Valve Prolapse Abnormalities and Catecholamine Activity in Anxious Patients." *Psychiatry Research* (1987); 20, 13–18.

De Moor, W. "The Topography of Agoraphobia." *American J of Pyschotherapy,* vol. XXXVIX, no. 3, July (1985), 371–88.

Demisch, L. Georgi, K, Patzke, B, et al. "Correlation of Platelet MAO Activity with Introversion: A Study on a German Rural Population." *Psychiatry Research* (1982), 6, 303–11.

Diamond, S, Millstein, E. "Current Concepts of Migraine Therapy," *J Clin Pharmacology* (1988); 28; 194.

Dijkman, CIM, deVries, MW. "The Social Ecology of Anxiety: Theoretical and Quantitative Perspectives." *J of Nervous and Mental Disease* vol. 175, no. 19 (1987), 550–57.

Dillon, DJ, Gorman, JM, Liebowitz, MR et al. "Measurement of Lactate-Induced Panic and Anxiety." *Psychiatry Research* (1987), vol. 20, 97–105.

Dwyer, BJ. "Experts Update Management of Phobia, Panic Disorders." *The Psychiatric Times.* February 1988, 34–36. Eaton, WW, Ritter, C. "Distinguishing Anxiety and Depression with Field Survey Data." *Psychological Medicine* (1988), 18, 155–66.

Eisenberg, L. "Mindlessness and Brainlessness in Psychiatry." *British J of Psychiatry,* vol. 148, 1986, 497–508.

Eriksson, E. "Brain Neurotransmission in Panic Disorder." *Acta Psychiatr Scand,* vol. 76, suppl. 335, (1987), 31–37.

Estroff, TW, Gold, MS. "Psychiatric Misdiagnosis." Chapter 2 in *Advances in Psychopharmacology: Predicting and Improving Treatment Response.* MS Gold, RB, Lydiard, JS Carman, eds. Boca Raton, FL: CRC Press, Inc. 1984.

Estroff, TW, Gold, MS. "Medical Evaluation of the Psychiatric Patient." Chapter 2 in *Diagnostic and Laboratory Testing in Psychiatry.* MS Gold and ALC Pottash, eds. New York: Plenum Publishing, 1986.

Estroff, TW, Gold, MS. "Medication-Induced and Toxin-Induced Psychiatric Disorders." Chapter 7 in *Medical Mimics of Psychiatric Disorders.* IL Extein and MS Gold, eds. Washington: American Psychiatric Press, 1986.

Ettedgui, E, Bridges, M. "Posttraumatic Stress Disorder." *Psychiatric Clinics of North America* (March, 1985), vol. 8, no. 1, 89–103.

Evans, L, Kenardy, J, Schneider, Hoey, H. "Effect of a Selective Serotonin Uptake Inhibitor in Agoraphobia with Panic Attacks: A Double-Blind Comparison of Zimeldine, Imipramine, and Placebo." *Acta Psychiatr Scand* 186: 73: 49–53.

Extein, I, Gold, MS, eds. *Medical Mimics of Psychiatric Disorders.* Washington DC: American Psychiatric Press, 1986.

Fabrega, Jr., H. "Psychiatric Diagnosis: A Cultural Perspective." *Journal of Nervous and Mental Disease,* (July, 1987), vol. 175, no. 7, Serial no. 1256, 383–94.

Fava, GA, Kellner, R, Zielezny, M, Grandi, S. "Hypochrondrial Fears and Beliefs in Agoraphobia." *J Affective Disorders* (1988), 14, 239–44.

Fawcett, J, Kravitz, HM. "Anxiety Syndromes and Their Relationship to Depressive Illness." *J Clin Psychiatry.* 44 (1983), 8–11.

Feighner, JP, Boyer, WF, Herbstein, J. "New Antidepressants." *Fair Oaks Hospital Psychiatry Letter* (Spring/Summer 1988); vol. VI, no. 1–6, 1–4.

File, SE. "The Benzodiazepine Receptor and Its Role in Anxiety." *British J of Psychiatry* (1988), 15, 599–600.

Fishman, SM, Sheehan, DV. "Anxiety and Panic: Their Cause and Treatment." *Psychology Today.* April 1985, 26–29.

Foley, MJ. "Portrait of a Disorder: The Hand-Washing Syndrome." *George Street Journal,* September 2, 1987, 5.

Ford, MJ, McMiller, P, Eastwood, J, Eastwood, MA. "Life Events, Psychiatric Illness and the Irritable Bowel Syndrome." *Gut,* vol. 28, (1987), 160–65.

Frances, A, Dunn, P. "The Attachment-Autonomy Conflict in Agoraphobia." *Int J Psycho-Anal.* 56(1975); 435–39.

Freedman, AM. "Psychopharmacology and Psychotherapy in the Treatment of Anxiety." Chapter in *Current Psychiatric Therapies: 1986.* New York: Grune & Stratton, 1986.

Freedman, M. "Post-Vietnam Syndrome: Recognition and Management." *Psychosomatics* (1981); 22(11): 931–43.

Freud, S. "Obsessive Acts and Religious Practices (1907)." Chapter in *Sigmund Freud Character and Culture.* P. Rieff, ed. New York: Collier Books, div. of Macmillan Publishing Co. (1963).

Freud, S. "Turnings in the Ways of Psychoanalytic Therapy (1919)." Reprinted as Chapter 34 in *Collected Papers,* vol. 2. London: Hogarth Press, 1974.

Freud, S. *Introductory Lectures on Psychoanalysis.* Translated and edited by James Strachey. New York: W.W. Norton, 1966.

Friedman, HS, Booth-Kewley, S. "The 'Disease-Prone Personality': A Meta-Analytic View of the Construct." *J of the American Psychological Assoc,* vol. 42, no. 6, June (1987), 539–53.

Friedman, MJ. "Toward Rational Pharmacotherapy for the Posttraumatic Stress Disorder." *Am J Psychiatry* (March 1988) 145: 281–85.

Fuller, RW. "The Brain's Three Catecholamines." *Trends in Pharmaceutical Diseases,* September 4, 1983, 394–97.

Fyer, AJ, Liebowitz, MR, Gorman, JM, et al. "Discontinuation of Alprazolam Treatment in Panic Patients." *Am J Psychiatry* (March 1987); 144: 303–8.

Fyer, AJ, Liebowitz, MR, Gorman, JM, et al. "Lactate Vulnerability of Remitted Panic Patients." *Psychiatry Research.* 14, (1985), 143–48.

Fyer, AJ, Mannuzza, S, Endicott, J. "Differential Diagnosis and Assessment of Anxiety: Recent Developments." Chapter 121 in *Psychopharmacology: The Third Generation of Progress.* HY Meltzer, ed. New York: Raven Press, 1987.

Fyer, AJ, Sandberg, D. "Pharmacologic Treatment of Panic Disorder." Chapter 5 in *Review of Psychiatry: Volume 7.* RE Hales and AJ Frances, eds. Washington: American Psychiatric Press, 1988.

Gaffney, FA, Fenton, BJ, Lane, LD, Lake, CR. "Hemodynamic, Ventilatory and Biochemical Responses of Panic Patients and Normal Controls with Sodium Lactate Infusion and Spontaneous Panic Attacks." *Arch Gen Psychiatry* (January 1988), vol. 45, 53–60.

Gallagher, W. "High Anxiety: More Than a Million Americans Suffer from Obsessive-Compulsive Disorder. At Last, Real Help is Available." *Rolling Stone,* (March 12, 1987), issue 495, 34.

Garssen, B, van Veenendall, E, Bloemink, R. "Agoraphobia and the Hyperventilation Syndrome." *Behav Res Ther* (1983), vol. 21, no. 6, 643–49.

George, DT, Ladenheim, JA, Nutt, DJ. "Effect of Pregnancy on Panic Attacks." *Am J Psychiatry.* 14(1987); 1078–79.

George, DT, Zerby, A, Noble, S, Nutt, D. "Panic Attacks and Alcohol Withdrawal: Can Subjects Differentiate the Symptoms?" *Biol Psychiatry* 1988; 24: 240–43.

Gershon, S, Eison, AE. "The Ideal Anxiolytic." *Psychiatric Annals* (March 1987); 17: 3: 156–70.

Giannini, AJ, ed. *The Biological Foundations of Clinical Psychiatry.* New York: Medical Examination Publishing Company, 1986.

Glanze, WD, Anderson, KN, Anderson, LE, eds. *The Signet/Mosby Medical Encyclopedia.* New York: New American Library, 1985.

Gold, MS, Estroff, TW, Pottash, ALC. "Substance Induced Organic Mental Disorders." Chapter 12 in *Annual Review-Volume 4.* RE Hales and AJ Frances, eds. Washington: American Psychiatric Press, 1985.

Gold, MS, Fox, CF. "Antianxiety and Opiates." *Behavioral and Brain Sciences* 1982, 5(3): 486–87.

Gold, MS, Lydiard, RB, Carman, JS, eds. *Advances in Psychopharmacology: Predicting and Improving Treatment Response.* Boca Raton, FL: CRC Press, 1984.

Gold, MS, Pottash, AC, Extein, I. "Endorphin Dysfunction in Panic Anxiety and Primary Affective Illness." Chapter 20 in *Endorphins and Opiate Antagonists in Psychiatric Research.* Shah, NS, Donald, AG, eds. New York: Plenum Publishing, 1982.

Gold, MS, Pottash, ALC, eds. *Diagnostic and Laboratory Testing in Psychiatry.* New York: Plenum Publishing, 1986.

Gold, MS, Pottash, ALC, Estroff, TW, Extein, I. "Laboratory Evaluation in Treatment Planning." In *The Somatic Therapies,* Part I of *The Psychiatric Therapies,* TB Karasu, ed. APA Commission on Psychiatric Therapies, 1984, 31–50.

Gold, MS, Pottash, ACL, Extein, I, Sweeney, DR. "Diagnosis of Depression in the 1980s." *JAMA* (1981) 245(15): 1562–64.

Gold, MS, Pottash, ALC, Sweeney, DR, et al. "Antimanic, Antidepressant, and Antipanic Effects of Opiates: Clinical, Neuroanatomical, and Biochemical Evidence." *Ann NY Acad Sci* (1982), 398: 140–50.

Gold, MS, Pottash, ALC, Extein, I, et al. "Endorphin Dysfunction in Panic Anxiety and Primary Affective Illness." In *Endorphins and Opiate Antagonists in Psychiatric Research.* NS Shah and AG Donald, eds. New York: Plenum Publishing, 1982. 355–74.

Gold, MS, Pottash, ALC, Sweeney, DR, et al. "Rapid Opiate Detoxification: Clinical Evidence of Antidepressant and Antipanic Effects of Opiates." *Am J Psychiatry* (1979), 136(7): 982–83.

Gold, MS, Redmond, DE Jr. "Pharmacological Activation and Inhibition of Noradrenergic Activity After Specific Behaviors in Nonhuman Primates." *Society of Neuroscience Abstract* (1977), 3(783): 250.

Gold, MS. *The Good News About Depression.* New York: Villard Books, 1987.

Gold, PW, Pigott, TA, Kling, MA, et al. "Basic and Clinical Studies with a Corticotropin-Releasing Hormone: Implications for a Possible Role in Panic Disorder." *Psychiatric Clinics of North America* (June 1988); vol. 11, no. 2: 327–34.

Goldstein, S, Halbreich, U, Asnis, G, et al. "The Hypothalamic-Pituitary-Adrenal System in Panic Disorder." *Am J Psychiatry,* (October, 1987) vol. 144: 10, 1320–23.

Goleman, D. "New Studies Report Health Danger of Repressing Emotional Turmoil." *New York Times,* March 3, 1988; B7.

Goleman, D. "Study Affirms Link of Personality to Illness." *New York Times,* January 19, 1988.

Goleman, D. "Little Fears That Grow With Age." *New York Times,* April 21, 1988, B8.

Goodman, WK. Fluvoxamine in Treatment of OCD. Personal communications, 1988.

Goodman, WK, Price, CH, Heninger, GR, Charney, DS. "Pharmacological Treatment of Obsessive-Compulsive Disorder." APA Symposium (1988), 47F, 190.

Gorman, JM, Liebowitz, MR, Fyer, AJ, et al. "Possible Respiratory Abnormalities in Panic Disorder." *Psychopharmacology Bulletin,* vol. 22, no. 3 (1986), 797–801.

Gorman, JM, Askanazi, J, Liebowitz, MR, et al. "Response to Hyperventilation in a Group of Patients with Panic Disorder." *Am J Psychiatry* (July 1984), 141: 857–61.

Gorman, JM, Davies, M, Steinman, R, et al. "An Objective Marker of Lactate-Induced Panic." *Psychiatry Research* (1987), vol. 22, 341–48.

Gorman, JM, Dillon, D, Fyer, AJ, et al. "The Lactate Infusion Model." *Psychopharmacology Bulletin* (1985), vol. 21, no. 3, 428–33.

Gorman, JM, Fyer, MR, Goetz, R, et al. "Ventilatory Physiology of Patients with Panic Disorder." *Amer Gen Psychiatry* (Jan 1988); 45: 31–39.

Gorman, JM, Fyer, MR, Liebowitz, MR, Klein, DF. "Pharmacologic Provocation of Panic Attacks." Chapter in *Psychopharmacology: The Third Generation of Progress.* Meltze, HY, ed. New York: Raven Press. 1987.

Gorman, JM, Gorman, LK. "Drug Treatment of Social Phobia." *J Affective Disorders* (1987), 13, 183–92.

Gorman, JM, Liebowitz, MR, Fyer, AJ, et al. "Lactate Infusions in Obsessive-Compulsive Disorder." *Am J Psychiatry* (July 1985); 142: 864–66.

Gorman, JM, Liebowitz, MR, Dillon, D, et al. "Antipanic Drug Effects During Lactate Infusion in Lactate-Refractory Panic Patients." *Psychiatry Research,* 21 (1986), 205–12.

Gorman, JM, Shear, MK, Devereux, RB, et al. "Prevalence of Mitral Valve Prolapse in Panic Disorder: Effect of Echocardiographic Criteria." *Psychosomatic Medicine* (March/April 1986); vol. 48; no. 3–4; 167–70.

Gottlieb, SH. "Mitral Valve Prolapse." *Am J Cardiol* (December 28, 1987); 60: 53J–58J.

Gray, B. "Some Haunting Memories of Stage Fright." *Los Angeles Times,* October 31, 1985; section 6, page 1.

Greenblatt, D, Shader, R, Abernathy, D. "Current Status of Benzodiazepines." *N Engl J Med* 309(1983): 354–59; 410–15 (second of two parts).

Greene, R. "The Mellow Market," *Forbes,* October 31, 1988, 106.

Greist, JH, Jefferson, JW, Marks, IM. *Anxiety and its Treatment: Help Is Available.* New York: Warner Books, 1987.

Griez, E, van den Hout, MA, "CO₂ Inhalation in the Treatment of Panic Attacks." *Behav Res Ther;* vol. 24, no. 2, 145–50.

Gross, DA, Extein, I, Gold, MS. "The Psychiatrist as Physician." Chapter 1 in *Medical Mimics of Psychiatric Disorders.* I Extein and MS Gold, eds. Washington: APA Press, 1986, 1–12.

Hall, CS. *A Primer of Freudian Psychology.* New York: New American Library, 1954.

Hamlin, CL, Dackis, CA, Martin D. et al. "Blunted Thyrotropin Releasing Hormone Stimulation Test in Panic Disorder." APA Abstract (1984), 13: 231.

Hamlin, CL, Gold, MS. "Anxiolytic: Predicting Response/Maximizing Efficacy." Chapter 9 in *Advances in Psychopharmacology: Predicting and Improving Treatment Response.* MS Gold, RB, Lydiard, JS Carman, eds. Boca Raton, FL: CRC Press, Inc. 1984.

Hamlin, CL, Lydiard, RB, Martin D. et al. "Urinary Excretion of Noradrenaline Metabolite Decreased in Panic Disorder." *Lancet,* 1983, 2(8352): 740–41.

Hamlin, CL, Pottash, ALC. "Evaluation of Anxiety Disorders." Chapter 16 in *Diagnostic and Laboratory Testing in Psychiatry.* MS Gold and ALC Pottash, eds. New York: Plenum Publishing, 1986.

Hanson, Kitty, "Why Live with Your Fears When You Can Overcome Them?" New York *Daily News* 1981, reprinted by permission in *Woman,* September 1982, 40–42.

Hays, PE, Dommisse, CS. "Current Concepts in Clinical Therapeutics: Anxiety Disorders, Part 1." *Clinical Pharmacy,* vol. 6, February, 1987.

Herman, JB, Brotman, AW, Rosenbaum, JF. "Rebound Anxiety in Panic Disorder Patients Treated with Shorter-Acting Benzodiazepines." *J Clin Psychiatry* (October 1987) 48: 10 (Suppl), 22–28.

Herman, R. "Nocturnal Panic in a Depressed Patient: Pathophysiological Implications." *Biol Psychiatry* (1988); 24: 432–36.

Herrington, BS. "Clomipramine May Be Approved for Use in Selected Patients." *Psychiatric News,* June 3, 1988. p. 4.

Hibbert, G, Pilsbury, D. "Hyperventilation in Panic Attacks: Ambulant Monitoring of Transcutaneous Carbon Dioxide." *Brit J Psychiatry,* (1988) 153, 76–80.

Himadi, WG, Boice, R, Barlow, DH. "Assessment of Agoraphobia—II: Measurement of Clinical Change." *Behav Res Ther* (1986); vol. 24, no. 3, 321–32.

Hoehn-Saric, R, McLeod, DR. "Generalized Anxiety Disorder." *Psychiatric Clinics of North America* (March 1985), vol. 8, no. 1, 73–87.

Hoehn-Saric, R, McLeod, DR. "The Peripheral Sympathetic Nervous System: Its Role in Normal and Pathologic Anxiety." *Psychiatric Clinics of North America* (June 1988); vol. 11, no. 2: 375–86.

Hoehn-Saric, R. "Pharmacotherapy of Generalized Anxiety." Presentation for the Annual Meeting of the American Psychiatric Association, Chicago, May 1987.

Holden, S. "Carly Simon Triumphs Over Her Own Panic." *New York Times.* June 17, 1987, C19.

Hollander, E, Fay, M, Cohen, B, et al. "Serotonergic and Noradrenergic Sensitivity in Obsessive-Compulsive Disorder: Behavioral Findings." *Am J Psychiatry* 145: 8 (August 1988) 1015–17.

Hollister, LE. "Anxiety: Drug Treatments for Biologically Determined Disorders." Rational Drug Therapy (April 1986), vol. 20, no. 4, 1–6.

Hollister, LE. "Pharmacotherapeutic Considerations in Anxiety Disorders." *J Clin Psychiatry* 47 [6, Suppl] (June 1986), 33–36.

Hollister, LE. "New Antidepressants: Weighing the Pros and Cons." *Drug Therapy* (March, 1986) 133–40.

Hu, SS. "P.E.T. Scans Hint Panic Attack Traces to a Cerebral Focus." *Medical Tribune.* February 2, 1985.

Huang, YH, Redmond, DE Jr, Synder, DR, Maas, JW. "In Vivo Location and Destruction of the Locus Coeruleus in the Stumptail Macaque (Macaca arctoides)." *Brain Research* (1975), 100; 157–62.

Humble, M. "Aetiology and Mechanisms of Anxiety Disorders." *Acta Psychiatr Scand* (1987), vol. 76, suppl. 335, 15–30.

Insel, TR. "Obsessive-Compulsive Disorder." *Psychiatric Clinics of North America* (March 1985), vol. 8, no. 1, 105–17.

Jacob, RG, Turner, SM. "Panic Disorder: Diagnosis and Assessment." Chapter 4 in *Review of Psychiatry: Volume 7.* RE Hales and AJ Frances, eds. Washington: American Psychiatric Press, 1988.

Jacobsen, FM, Wehr, TA, Skwerer, RA, et al. "Morning Versus Midday Phototherapy of Seasonal Affective Disorder." *Am J Psychiatry* (October, 1987) vol. 144: 10, 1301–5.

Jefferson, JW. "Biologic Systems and Their Relationship to Anxiety: Summary." *Psychiatric Clinics of North America* (June 1988), vol. 11, no. 2: 463–72.

Jefferson, JW. "Beta-Adrenergic Receptor Blocking Drugs in Psychiatry." *Arch Gen Psychiatry.* (1976); 133; 1389–94.

Jenike, MA, Baer, L. "Behavior Therapy Techniques in Treating OCD." *The Psychiatric Times,* August 1988; page 1, continued on 15–17.

Jenike, MA. "Obsessive-Compulsive Disorders: Treatment with Drugs, ECT, and Psychiatric Surgery." *The Psychiatry Times,* July 1988. Vol V, no. 7.

Johnson, G. "Scientists Identify 'Gate' in Brain as Crucial to Memory." *New York Times* (May 10, 1988), C1.

Kahn, JP, Gorman, JM, King, DL, et al. "Increased Variance of Cardiac Size in Panic Disorder." Paper presented at the American Psychiatric Association Annual Meeting, San Francisco, May 1989.

Kahn, RS, van Praag, HM, Wetzler, S, et al. "Serotonin and Anxiety Revisted." *Biol Psychiatry* (1988); 23: 189–208.

Kathol, RG, Delahunt, JW. "The Relationship of Anxiety and Depression to Symptoms of Hyperthyroidism Using Operational Criteria." *General Hospital Psychiatry* (1986) vol. 8, 23–28.

Kathol, RG, Noyes, Jr., R, Lopez, AL, Reich, JH. "Relationship of Urinary Free Cortisol Levels in Patients with Panic Disorder to Symptoms of Depression and Agoraphobia." *Psychiatry Research* (1987), vol. 24, 211–21.

Kathol, RG, Noyes, R, Lopez, A. "Similarities in Hypothalamic-Pituitary-Adrenal Axis Activity Between Patients with Panic Disorder and Those Experiencing External Stress." *Psychiatric Clinics of North America* (June 1988), vol. 11, no. 2, 335–47.

Karno, M, Golding, JM, Sorenson, SB, Burnam, A. "The Epidemiology of Obsessive-Compulsive Disorder in *Five* U.S. Communities." *Arch Gen Psychiatry,* December 1988, 45: 1094–99.

Katon, W. "Unexplained Cardiac Symptoms May Be Related to Panic." *The Psychiatric Times,* August, 1988, 21–22.

Kauffman, CD, Reist, C, Djenderedijian, A, et al. "Biological Markers of Affective Disorders and Posttraumatic Stress Disorder: A Pilot Study with Desipramine." *J Clin Psychiatry* (Sept 1988); 48: 366–67.

Kendler, KS, Heath, AC, Martin, NG, Eaves, LJ. "Symptoms of Anxiety and Symptoms of Depression: Same Genes, Different Environments?" *Arch Gen Psychiatry,* vol. 44, May 1987, 451–57.

Klein, DF, Ross, DC, Cohen, P. "Panic and Avoidance in Agoraphobia: Application of Path Analysis to Treatment Studies." *Arch Gen Psychiatry* (April 1987), vol. 44: 377–85.

Klein, DF. "Anxiety Reconceptualized." In *Anxiety: New Research and Changing Concepts."* DF Klein and J Rabkin, eds. New York: Raven: 1981.

Klein, DF. "Medication in the Treatment of Panic Attacks and Phobic States." *Psychopharmacology Bulletin* (1982); 18: 85–90.

Klein, DF, Zitrin, CM, Woerner, MG. "Imipramine and Phobia." *Psychopharmacology Bulletin,* (1977); 13: 24–27.

Klein, DF. "Panic Attacks and Agoraphobia." The Expert Speaks supported through an education grant from Merrell Dow Pharmaceuticals, Cincinnati, OH.

Klein, DF. "Importance of Psychiatric Diagnosis in Prediction of Clinical Drug Affects." *Arch Gen Psychiatry* (1967), 16: 118–26.

Klerman, GL. "Overview of the Cross-National Collaborative Panic Study." *Arch Gen Psychiatry* (May 1988), 45: 407–12.

Klien, E, Uhde, TW. "Controlled Study of Verapamil for Treatment of Panic Disorder." *Am J Psychiatry* (April 1988), vol. 145: 4, 431–34.

Ko, GN, Elsworth, JD, Roth, RH, et al. "Panic-Induced Elevation of Plasma MHPG Levels in Phobic-Anxious Patients: Effects of Clonidine and Imipramine." *Arch Gen Psychiatry.* (April 1983); 40: 425–30.

Konner, M. "New Keys to the Mind." *The New York Times Magazine,* July 17, 1988, 49–50.

Kumar, R, Mac, DS, Gabrielli, WF Jr, Goodwin, DW. "Anxiolytics and Memory: A Comparison of Lorazepam and Alprazolam." *J Clin Psychiatry* (April 1987) 48: 158–60.

Langer, SF, Feighner, JP, Pambakian, R, et al. "Pilot Study of Alpidem, a Novel Imidazopyridine Compound, in Anxiety." *Psychopharmacology Bulletin,* vol. 24, no. 1, 1988.

Leckman, JF, Gershon, ES, Murphy, DL, paper presented at the APA annual convention at Miami Beach on MAO Levels in patients and relatives of manic depressive.

Lee, JE. "Affective Disorders and Molecular Genetics." *Abbot Diagnostic Ed-*

ucational Services' Diagnostic Update: Mental Illness and Neurological Disorders. vol. 2, no. 5, 5–7.

Lee, MA, Cameron, OG, Greden, JF. "Anxiety and Caffeine Consumption in People with Anxiety Disorders." *Psychiatry Research* (1985), 15, 211–17.

Leonard, H, Swedo, S, et al. "Treatment of Childhood Obsessive-Compulsive Disorder with Clomipramine and Desmethylimipramine: A Double-Blind Crossover Comparison." *Psychopharmacology Bulletin,* 1988, vol. 24, no. 1, 93–95.

Lesser, IM, Rubin, RT, Lydiard, RB, et al. "Past and Current Thyroid Function in Subjects with Panic Disorder." *J Clin Psychiatry* 48: 12 (December 1987), 473–76.

Lesser, IM, Rubin, RT, Pecknold, JC, et al. "Secondary Depression in Panic Disorder and Agoraphobia: I. Frequency, Severity, and Response to Treatment." *Arch Gen Psychiatry.* Vol. 45 (May 1988), 437–43.

Lesser, IM, Rubin, RT. "Diagnostic Consideration in Panic Disorders." *J Clin Psychiatry* 47 [6, Suppl] (June 1986), 4–10.

Levin, AP, Liebowitz, MR. "Drug Treatment of Phobias: Efficacy and Optimum Use." *Drugs* 34: 504–14 (1987).

Liebowitz, MR, Fyer, AJ, Gorman, J, Klein, DF. "Recent Developments in the Understanding and Pharmacotherapy of Panic Attacks." *Psychopharmacology Bulletin,* vol. 22, no. 3, 1986, 792–96.

Liebowitz, MR, Fyer, AJ, Gorman, JM, et al. "Lactate Provocation of Panic Attacks." *Arch Gen Psychiatry,* vol. 41, August 1984, 764–69.

Liebowitz, MR, Fyer, AJ, McGrath, P, Klein, DF. "Clonidine Treatment of Panic Disorder." *Psychopharmacology Bulletin,* (1981), 17: 122–23.

Liebowitz, MR, Gorman, JM, Fyer, A, et al. "Possible Mechanisms for Lactate's Induction of Panic." *Am J Psychiatry.* 143: 4 (April 1986). 495–502.

Liebowitz, MR, Gorman, JM, Fyer, AJ, et al. "Lactate Provocation of Panic Attacks: II. Biochemical and Physiological Findings." *Arch Gen Psychiatry* (July 1985); 42: 702–19.

Liebowitz, MR, Klein, DF. "Assessment and Treatment of Phobic Anxiety." *J Clin Psychiatry* (November 1979) 40: 486–92.

Liebowitz, MR, "DSM-III-R Anxiety Classification: Impact on Psychopharmacology Clinical Trials." *Psychopharmacology Bulletin* (1988). Vol. 24, no. 1, 21–24.

Liebowitz, MR. "Antidepressants in Panic Disorder." *British Journal of Psychiatry* (1989), 155 (suppl. 6), 46–52.

Liebowitz, MR. "Panic Disorders Update." *Fair Oaks Hospital Psychiatry Letter.* (May 1986), vol. IV, no. 5; 25–28.

Lindemann, CG, Zitrin, CM, Klein, DF. "Thyroid Dysfunction in Phobic Patients." *Psychosomatics* (August 1984), vol. 25, no. 8, 603–6.

Lindenbaum, J, Healton, EB, Savage, DG, et al. "Neuropsychiatric Disorders Caused by Cobalamin Deficiency in the Absence of Anemia or Macrocytosis." *New England J of Medicine* (June 30, 1988), vol. 318, no. 26, 1720–28.

Lustman, PJ. "Anxiety Disorders in Adults with Diabetes Mellitus. *Psychiatric Clinics of North America* (June 1988); vol. 11, no. 2: 419–32.

Lydiard, RB, Ballenger, JC. "Antidepressants in Panic Disorder and Agoraphobia." *J Affective Disorders* (1987), 13, 153–68.

Lydiard, RB, Pottash, ALC, Gold, MS. "Speed of Onset of Action of the Newer

Antidepressants." *Psychopharmacologic Bulletin,* 1984, 20(2): 258–71.

Margraf, J, Ehlers, A, Roth, WT. "Biological Models of Panic Disorder and Agoraphobia—A Review." *Behav. Res. Ther.,* vol. 24, no. 5, (1986), 553–67.

Marks, IM, Lelliott, P, Basoglu, M, et al. "Clomipramine, Self-Exposure and Therapist-Aided Exposure for Obsessive-Compulsive Rituals." *British J Psychiatry* (1988), 152, 522–34.

Marks, IM. "Epidemiology of Anxiety." *Soc Psychiatry* (1986) 21: 167–71. Summary of chapter in Marks, IM. *Fears, Phobias and Rituals.* New York: Oxford University Press (1987).

Marks, IM. "Genetics of Fear and Anxiety Disorder." *British J Psychiatry* (1986), 149, 406–18.

Marks, IM. *Living with Fear: Understanding and Coping with Anxiety.* New York: McGraw-Hill, 1978.

Mavissakalian M, Salerni, R, Thompson, ME, Michelson, L. "Mitral Valve Prolapse and Agoraphobia." *Am J Psychiatry* (December 1983); 140: 1612–14. McFarlane, AC. "The Aetiology of Post-traumatic Stress Disorders Following a Natural Disaster." *British J of Psychiatry* (1988), 152, 116–21.

Mavissakalian, M, Michelson, L, Dealy, RS. "Pharmacological Treatment of Agoraphobia: Imipramine Versus Imipramine with Programmed Practice." *Brit J Psychiat* (1983), 143, 348–55.

McDaniel, KD. "Clinical Pharmacology of Monoamine Oxidase Inhibitors." *Clinical Neuropharmacology* (1987). vol. 9, no. 3: 207–34.

McGrath, PJ, Stewart, JW, Harrison, W, et al. "Lactate Infusion in Patients with Panic and Anxiety." *Psychopharmacology Bulletin* (1985), vol. 21, no. 3, 555–57.

Meibach, RC, Dunner, D, Wilson, LG, et al. "Comparative Efficacy of Propranolol, Chlordiazepoxide and Placebo in the Treatment of Anxiety: A Double-Blind Trial." *J Clin Psychiatry* (September 1987), vol. 48: 9, 355–58.

Meyer, BC. "Notes on Flying and Dying." *Psychoanalytic Quarterly,* LII, 1983, 327–51.

Michelson, L, Mavissakalian, M, Marchione, K. "Cognitive and Behavioral Treatments of Agoraphobia: Clinical, Behavioral, and Psychophysiological Outcomes." *J of Consulting and Clinical Psychology* (1985), vol. 53, no. 6, 913–25.

Modell, JG, Mountz, JM, Curtis, GC. "Positron Emission Tomographic Evaluation of Cerebral Blood Flow During State-Anxiety." Presented at the American Psychiatric Association Annual Meeting, Montreal, May 12, 1988.

Mohl, PC. "Should Psychotherapy Be Considered A Biological Treatment." *Psychosomatics,* vol. 28, no. 6 (June 1987), 320–26.

Montz, JM, Modell, JG, Wilson, MW, et al. "Positron Emission Tomographic Evaluation of Cerebral Blood Flow During State Anxiety in Simple Phobia." *Archives of General Psychiatry* (June 1989) vol 46, 501–504.

Mullaney, JA, Trippert, CJ. "Alcohol Dependence and Phobias; Clinical Description and Relevance." *J Psychiatry* (1979) 135: 565–73.

Munjack, DJ, Moss, HB. "Affective Disorder and Alcoholism in Families of Agoraphobics." *Arch Gen Psychiatry* (August 1981) vol. 38, 869–71.

Norman, TR, Burrows, GD. "Anxiety and the Benzodiazepine Receptor." In *Progress in Brain Research.* JM van Ree and S Matthysse, eds. Vol 65, Elsevier Science Publishers, 1986.

Noyes, R Jr, Crowe, RR, Harris, EL, et al. "Relationships Between Panic Disorder and Agoraphobia: A Family Study." *Arch Gen Psychiatry* (March 1986); 43: 227–232.

Noyes, R Jr. "Beta-Adrenergic Blocking Drugs in Anxiety and Stress." *Psychiatric Clinics of North America* (March 1985); vol. 8, no. 1, 119–32.

Noyes, R Jr. "Drug Treatment of Anxiety Disorders: Update 1987." *J Affective Disorders:* Update 1987. 13 (1987), 95–98.

Öst, LG, Hugdahl, K. "Acquisition of Agoraphobia, Mode of Onset and Anxiety Response Patterns." *Behav Res Ther* (1983), vol. 21, no. 6, 623–31.

Palumbo, JM. Evaluation and treatment of Panic Disorder and OCD. Personal communication.

Papp, LA, Gorman, JM, Liebowitz, MR, et al. "Epinephrine Infusion in Patients with Social Phobia." *Am J Psychiatry* 145: 6 (June 1988), 733–36.

Paul, SM, Skolnick, P. "The Biochemistry of Anxiety: From Pharmacotherapy to Pathophysiology." In *Psychiatric Update-Volume III.* L. Grinspoon, ed. Washington: American Psychiatric Press, 1984.

Pecknold, JC, Swinson, RP. "Alprazolam in Panic Disorder and Agoraphobia." *Am J Psychiatry* (March 1987) 144: 3: 303–8.

Perris, H, von Knorring, L, Oreland, L, Perris, C. "Life Events and Biological Vulnerability: A Study of Life Events and Platelet MAO Activity in Depressed Patients." *Psychiatry Research,* vol. 12, 111–20.

Physicians' Desk Reference. 42nd edition. Oradell, NJ: Medical Economics Company, Inc. 1988.

Pines, M. "When Your Body Is Afraid." *American Health,* June 1984.

Pohl, R, Berchou, R. Rainey, JM Jr. "Tricyclic Antidepressants and Monoamine Oxidase Inhibitors in the Treatment of Agoraphobia." *J Clin Psychopharmacol* (1982), vol. 2, no. 6, 399–406.

Popkin, MK, Callies, AL, Lentz, RD, et al. "Prevalence of Major Depression, Simple Phobia, and Other Psychiatric Disorders in Patients with Long-Standing Type I Diabetes Mellitus." *Arch Gen Psychiatry* (January 1988); 45: 64–68.

Porro, CA, Facchinetti, F, Bertellini, E, et al. "Beta-Lipotropin Is the Major Component of the Plasma Opioid Response to Surgical Stress in Humans." *Life Sciences* (1987), vol. 41, 2581–88.

Rafuls, WA, Extein, I, Gold, MS, Goggans, FC. "Neuropsychiatric Aspects of Endocrine Disorders." In *Textbook of Neuropsychiatry.* RE Hales and SC Yudofsky, eds. Washington: American Psychiatric Press, 1987, 307–25.

Rahe, R. "Anxiety and Physical Illness." *Journal of Clinical Psychiatry* (October, 1988), vol 49, no. 10, 26–29.

Rainey, JM, Nesse, RM. "Psychobiology of Anxiety and Anxiety Disorders." Psychiatric Clinics of North America (March 1985), vol. 8, no. 1, 133–43.

Rea, WS, Extein, IL, Gold, MS. "Biological Markers." Chapter 6 in *Issues in Diagnostic Research,* CG Last & M Hersen, eds. New York: Plenum Press 1987.

Redmond, DE, Jr. Huant, YH, Baulu, J, Gold, MS. "Evidence for the Involvement of a Brain Norepinephrine System in Anxiety." In *Catecholamines: Basic and Clinical Frontiers.* E. Usdin, I. Kopin, J. Barchas, eds. New York: Pergamon Press. 1979, 2: 1693–95.

Redmond, DE, Jr, Hwang, Y, Gold, MS. "Anxiety: The Locus Coeruleus Connection." *Society of Neuroscience Abstract* (1977) 3: 258.

Redmond, DE, Jr. "Clonidine and the Primate Locus Coeruleus: Evidence

Suggesting Anxiolytic and Anti-Withdrawal Effects." Chapter in *Psychopharmacology of Clonidine.* New York: Alan R. Liss, Inc. (1981).

Redmond, DE Jr. "Studies of the Nucleus Locus Coeruleus in Monkeys and Hypotheses for Neuropsychopharmacology." Chapter 95 in *Psychopharmacology: The Third Generation of Progress.* HY Meltzer, ed. New York: Raven Press 1987.

Reich, J. The Epidemiology of Anxiety. *J of Nervous and Mental Disease.* vol. 174, no. 3 (March 1986), 129–36.

Reiman, EM, Raichle, ME, Robins, E, et al. "The Application of Positron Emission Tomography to the Study of Panic Disorder." *Am J Psychiatry* (April 1986), vol. 143: 4: 469–77.

Reiman, EM, Raichle, ME, Robins, E, et al. "Neuroanatomical Correlates of a Lactate-Induced Anxiety Attack." *Archives of General Psychiatry* (June 1989) vol 46, 493–499.

Reiman, EM. "The Quest to Establish the Neural Substrates of Anxiety." *Psychiatric Clinics of North America* (June 1988); vol. 11, no. 2: 295–307.

Rickels, K, Schweizer, EE. "Current Pharmacotherapy of Anxiety and Panic." Chapter 122 in *Psychopharmacology: The Third Generation of Progress.* HY Meltzer, ed. New York: Raven Press, 1987.

Rifkin, A, Klein, DF, Dillon, D. "Blockade by Imipramine or Desipramine of Panic Induced by Sodium Lactate." *Am J Psychiatry* (1981); 138(5): 676–77.

Riskind, JH, Beck, AT, Brown, G, Steer, RA. "Taking the Measure of Anxiety and Depression: Validity of the Reconstructed Hamilton Scales." *J of Nervous and Mental Disease,* (1987), 474–79.

Robinson, DS, Nies, A, Ravaris, CL, et al. "Clinical Pharmacology of Phenelzine." *Arch Gen Psychiatry* (May 1978), vol. 35.

Rose, RJ, Miller, JZ, Pogue-Geile, MF, Cardwell, GF. "Twin-Family Studies of Common Fears and Phobias." Pages 169–74 in *Twin Research 3: Intelligence, Personality and Developments.* New York: Alan R. Liss, Inc., 1981.

Rosenbaum, JF, Biederman, J, Gertsen, M, et al. "Behavioral Inhibition in Children of Parents with Panic Disorder and Agoraphobia." *Arch Gen Psych* (May 1988), 45: 463–70.

Roy-Byrne, PP, Mellman, TA, Uhde, TW. "Biologic Findings in Panic Disorder: Neuroendocrine and Sleep-Related Abnormalities." *J of Anxiety Disorders* (1988), vol. 2, 17–29.

Roy-Byrne, PP, Uhde, TW, Gold, PW, et al. "Neuroendocrine Abnormalities in Panic Disorder." *Psychopharmacology Bulletin* (1985), 21: 546–50.

Royner, S. "Understanding the Fear of People." *Washington Post,* January 13, 1987. P17.

Rubinow, DR, Roy-Byrne, PP. "Premenstrual Syndrome: Overview from a Methodologic Perspective." *Am J Psychiatry* (1984), 141: 163–72.

Rudorfer, MV, Potter, WZ. "The New Generation of Antidepressants." In press (submitted to *Treatment of Tricyclic Resistant Depression.* Extein, I, ed. APA Press Progress in Psychiatric Series).

Sarason, IG. "Anxiety, Self-Preoccupation and Attention." *Anxiety Research,* 1988, vol. 1, 3–7.

Saravay, SM, Marke, J, Steinberg, MD, Rabiner, CJ. " 'Doom Anxiety' and Delirium in Lidocaine Toxicity." *Am J Psychiatry* (February 1987); 144: 159–163.

Sarnoff, D, with Moore, G. *Never Be Nervous Again.* New York: Crown Publishers, 1987.

Sattaur, O. "Breathing Correctly Stops Agoraphobic Panic." *New Scientist,* February 28, 1985, 22.

Schatzberg, AF, Cole, JO. *Handbook of Clinical Psychopharmacology.* Washington: American Psychiatric Press, 1986.

Schatzberg, AF, Dessain, E, O'Neil, P, et al. "Recent Studies on Selective Serotonergic Antidepressants: Trazodone, Fluoxetine, Fluvoxamine." *J Clin Psychopharmacol* (1987) 7: 445–95.

Schmidt, SB. "Mitral Valve Prolapse: Practical Aspects of Diagnosis and Management." *Postgraduate Medicine* (April 1988); vol. 83, no. 5: 225–28.

Seagrave, A. Covington, F. *Free From Fears: New Help for Anxiety, Panic and Agoraphobia.* New York: Poseidon Press, 1987.

Shader, R. Goodman, M, Giver, M. "Panic Disorder: Current Perspectives." *J Clin Psychopharmacol* (1982), 2(6S): 2S–10S.

Sharfstein, SS. "The Economics of Anxiety. Consequences of Anxiety: Management Strategies for the Primary Care Physician." A clinical monograph based on a symposium held October 8–11, 1987, in Orlando, Florida, and supported by a grant from The Upjohn Company.

Shear, MK, Fyer, MR. "Biological and Psychopathologic Findings in Panic Disorder." Chapter 2 in *Review of Psychiatry: Volume 7.* RE Hales and AJ Frances, eds. Washington: American Psychiatric Press, 1988.

Shear, MK. "Pathophysiology of Panic: A Review of Pharmacologic Provocative Tests and Naturalistic Monitoring Data." *J Clin Psychiatry* 47 [6, Suppl] (June 1986), 18–26.

Sheehan, DV, Carr, DB, Fishman, SM, et al. "Lactate Infusion in Anxiety Research: Its Evolution and Practice." *J Clin Psychiatry* (May 1985), 46: 5: 158–65.

Sheehan, DV, Coleman, JH, Greenblatt, DJ, et al. "Some Biochemical Correlates of Panic Attacks with Agoraphobia and Their Response to a New Treatment." *J Clin Psychopharmacol* (April 1984), vol. 4, no. 2, 66–75.

Sheehan, DV, Davidson, J, Manschreck, T, Van Wyck Fleet, J. "Lack of Efficacy of a New Antidepressant (Buproprion) in the Treatment of Panic Disorder with Phobias." *J Clin Psychopharmacology* (February 1983), vol. 3: 28–31.

Sheehan, DV, Sheehan, KH. "Pharmacological Treatment of Panic and Anxiety Disorders." *ISI Atlas of Science Pharmacology,* 1987, 254–56.

Sheehan, DV. "Monoamine Oxidase Inhibitors and Alprazolam in the Treatment of Panic Disorder and Agoraphobia." *Psychiatric Clinics of North America* (March 1985), vol. 8, no. 1, 46–62.

Sheehan, DV. *The Anxiety Disease.* New York: Bantam Books, 1986.

Speigel, D, Hunt, T, Dondershine, HE. "Dissociation and Hypnotizability in Posttraumatic Stress Disorder." *Am J Psychiatry* (March 1988), 145: 301–5.

Simon, P, Soubrie, P, Wildlocher, D. *Selected Models of Anxiety, Depression and Psychosis.* Volume 1 of *Animal Models of Psychiatric Disorders.* Basel: Krager, 1988.

Siwolop, Sana, with Evert Clark. "What's Everybody So Afraid Of? Almost Anything." *Business Week,* April 21, 1986, 44–46.

Slaby, AE, Lieb, J, Tancredi, LR. *Handbook of Psychiatric Emergencies,* 2nd edition. Garden City, New York: Medical Examination Publishing (1975).

Sobel, D. "For Stage Fright, A Remedy Proposed," *New York Times* (November 20, 1979), C1.

Solomon, HS, Chilnick, LD. *Beat the Odds.* New York: Villard Books, 1986.

Spitzer, R. "New Approaches to Classification." Panic Disorders Clinical Update. Presented at the 137th Annual Meeting of the American Psychiatric Association, Los Angeles, Abstr 12B, May 1984.

Starkstein, SE, Robinson, RG, Berthier, ML, et al. "Differential Mood Changes Following Basal Ganglia vs Thalamic Lesions." *Arch Neurol* (July 1988), 45: 725–30.

Stavrakaki, C, Vargo, B. "The Relationship of Anxiety and Depression: A Review of the Literature." *British J of Psychiatry,* vol. 149, (1986), 7–16.

Stein, M, Keller, SE, Schleifer, SJ. "Immune System: Relationship to Anxiety Disorders." *Psychiatric Clinics of North America* (June 1988), vol. 11, no. 2: 349–60.

Stein, MB, Shea, CA, Uhde, TW. "Social Phobic Symptoms in Patients With Panic Disorder: Practical and Theoretical Implications." Submitted to *The American Journal of Psychiatry* as a Brief Communication, March 1988.

Stein, MB. "Panic Disorder and Medical Illness." *Psychosomatics* (December 1986), vol. 27, no. 12, 833–38.

Stillman, RC, Wyatt, RJ, Murphy, DL, Rauxhcer, FP. "Low Platelet Monoamine Oxidase Activity and Chronic Marijuana Use." *Life Sciences* (1978), vol. 23: 1577–82.

Stockwell, T, Smail, P, Hodgson, R, Canter, S. "Alcohol Dependence and Phobic Anxiety States: II. A Retrospective Study." *Brit J Psychiatry* (1984), 144, 58–63.

Stone, E, ed. *American Psychiatric Glossary,* 6th edition. Washington: American Psychiatric Press, 1988.

Sullivan, JL, Cavenar Jr., JO, Maltbie, AA, et al. "Familial Biochemical and Clinical Correlates of Alcoholics with Low Platelet Monoamine Oxidase Activity." *Biological Psychiatry* (1979), vol. 14, no. 2.

Sussman, N. "Treatment of Anxiety with Buspirone." *Psychiatric Annals* (February 1987), vol. 17: 2, 114–20.

Swedo, SE, Schapiro, MB, Grady, CL, et al. "Cerebral Glucose Metabolism in Child-Onset Obsessive-Compulsive Disorder." *Archives of General Psychiatry* (June 1989) vol 46, 518–523.

Sweeney, DR, Gold, MS, Pottash, ALC, Martin, D. "Plasma Levels of Tricyclic Antidepressants in Panic Disorder." *Int J Psychiatry Med,* 1983, 13(2): 93–96.

Sweeney, DR, Gold, MS, Martin, DM, et al. "Opiate Withdrawal and Panic Anxiety." *APA Abstract* (1980) 49: 123–24.

Sweeney, DR, Gold, MS, Pottash, ALC, Davies, RK. "Neurobiological Theories." In *The Handbook of Stress and Anxiety: Current Knowledge, Theory, and Treatment.* IL Kutash and LB Schlessinger, eds. San Francisco: Jossey Bass, 1980, 112–22.

Sweeney, DR, Gold, MS, Pottash, ALC, Martin, D. "Plasma Levels of Tricyclic Antidepressants in Panic Disorder." *Int'l J Psychiatry in Medicine* (1983–84), vol. 13(2): 93–96.

Swenson, TH. "Peripheral, Autonomic Regulation of Locus Coeruleus Noradrenergic Neurons in Brain: Putative Implications for Psychiatry and Psychopharmacology." *Psychopharmacology* (1982) 92: 1–7.

Tavris, C. "Coping with Anxiety." *Science Digest,* February, 1986. 46–81.

Tearnan, BH, Telch, MJ, Keefe, P. "Etiology and Onset of Agoraphobia: A Critical Review." *Comprehensive Psychiatry* (January/February 1984), vol. 25, no. 1, 51–62.

Telch, MJ, Tearnan, BH, Taylor, CB. "Antidepressant Medication in the Treatment of Agoraphobia: A Critical Review." *Behav Res Ther* (1983), vol. 21, no. 5, 505–17.

"Thirty-five-Year Follow-Up Study Finds Severe Anxiety Best Masker for Future Disease." *Psychiatric News,* September 2, 1988.

Thyer, BA, Parrish, RT, Himle, J, et al. "Alcohol Abuse Among Clinically Anxious Patients." *Behav Res Ther* (1986), vol. 24, no. 3, 357–59.

Tyrer, P, Candry, J. Kewlly, D. "A Study of the Clinical Effects of Phenelzine and Placebo in the Treatment of Phobic Anxiety." *Psychopharmacologia* (1973), 32, 237–54.

Uhde, TE, Boulenger, JP, Vittone, B, et al. "Human Anxiety and Noradrenergic Function: Preliminary Studies with Caffeine, Clonidine and Yohimbine." *Proceedings on the Neurobiology of Anxiety—VIIth World Congress of Psychiatry.* New York: Plenum Press.

Uhde, TW, Joffe, RT, Jimerson, DC, Post, RM. "Normal Urinary Free Cortisol and Plasma MHPG in Panic Disorder: Clinical and Theoretical Implications." *Society of Biological Psychiatry,* vol. 23, 1988, 575–85.

Uhde, TW, Stein, MB, Post RM. "Lack of Efficacy in the Treatment of Panic Disorder." *Am J Psychiatry,* 145: 9 (September 1988), 1104–9.

Van Den Hout, MA, Griez, E. "Panic Symptoms After Inhalation of Carbon Dioxide." *British J of Psychiatry* (1984), 144, 503–7.

van der Kolk, BA. "The Drug Treatment of Post-Traumatic Stress Disorder." *J of Affective Disorders,* 13 (1987), 203–13.

Veith, RC, Raskind, MA. "The Neurobiology of Aging: Does It Predispose to Depression?" *Neurobiology of Aging* (1988), vol. 9, 101–17.

Verebey, K, Gold, MS. "Endorphins and Mental Disease." In *Handbook of Neurochemistry,* A. Lajtha, ed. New York: Plenum Publishing, 1984, 10: 589–615.

Victoroff, VM, Mantel, SJ, et al. "Physical Examinations in Psychiatric Practice." *Ohio Hosp Comm Psychiatry* (1979), 30: 536–40.

Vittone, BJ, Uhde, TW. "Differential Diagnosis and Treatment of Panic Disorder: A Medical Model Perspective." *Australian and New Zealand J of Psychiatry,* vol. 19, (1985), 330–41.

Wall, M, Tuchman, M, Mielke, D. "Panic Attacks and Temporal Lobe Seizures Associated with a Right Temporal Lobe Arteriovenous Malformation: Case Report." *J Clin Psychiatry* (April 1985), 46: 143–45.

Wallace, ER, IV. "Mind-Body: Monistic Dual Aspect Interactionism." *J of Nervous and Mental Disease,* vol. 176, no. 1 (1986), 4–21.

Warwick, HMC, Marks, IM. "Behavioural Treatment of Illness Phobia and Hypochondriasis: A Pilot Study of Seventeen Cases." *British J Psychiatry* (1988), 152, 239–41.

Weissman, MM, Leaf, PJ, Blazer, DG, et al. "Panic Disorder: Clinical Characteristics, Epidemiology, and Treatment." *Psychopharmacology Bulletin* (1986), vol. 22, no. 3, 787–91.

Weissman, MM. "Anxiety Disorders in the Community and Family." Cross National Perspective on Treatment of Anxiety Disorders: Scientific Foundation for Clinical Practice. Presented at the Annual Meeting of the

American Psychiatric Association, Montreal, May 8, 1988, and supported by a grant from The Upjohn Company.

Weissman, MM. "The Epidemiology of Panic Disorder and Agoraphobia." Chapter 3 in *Review of Psychiatry: Volume 7.* RE Hales and AJ Frances, eds. Washington: American Psychiatric Press, 1988.

Winokur, G. "Anxiety Disorders: Relationships to Other Psychiatric Illness." *Psychiatric Clinics of North America* (June 1988), vol. 11, no. 2, 287–93.

Wolkowitz, OM, Paul, SM. "Neural and Molecular Mechanisms in Anxiety." *Psychiatric Clinics of North America,* vol. 8, no. 1 (March 1985), 145–58.

Wood, G. *The Myth of Neurosis: Overcoming the Illness Excuse.* New York: Harper and Row, 1986.

Woods, SW, Charney, DS, Goodman, WK, Heninger, GR. "Carbon Dioxide-Induced Anxiety: Behavioral, Physiologic, and Biochemical Effects of Carbon Dioxide in Patients with Panic Disorder and Healthy Subjects." *Arch Gen Psychiatry* (January 1988), 45: 43–52.

Woods, SW, Charney, DS, Loke, J, et al. "Carbon Dioxide Sensitivity in Panic Anxiety." *Arch Gen Psychiatry* (September 1986), vol. 23, 900–909.

Woods, SW, Charney, DS, McPherson, CA, et al. "Situational Panic Attacks." *Arch Gen Psychiatry* (1987), 44: 365–75.

Yeragani, VK, Pohl, R, Balon, R, et al. "Lactate Infusions: The Role of Baseline Anxiety and Autonomic Measures." Letter to the editor, *Psychiatry Research* (1987), 22, 263–64.

Zal, HM. "Panic Disorder: Is It Emotional or Physical?" *Psychiatric Annals* (July 1987), vol. 17: 7, 497–505.

Zane, MD, Milt, H. *Your Phobia: Understanding Your Fears Through Contextual Therapy.* Washington: American Psychiatric Press, 1984.

Zitrin, CU, Klein, DF, Woerner, MG, Ross, D. "Treatment of Phobias. I. Comparison of Imipramine Hydrochloride and Placebo." *Arch Gen Psychiatry* (1983), 40: 125–38.

Zohar, J, Insel, TR. "Biological Approaches to Diagnosis and Treatment of Obsessive-Compulsive Disorder." Chapter in *The Art of Psychopharmacology.* SC Risch and RD Hanowsky, eds. New York: Guilford Publications, 1987.

Zohar, J, Insel, TR. "Diagnosis and Treatment of Obsessive-Compulsive Disorder." *Psychiatric Annals* (March 1988), 18: 3: 168–71.

Zohar, J. Insel, TR. "Obsessive-Compulsive Disorder: Psychobiological Approaches to Diagnosis, Treatment, and Pathophysiology." *Biol Psychiatry* (1987), 22: 667–87.

———"Adult Children of Alcoholics Like PTSD Victims? *Psychiatric News* (July 1, 1988), 11.

———"An Update on Panic Disorders. An Interview with Donald F. Klein." *Currents,* vol. IV, no. 10 (October), 5–10.

———"Brain Metabolism Studied." *American Medical News,* (March 20, 1987), 33.

———"Brain Wound Eliminates Man's Mental Illness." *New York Times,* February 25, 1988.

———"Diagnosing and Treating the Anxiety Disorders. An Interview with David V. Sheehan." VI(4), April 1987, 5–10.

———"Medical School Enrollment Continues to Drop: Psychiatry Holds Steady in Attracting New Trainees." *Psychiatric News* (September 18, 1987), 2.

————"New Anxiolytic Still in Limbo." *Medical World News* (February 10), 1986.

————"Panic Attacks Linked With Aspartame (Nutrasweet)." *Currents* (December 1986), vol. V, no. 12.

————"Panic Can Be Suicide Omen." *The New York Times* (from the Associated Press), November 2, 1989, p. B20.

————"Panic Out of the Blue." *Emergency Medicine* (January 30, 1984), 61–63.

————"The Fight to Conquer Fear: Phobias Afflict Millions of Americans—But New Therapies Are Providing Help." *Newsweek,* April 23, 1984. 66–72.

————"U.C.L.A. Educator Sees Hopeful Prospects For Those Entering Psychiatry." *Psychiatric News,* June 3, 1988.

INDEX

meditation, 256
Menninger, Karl, 23
mercury poisoning, 103–4, 183,
    185
metabolic diseases, 167–69
methadone, 180
mianserin, 279–80
midsystolic apical murmur
    (heart murmur), 171
mimickers of anxiety disorders,
    149–86
  categories of, 155
  defined, 10, 12
  list of (chart), 152–53
  psychiatric symptoms caused
    by, 154–55
  psychiatric vs. physical, 174–
    76
mitral valve prolapse (MVP), 7,
    31–32, 108, 171–72, 184,
    195, 196
moclobemide, 282–83
mononeucleosis, 166
multiple sclerosis (MS), 165
myocardial infarction (MI)
    (heart attack), 5, 35–36,
    172

nalorphine, 182
Napoleon I, Emperor of the
    French, 39
neurobiology, 128–30, 142–43
neurocirculatory asthenia, 135
neurons, 128, 142, 186
neurotransmitters, 128–32
  GABA, 142–43, 274
    noradrenergic, 129–31
    serotonin, 143, 240, 281–82
niacin deficiency, 117, 167–68
nicotine, 261–62
NIMH (National Institute of
    Mental Health), 8
nitrous oxide, 186
norepinephrine, 129
nortriptyline, 218
nuclear magnetic resonance
    (NMR) imaging, 32, 165

obesity, 18
obsessions:
  defined, 40, 41, 76
  pure, 78
obsessive-compulsive disorder
    (OCD), 58, 76–80, 88–89,
    132, 203, 204, 268–69
  age for onset of, 240
  defined, 40
  obsessive-compulsive
    personality disorder vs., 176
  statistics on, 77
  treatment of, 80, 239–40, 282
Olivier, Sir Laurence, 39

pancreatic carcinoma, 170
panhypopituitarism, 161
panic attacks (PAs), 5–13, 17–
    18, 31–32, 33, 34, 53–54,
    75, 89, 100–101, 103, 106,
    118, 147, 203, 207, 209,
    233, 237, 270, 281
  age for onset of, 39
  agoraphobia caused by, 71,
    163
  anticipatory anxiety before,
    94–95, 119, 122, 127, 214–
    15, 221, 223, 226
  brain mapping and, 130–32
  diagnostic criteria for, 110–
    13, 204
  dread of recurrence of, 36,
    45–46, 54, 69–70, 94–95
  drug abuse and, 177–78, 179,
    193
  drugs and, 43–44, 101, 120–
    21, 122, 142, 157, 163, 177,
    179, 182, 193, 215–31
  duration and intensity of, 214
  Freudian view of, 83–84
  hyperventilation and, 132–34,
    138, 165
  mimickers of, 156, 160, 162,
    163, 164, 165, 171–72,
    183–86
  phobias caused by, 38, 45–47,
    69, 71, 214

ABOUT THE AUTHOR

MARK S. GOLD, M.D., is Director of Research at Fair Oaks Hospital in Summit, New Jersey, and Delray Beach, Florida. He is the founder of both the National Cocaine Hotline (800-CO-CAINE) and Psychiatric Diagnostic Laboratories of America.

Dr. Gold and his colleagues at Yale and Fair Oaks have been granted three patents for the invention of new psychiatric treatments. Dr. Gold has received numerous awards for his pioneering research involving the use of laboratory tests in psychiatric diagnosis and treatment; brain mechanisms that produce fear, anxiety, and panic; and the use of medicines in treatment of patients with anxiety or depression. He has written extensively for physicians and other professional audiences. In addition, Dr. Gold is the author of four books for general audiences: *The 800-COCAINE Book, The Good News About Depression, The Facts About Drugs and Alcohol,* and *Wonder Drugs.*